NOTES ON THE
MIRACLES OF OUR LORD

NOTES

ON THE

MIRACLES OF OUR LORD

BY

RICHARD CHENEVIX TRENCH

POPULAR EDITION

BAKER BOOK HOUSE
Grand Rapids, Michigan

ISBN: 0-8010-8776-7

First printing, November, 1949
Second printing, August, 1951
Third printing, February, 1953
Fourth printing, August, 1956
Fifth printing, November, 1958
Sixth printing, September, 1962
Seventh printing, November, 1965
Eighth printing, March, 1967
Ninth printing, October, 1968
Tenth printing, October, 1969
Eleventh printing, March, 1972
Twelfth printing, April, 1974

PHOTOLITHOPRINTED BY CUSHING - MALLOY, INC.
ANN ARBOR, MICHIGAN, UNITED STATES OF AMERICA
1974

PREFACE

Trench's NOTES ON THE MIRACLES is widely acknowledged as being the most comprehensive and penetrating study of the subject in the English language. The author manifests a keen sensitivity to the meaning and interpretation of the Biblical text — insisting that God's Word shall speak for itself. Yet, he marshalls the opinions of a wide array of recognized authorities on the subject — realizing that the full light of revelation is focused on no single mind. Trench succeeds admirably in suggesting the practical lessons which are embedded in the miracles of our Lord.

This *Popular Edition* of the NOTES ON THE MIRACLES is a companion volume to a similar edition of Trench's NOTES ON THE PARABLES. In preparing this edition the numerous notes in the foreign language — Greek, Latin, German, and French — have been carefully translated and evaluated. Those considered valuable have been retained as footnotes. Lengthy passages of a polemic nature, of particular significance to the time of Trench, have been reduced in length or eliminated entirely. A number of other alterations have been made in the interest of clarity and directness of presentation.

All those who appreciate the scholarship of Archbishop Trench will be pleased that his practical exposition of the miracles is once more available. The general Christian public will be grateful that this new edition makes this study available for its ready use.

CONTENTS

Preliminary Essay:

Miracles:

PRELIMINARY ESSAY

CHAPTER I.

On the Names of the Miracles

EVERY inquiry about a thing will best begin with an investigation of the name or names which it bears; for the name seizes and presents the most distinctive features, the innermost nature of the thing which we desire to understand, and embodies this in a word. What we usually term *miracles,* are in the sacred Scriptures termed sometimes "wonders," sometimes "signs," sometimes "powers," sometimes simply "works." Other titles also they bear, but of rarer occurrence; such as will easily range themselves under one or other of these. On each of these it will be worth while to say something, before making any further advance in our study of the subject.

1. In the name *wonder,* the astonishment which the work produces upon the beholders (Mark ii. 12; iv. 41; vi. 51; vii. 37; cf. Acts iii. 10, 11), is transferred to the work itself. This word, as will at once be felt, does but touch the outside of the matter. The ethical meaning of the miracle would be wholly lost, were blank astonishment or mere amazement *all* which it aroused; since the same effect might be produced by a thousand meaner causes. Indeed it is not a little remarkable, rather is it profoundly characteristic of the miracles of the New Testament, as Origen noted long ago,[1] that this name *wonders* is never applied to them but in connexion with some other name. They are "signs *and* wonders" (Acts xiv. 3; Rom. xv. 19; Matt. xxiv. 24; Heb. ii. 4); or "signs" alone (John ii. 11; Acts viii. 6; Rev. xiii. 13); or "powers" alone (Mark vi. 14; Acts xix. 11);

---

[1] Godet: "The Miracles of Jesus are not mere prodigies intended to strike the imagination. There is a close relation between these marvellous facts and the person of Him who does them. They are visible emblems of what He is and what He comes to do, images which spring as rays from the abiding miracle of the manifestation of the Christ."

but never "wonders" alone. Not that the miracle, considered
simply as a wonder, as an astonishing event which the beholders
can reduce to no law with which they are acquainted, is even
as such without its meaning and its purpose; that purpose being
forcibly to startle men from the dull dream of a sense-bound
existence, and, however it may not be itself an appeal to the
spiritual in man, yet to act as a summons to him that he now
open his eyes to the spiritual appeal which is about to be addressed to him (Acts xiv. 8-18).

2. But the miracle is not a "wonder" only; it is also a *sign,*
a token and indication of the near presence and working of
God. In this word the ethical purpose of the miracle comes out
the *most* prominently, as in "wonder" the least. They are *signs*
and pledges of something more than and beyond themselves
(Isai. vii. 11; xxxviii. 7) ;[2] valuable, not so much for what they
are, as for what they indicate of the grace and power of the
doer, or of the connexion in which he stands with a higher
world. Oftentimes they are thus seals of power set to the person
who accomplishes them ("the Lord confirming the word with
signs following," Mark xvi. 20; Acts xiv. 3; Heb. ii. 4);
legitimating acts, by which he claims to be accepted as a messenger from God. "What *sign* shewest thou?" (John ii. 18) was
the question which the Jews asked, when they wanted the Lord
to justify the things which He was doing, by showing that He
had especial authority to do them. St. Paul speaks of himself as
having "the *signs* of an apostle" (2 Cor. xii. 12), in other
words, the tokens which designate him as such. Thus, too, in the
Old Testament, when God sends Moses to deliver Israel He
furnishes him with two *signs.* He warns him that Pharaoh will
require him to legitimate his mission, to produce his credentials
that he is indeed God's ambassador; and equips him with the
powers which shall justify him as such, which, in other words,

---

[2] Basil: "A *sign* is an evident thing, which bears within it the indication of some
other thing which is obscure."

shall be his *signs* (Exod. vii. 9, 10). He "gave a sign" to the prophet, whom He sent to protest against the will-worship of Jeroboam (1 Kin. xiii. 3).

With all this it is well worth observing that the *sign* is not of necessity a miracle, although only as such it has a place in our discussion. Many a common matter may be a *sign* or seal set to the truth of some word, the announcement of which goes along with it. Thus the Angels give to the shepherds for a *sign* their finding of the Child wrapt in swaddling clothes in a manger (Luke ii. 12; cf. Exod. iii. 12). Or it is possible for a man, under a strong conviction that the hand of God is leading him, to set such or such a contingent event as a *sign* to himself, the falling out of which in this way or in that he will accept as an intimation from God of what He would have him to do. Examples of this also are not uncommon in Scripture (Gen. xxiv. 14-21; Judg. vi. 36-40; 1 Sam. xiv. 8-13). Very curious, and standing by themselves, are the *signs* which shall only come to pass *after* that of which they were the signs has actually befallen; but which shall still serve to confirm it as having been wrought directly of God (Exod. iii. 12; 2 Kin, xix. 29).

3. Frequently also the miracles are styled *powers* or *mighty works,* that is, of God. As in the term "wonder" or "miracle," the effect is transferred and gives a name to the cause, so here the cause gives its name to the effect. The *power* dwells originally in the divine Messenger (Acts vi. 8; x. 38; Rom. xv. 19) ; is one with which he is himself equipped of God. Christ is thus in the highest sense that which Simon blasphemously suffered himself to be named, "The great *Power of God"* (Acts viii. 10). But then, by an easy transition, the word comes to signify the exertions and separate puttings forth of this power. These are *powers* in the plural, although the same word is now translated in our Version "wonderful works" (Matt. vii. 22), and now, "mighty works" (Matt. xi. 20; Mark vi. 14; Luke x. 13),

and still more frequently, "miracles" (Acts ii. 22; xix. 11; 1 Cor. xii. 10, 28; Gal. iii. 5); in this last case giving such tautologies as this, "miracles *and* wonders" (Acts ii. 22; Heb. ii. 4); and obscuring for us the express purpose of the word, pointing as it does to new *powers* which have entered, and are working in, this world of ours.

These three terms, *wonders, signs,* and *powers,* occur three times in connexion with one another (Acts ii. 22; 2 Cor. xii. 12; 2 Thess. ii. 9), although on each occasion in a different order. They are all, as has already been noted in the case of two, rather descriptive of different aspects of the same works, than themselves different classes of works. An example of one of our Lord's miracles will illustrate what I say. The healing of the paralytic (Mark ii. 1-12) was a *wonder,* for they who beheld it "were all *amazed";* it was a *power,* for the man at Christ's word "arose, took up his bed, and went forth before them all"; it was a *sign,* for it gave token that One greater than men deemed was among them; it stood in connexion with a higher fact of which it was the seal and sign (cf. 1 Kin. xiii. 3; 2 Kin. i. 10), being wrought that they might "know that the Son of man hath power on earth to forgive sins."[3]

4. Eminently significant is another term by which St. John very frequently names the miracles. They are constantly for him simply *works* (v. 36; vii. 21; x. 25, 32, 38; xiv. 11, 12; xv. 24; cf. Matt. xi. 2); as though the wonderful were only the natural form of working for Him who is dwelt in by all the fulness of God; He must, out of the necessity of his higher being, put forth these works greater than man's. They are the periphery of that circle whereof He is the centre. The great miracle is the Incarnation; all else, so to speak, follows naturally and of course. It is no wonder that He whose name is "Wonder-

---

[3] Cf. Calvin on 2 Cor. xii. 12: "They are called *signs* because they are no idle spectacles, but are designed to teach. *Prodigies,* because by their unwontedness they should rouse and strike. Powers or virtues, because they are greater indications of divine power than the things which are seen in the ordinary course of nature."

ful (Isai. ix. 6) does works of wonder; the only wonder would be if He did them not. The sun in the heavens is itself a wonder; but it is not a wonder that, being what it is, it rays forth its effluences of light and heat. These miracles are the fruit after its kind which the divine tree brings forth; and may, with a deep truth, be styled the *works* of Christ, with no further addition or explanation.

CHAPTER II.

Miracles and Nature

WHEREIN, it may be asked, does the miracle differ from any event in the ordinary course of nature? For that too is wonderful; the fact that it is a marvel of continual recurrence may rob it, subjectively, of our admiration; yet it does not remain the less a marvel still.[1]

To this question some have answered, that since all is thus marvellous, since the seed sprouting, the sun rising, are as much the result of powers which we cannot trace or measure, as the water turned into wine, or the sick healed by a word, there is therefore no such thing as a miracle, eminently so called.

But this is indeed most shallow and fallacious. There is quite enough in itself and in its purposes to distinguish that which we call by this name, from all with which it is thus sought to be confounded. The distinction which is sometimes drawn, that in the miracle God is immediately working, and in other events is leaving it to the laws which He has established to work, cannot at all be allowed: for it rests on a dead mechanical view of the universe, altogether remote from the truth. The world is no curious piece of mechanism which its Maker constructs, and then dismisses from his hands, only from time to time reviewing and repairing it, but, as our Lord says, "My Father worketh hitherto, and I work" (John v. 17); He "upholdeth all things by the word of his power"[2] (Heb. i. 3). And to speak of "laws of God,"

---

[1] See Augustine, *De Gen. ad Lit. xii.* 18: *De Civ. Dei,* xxi. 8, 3; and Gregory the Great (*Hom. xxvi. in Evang.*): "The daily miracles of God have grown cheap by repetition."

[2] Melanchthon (*In loc. de Creatione*): "Human infirmity, although it deem God the Creator, can yet imagine afterwards, that as the workman departs from the ship which he has built and leaves it to the sailors, so God withdraws from his work and leaves it to the sole government of creatures. Such an imagination plunges souls into deep darkness and begets doubts."

"laws of nature," may become to us a language altogether deceptive, and hiding the deeper reality from our eyes. *Laws* of God exist only for us. It is a *will* of God for Himself.[3] Each *law*, as we term it, *of nature* is only that which we have learned concerning this will in that particular region of its activity. To say then that there is more of the will of God in a miracle than in any other work of his, is insufficient.

Yet while we deny the conclusion, that since all is wonder, therefore the miracle, commonly so called, is only in the same way as the ordinary processes of nature a manifestation of the presence and power of God, we must not with this deny the truth which lies in this statement. All *is* wonder; to make a man is at least as great a marvel as to raise a man from the dead. The miracle is not a *greater* manifestation of God's power than those ordinary and ever-repeated processes; but it is a *different* manifestation. By those other God is speaking at all times and to all the world; they are a vast unbroken revelation of Him. "The invisible things of Him from the creation of the world are clearly seen, being understood by the things that are made, even his eternal power and Godhead" (Rom. i. 20). This speaking is diffused over all time, and is addressed unto all men. But in the miracle, wrought in the sight of some certain men, and claiming their special attention, there is a speaking to them in particular. There is then a voice in nature which addresses itself directly to them, a singling of them out from the multitude. It is plain that God has now a peculiar word which they are to give heed to, a message to which He is bidding them to listen.

An extraordinary divine causality, and not that ordinary which we acknowledge everywhere and in everything, belongs, then, to the essence of the miracle. The unresting activity of God, which at other times hides and conceals itself behind the veil of what

---

[3] Augustine (*De Civ. Dei*, xxi. 8): "The will of God is the nature of each created thing."

we term natural laws, does in the miracle unveil itself; it steps out from its concealment, and the hand which works is laid bare.

It is indeed true that aught which is perfectly explicable from the course of nature and history is assuredly no miracle in the most proper sense of the word. At the same time the finger of God may be so plainly discernible in it that even while it is plainly explicable by natural causes, we yet may be entirely justified in terming it a miracle, a *providential,* although not an absolute, miracle. Absolute it cannot be called, since there were known causes perfectly capable of bringing it about. Yet the natural may in a manner lift itself up into the miraculous, by the moment at which it falls out, by the purposes which it is made to fulfil. It is a subjective wonder, a wonder *for us,* though not an objective, not a wonder in itself.

Thus many of the plagues of Egypt were the natural plagues of the land. None of these visitations were, or are, unknown in that land; but the intensity of *all* these plagues, the dread succession in which they followed on one another, their connexion with the word of Moses which went before, with Pharaoh's trial which was proceeding, with Israel's deliverance which they helped onward, the order of their coming and going, all these entirely justify us in calling them "the signs and wonders of Egypt," even as such is evermore the scriptural language about them (Deut. iv. 34; Ps. lxxviii. 43; Acts vii. 36). In the same manner it is no absolute miracle that a coin should be found in a fish's mouth (Matt. xvii. 27), or that a lion should meet a man and slay him (1 Kin. xiii. 24), or that a thunderstorm should happen at an unusual period of the year (1 Sam. xii. 16-19) ; and yet these circumstances may be so timed for strengthening faith, for punishing disobedience, for awakening repentance, they may serve such high purposes in God's moral government, that we at once range them in the catalogue of miracles, without seeking to make an anxious discrimination between the miracle absolute and providential. Especially have they a right to their place among these, when (as in each of the instances alluded to above) the final event is the sealing of a foregoing word from the Lord; for so, as miracles of his *foreknowledge* they claim that place, even if not as miracles of his *power*. It is true, of course, of these even more than of any other, that they exist only for the religious mind, for the man who believes that God rules; for him they will be eminently *signs,* signs of a present working God. In the case of the more absolute miracle it will be sometimes possible to extort from the ungodly, as of old from the magicians of Egypt, the unwilling confession, "This is the finger of God" (Exod. viii. 19) ; but this in the case of these will be well nigh impossible; since there is always the natural solution in which they may take refuge.

But while the miracle is not thus nature, so neither is it *against* nature. *Beyond* nature, *beyond* and *above* the nature which we know, they are, but not contrary to it. The miracle is not *unnatural*. The true miracle is a higher and a purer nature, coming down out of the world of untroubled harmonies into this world of ours which so many discords have jarred and disturbed, and bringing this back again, though it be but for one mysterious prophetic moment, into harmony with that higher. The healing of the sick can in no way be termed against nature, seeing that it is sickness which is abnormal, and not health. The healing is the restoration of the primitive order. We should see in the miracle not the infraction of a law, but the neutralizing of a lower law, the suspension of it for a time by a higher. Of this abundant analogous examples are evermore going forward before our eyes. Continually we behold in the world around us lower laws held in suspense by higher, mechanic by dynamic, chemical by vital, physical by moral; yet we do not say, when the lower thus gives place in favour of the higher, that there was any violation of law, or that anything contrary to nature came to pass; rather we acknowledge the law of a greater freedom swallowing up the law of a lesser.

Miracles exceed the laws of *our* nature, but it does not therefore follow that they exceed the laws of *all* nature. The chemical laws which would bring about decay in animal substances still subsist, even when they are restrained and hindered by the salt which keeps those substances from corruption. The law of sin in a regenerate man is held in continual check by the law of the spirit of life; yet is it in his members still. What in each of these cases is wrought may be against one particular law, that law being contemplated in its isolation, and rent away from the complex of laws whereof it forms only a part. But no law does stand thus alone, and it is not against, but rather in entire harmony with the system of laws; for the law of those laws is, that where powers come into conflict, the weaker shall give place to the stronger, the lower to the higher. In the miracle, this world of ours is drawn into and within a higher order of things; laws are then working in it which are not the laws of its fallen condition, but laws of mightier range and higher perfection; they assert the preëminence and predominance which are rightly their own.

It is with these wonders which have been, exactly as it will be with those wonders which we look for in regard of our own mortal bodies, and this physical universe. We should not speak of the resurrection of the body as something contrary to nature; as unnatural; yet no power now working upon our bodies could bring it about; it must be wrought by some power not yet displayed, which God has kept in reserve. So, too, the mighty transformation which is in store for the outward world, out of which it shall come forth a new heaven and a new earth, "the regeneration" of Matt. xix. 28, far exceeds any energies now working in the world. Yet it so belongs to the true idea of the world, now so imperfectly realized, that when it does take place, it will be felt to be the truest nature, which only then at length shall have come perfectly to the birth. The miracles of earth, as Jean Paul has said, are the laws of heaven.

The miracles, then, not being against nature, however they may be beside and beyond it, are in no respect slights cast upon its ordinary and every-day workings; but rather, when contemplated aright, are an honouring of them, in the witness which they render to the source from which these also originally proceed. For Christ, healing a sick man by his word, is claiming herein to be the lord and author of all healing powers which have ever exerted their beneficent influence on the bodies of men.

If in one sense the orderly workings of nature reveal the glory of God (Ps. xix. 1-6), in another they may hide that glory from our eyes; if they ought to make us continually to remember Him, yet there is danger that they lead us to forget Him, until this world around us shall prove—not a translucent medium, through which we behold Him, but a thick impenetrable curtain, concealing Him wholly from our sight. Did miracles serve no other purpose than this, namely to testify the liberty of God, and to affirm his will, which, however, it habitually shows itself *in* nature, is yet more than and above nature, were it only to break a link in that chain of cause and effect, which else we should come to regard as itself God, as the iron chain of an inexorable necessity, binding heaven no less than earth, they would serve a great purpose, they would not have been wrought in vain. But there are other purposes than these, and purposes yet more nearly bearing on the salvation of men, to which they serve, and to the consideration of these we have now arrived.

CHAPTER III.

The Authority of Miracles

IS the miracle to command absolutely, and without further question, the obedience of those in whose sight it is done, or to whom it comes as an adequately attested fact, so that the doer and the doctrine, without further debate, shall be accepted as from God? It cannot be so, for side by side with the miracles which serve for the furthering of the kingdom of God, runs another line of wonders, the counterworkings of him, who is ever the ape of the Most High; who has still his caricatures of the holiest. For that Scriptures attributes *real* wonders to him, though miracles wrought in a sphere rigidly defined and shut in by the power of God, there seems to me no manner of doubt. The Egyptian magicians, his servants, stood in relation to a spiritual kingdom, as truly as did Moses and Aaron. Only when we recognize this, does the conflict between those and these come out in its true significance. It loses this nearly or altogether, if we contemplate their wonders as mere conjurers' tricks or dexterous sleights of hand. *The gods* of Egypt, the spiritual powers of wickedness which underlay, and were the informing soul of, that dark and evil kingdom, were in conflict with the God of Israel. Else, unless it had been such a conflict as this, what meaning would such passages have as that in Moses' Song, "Who is like unto thee, O Lord, among the gods?" (Exod. xv. 11); or that earlier, *"Against all the gods* of Egypt I will execute judgment: I am the Lord" (Exod. xii. 12; cf. Numb. xxxiii. 4)?

Yet while the works of Antichrist and his organs are not mere tricks and juggleries, neither are they miracles in the very

15

highest sense of the word; they only in part partake of the essential elements of the miracle. This they have, indeed, in common with it, that they are real works of a power which is suffered to reach thus far, and not merely dexterous feats of legerdemain; but this, also, which is most different, that they are abrupt, isolated, parts of no organic whole; not the highest harmonies, but the deepest discords, of the universe; not the omnipotence of God wielding his own worlds to ends of grace and wisdom and love, but evil permitted to intrude into the hidden springs of things just so far as may suffice for its own deeper confusion in the end, and, in the mean while, for the needful trial and perfecting of God's saints and servants.

This fact, however, that the kingdom of lies has its wonders no less than the kingdom of truth, is itself sufficient evidence that miracles cannot be appealed to absolutely and finally, in proof of the doctrine which the worker of them proclaims; and God's word expressly declares the same (Deut. xiii. 1-5). A miracle does not prove the truth of a doctrine, or the divine mission of him that brings it to pass. That which alone it claims for him at the first is a right to be listened to: it puts him in the alternative of being from heaven or from hell. The doctrine must first commend itself to the conscience as being *good*, and only then can the miracle seal it as *divine*.[1] For all revelation presupposes in man a power of recognizing the truth when it is shown him, — that he will trace in it the lineaments of a friend, though of a friend from whom he has been long estranged, and whom he has well nigh forgotten. "He that is of God, heareth God's word," and recognizes it for that which it proclaims itself to be.

---

[1] Jeremy Taylor (*Liberty of Prophesying*): "Although the argument drawn from miracles is good to attest a holy doctrine, which by its own worth will support itself after way is a little made by miracles; yet of itself and by its own reputation it will not support any fabric; for instead of proving a doctrine to be true, it makes that the miracles themselves are suspected to be illusions, if they be pretended in behalf of a doctrine which we think we have reason to account false."

It may be objected, indeed, If this be so, if there be this inward witness of the truth, what need then of the miracle? The miracle shall be credentials for the bearer that he has a special mission for the realization of the purposes of God with man. When the truth has found a receptive heart, he who brings it may thus show that he is to be heard not merely as one that is true, but as himself the Truth (see Matt. xi. 4, 5; John v. 36); or at least, as a messenger standing in direct connexion with Him who is the Truth (I Kin. xiii. 3); claiming unreserved submission, and the reception, upon his authority, of other statements which transcend the mind of man.

To demand such a sign from one who comes professing to be the utterer of a new revelation, the bringer of a direct message from God, is no mark of unbelief, but on the contrary is a duty upon his part to whom the message is brought. Else might he lightly be persuaded to receive that as from God, which, indeed, was only the word of man. Credulity is as real, if not so great, a sin as unbelief. It was no impiety on the part of Pharaoh to say to Moses and Aaron, "Shew a miracle for you" (Exod. vii. 9, 10); on the contrary, it was altogether right for him to require this. They came, averring they had a message for him from God: it was his duty to put them to the proof. His sin began, when he refused to believe their credentials.

But the purpose of the miracle being to confirm that which is good, so, upon the other hand, where the mind and conscience witness against the doctrine, not all the miracles in the world have a right to demand submission to the word which they seal. On the contrary, the supreme act of faith is to believe, against, and in despite of, them all, in what God has revealed, and implanted in the soul, of the holy and the true; not to believe another Gospel, though an Angel from heaven, or one transformed into such, should bring it (Deut. xiii. 3; Gal. i. 8); and instead of compelling assent, miracles are then rather warnings to us that we keep them and their workers aloof, for they tell us that not merely lies are here, but that he who utters them is more than a common deceiver, is eminently "a liar and an Antichrist," a false prophet, — standing in more immediate connexion than other deceived and evil men to the kingdom of darkness, so that Satan has given him his power (Rev. xiii. 2), is using him to be an especial organ of his, and to do a peculiar work for him.

But if these things are so, there may seem a twofold danger to which the simple and unlearned Christian would be exposed — the danger, first, of not receiving that which indeed comes from God, or secondly, of receiving that which comes from an evil source. But indeed these dangers do not beset the unlearned and the simple more than they beset and form part of the trial and temptation of every man; the safeguard from either of these fatal errors lying altogether in men's moral and spiritual, and not at all in their intellectual, condition. They only believe the lying wonders, in whom the moral sense is already perverted; they have not before received and embraced the love of the truth, that they might be saved from believing a lie. Thus, then, their believing this lie and rejecting that truth is, in fact, but the final judgment upon them that have had pleasure in unrighteousness. With this view exactly agree the memorable words of St. Paul (2. Thess. ii. 9-12), wherein he declares that it is the anterior state of every man which shall decide whether he shall receive the lying wonders of Antichrist or reject them (cf. John v. 43).[2] For while such come "with all deceivableness of unrighteousness" to them whose previous condition has fitted them to embrace them, there is ever some fault in these wonders which detects and lays them bare to a simple faith, and broadly differ-

---

[2] Augustine (*De Civ. Dei* xx. 19): "They shall be seduced by those signs and wonders who shall deserve to be seduced. . . Therefore, being judged they shall be seduced, and, being seduced, they shall be judged."

ences them and their doers from such as belong to the kingdom of the truth.

These differences have been often brought out. Such miracles are immoral; or if not immoral, they are idle, leading to and ending in nothing. This argument Origen continually uses, when plied with the alleged miracles of heathen saints and sages. He counts, and rightly, that he has abundantly convinced them of falsehood, when he has asked, and obtained no answer to, this question, "What came of these? In what did they issue? The miracles of Moses issued in a Jewish polity; those of Jesus Christ in a Christian Church; whole nations were knit together through their help. What have your boasted Apollonius or Æsculapius to show as the fruit of theirs? What traces of their greatness have they left behind them?" And not merely, he goes on to say, were Christ's miracles effectual, but effectual for good, while the first, whose own work is built upon fraud and lies, can have no such purpose of destroying that very kingdom out of which he himself grows.

These, too, are marks of the true miracle, and marks very nearly connected with the foregoing, that it is never a mere freak of power, done as in wantonness, with no need compelling, for display and ostentation.[3] With good right in that remarkable religious romance of earliest Christian times, *The Recognitions of Clement,* and in the cognate *Clementine Homilies,* Peter draws a contrast between the wonderful works of Christ and those alleged by the followers of Simon Magus to have been wrought by their master. What profit, he asks, or what significance was there in Simon's speaking statutes, his dogs of brass or stone that barked, which all even if he had done, and much more in the same fashion, the works possessed no meaning; they stood

---

[3] Gerson (*De Distinct. Ver. Mirac.*): "A miracle, if it be wanting in the note of pious usefulness or necessity, is suspect from that very act." And Pope Benedict XIV. in his learned work on Canonization says well: "False miracles are distinguished from true by their efficacy, their usefulness, the manner of their working, their end, their worker, and the occasion whereon they are wrought."

in relation to nothing; they were not, what each true miracle will always be more or less, *redemptive* acts; in other words, works not merely of power but of grace, each one an index and a prophecy of the inner work of man's deliverance, which it accompanies and helps forward. But, as we should justly expect, it was preëminently thus with the miracles of Christ. Only when regarded in this light do they appear not merely as illustrious examples of his might, but also as glorious manifestations of his holy love.

It is worth while to follow this a little in detail. What evils are they, which hinder man from reaching the true end and aim of his creation, and from which he needs a redemption? It may brieflly be answered that they are sin in its moral and in its physical manifestations. If we regard its moral manifestations, none were such fearful examples of its tyranny as the demoniacs; they were special objects, therefore, of the miraculous power of the Lord. Then if we ask ourselves what are the physical manifestations of sin; they are sicknesses of all kinds, fevers, palsies, leprosies, blindness, each of these death beginning, a partial death — and finally, the death absolute of the body. This region therefore is fitly another, as it is the widest region, of his redemptive grace. Even the two or three of his works which do not range themselves so readily under any of these heads, yet are not indeed exceptions. Take, for example, the multiplying of the bread. The original curse of sin was the curse of barrenness, — the earth yielding hard-won and scanty returns to the sweat and labour of man; but here this curse is removed, and in its stead the primeval abundance for a moment reappears.

The miracle, then, is an ethical act, and only to be received when it is so, and when it seals doctrines of holiness. If men are taught to believe in Christ upon no other grounds than because He attested his claims by works of wonder, while on these grounds they have no choice but so to do, how shall they consistently refuse belief to any other, who may come here after attesting his claims by the same? We have here a paving of the way of Antichrist; for as we know that he will have his "signs and wonders" (2 Thess. ii. 9; Matt. xxiv. 23-26), so, if this argument is good, he will have right on the score of these to demand the faith and allegiance of men. But no; the miracle must witness for itself, and the doctrine must witness for itself, and then, and then only, the first is capable of witnessing for the second.[4]

---

[4] Gerhard (*Loc. Theoll.* loc. xxiii. 11): "Miracles are the tokens and seals of doctrine; now as a seal torn from a document is of no avail as proof, so miracles avail nothing without doctrine."

CHAPTER IV.

The Evangelical, Compared With Other Cycles of Miracles

1. THE MIRACLES OF THE OLD TESTAMENT

THE miracles of our Lord and those of the Old Testament afford many interesting points of comparison, a comparison equally instructive, whether we trace the points of likeness, or of unlikeness, which exist between them. Thus, to note first a remarkable difference, we find oftentimes the holy men of the older Covenant bringing, if one man venture so to speak, hardly, and with difficulty, the wonder-work to pass; while the miracles of Christ are always accomplished with the highest ease; He speaks, and it is done. Thus Moses must plead and struggle with God, before the plague of leprosy is removed from his sister (Num. xii. 13-15); but Christ heals a leper by his touch (Matt. viii. 3). Elijah stretches himself thrice on the child and cries unto the Lord, and painfully wins back its life (1 Kin. xvii. 21, 22). Christ, on the other hand, shows Himself the Lord of the living and the dead, raising the dead with as much ease as He performs the commonest transactions of life. — In he miracles wrought by men, glorious acts of faith as they are, it is yet possible for human impatience and human unbelief to break out. Thus Moses, God's instrument though he be for the work of power, speaks hastily and acts unbelievingly (Num. xx. 11). It is needless to say of the Son, that his confidence ever remains the same, that his Father hears Him always.

Where the miracles are similar in kind, Christ's are larger, freer, and more glorious. Elisha, indeed, feeds a hundred men with twenty loaves (2 Kin. iv. 42-44), but He five thousand

23

with five.[1] Others have their instrument of power to which the wonder-working energy is linked. Thus Moses has his rod, his staff of wonder, wherewith to divide the Red Sea, and to accomplish his other mighty acts; without which he is nothing (Exod. vii. 19; viii. 5, 16; ix. 23; x. 13; xiv. 16. But Christ accomplishes his miracles simply by the agency of his word (Matt. xii. 13), or by a touch (Matt. viii. 3; xx. 34) ; or if he takes any material substance as the conductor of his healing power, it is from Himself He takes it (Mark vii. 33; viii. 23) ; or should He, as once He does, use any foreign medium in part (John ix. 6), yet by other miracles of like kind, in which He has recourse to no such extraneous helps, He declares plainly that this was of free choice, and not of necessity. Then too, while the miracles of Moses, or of the Apostles, are ever done in the name of another and with the attribution of the glory to another, "Stand still, and see the salvation of the Lord, which *He* will shew you" (Exod. xiv. 13), "In the name of Jesus Christ of Nazareth rise up and walk" (Acts iii. 6) ; his are ever wrought in his own name and by a power immanent and inherent in Himself: "*I will;* be thou clean" (Matt. viii. 3) ; "Thou dumb and deaf spirit, *I* charge thee, come out of him" (Mark ix. 25). When he prays, being about to perform one of his mighty works, his disciples shall learn even from his prayer itself that herein He is not asking for a power external to Himself, but indeed only testifying thus to the unbroken oneness of his life with his Father's (John xi. 41, 42). Thus needful was it for them, thus needful for all, that they should have high and exclusive thoughts of Him, and should not class Him with any other, even the greatest and holiest, of the children of men.

These likenesses, and these unlikenesses no less, are such as before hand we should naturally expect. We should expect the

---

[1] Tertullian (*Adv. Marc.* iv. 35): "The Lord works by Himself or by his Son after one manner, and by his servants the prophets after another manner, especially in the case of works evidencing power and might; for in these it is right that his own acts should be distinguished from those of his deputies by the greater brilliancy and strength which belong to them, as being his."

mighty works of either Covenant to be like, since the old and new form parts of one organic whole; and it is ever God's law that the lower should contain prophetic intimations and antici- pations of the higher. We should expect them to be unlike, since the very idea of God's kingdom is that of progress, of a gradually fuller communication and larger revelation of Himself to men, so that He who in times past spake unto the fathers by the prophets, did at length speak unto us by his Son; and it was only meet that this Son should be clothed with mightier powers than theirs, and powers which He held not from another, but such as were evidently his own in fee.

Those of the Old wear oftentimes a far severer aspect than those of the New. They are miracles, indeed, of God's grace, but yet also miracles of the Law, of that Law which worketh wrath, which will teach, at all costs, the lesson of the awful holiness of God. Miracles of the Law, they preserve a charac- ter that accords with the Law; being oftentimes fearful outbreaks of God's anger against the unrighteousness of men; such for instance are the signs and wonders in Egypt, many of those in the desert (Num. xvi. 31; Lev. x. 2), and some which the later prophets wrought (2 Kin. i. 10-12; ii. 23-25); leprosies are inflicted (Num. xii. 10; 2 Chr. xxvi. 19), not removed; a sound hand is withered and dried up (I Kin. xiii. 4), not a withered hand restored. Not but that these works also are for the most part what our Lord's are altogether and with no single exception, namely, works of evident grace and mercy. I affirm this of *all* our Lord's miracles; for that single one, which seems an exception, the cursing of the barren fig-tree, has no right really to be considered such. He needed to declare, not in word only but in act, what would be the consequences of an obstinate unfruitfulness and resistance to his grace, and thus to make manifest the severer side of his ministry, He chose for the showing out of this, not one among all the sinners who were about Him, but displayed his power upon a tree, which, itself incapable of feeling, might yet effectually serve as a sign and warning to men. He will allow no single exception to the rule of grace and love. When He blesses, it is men; but when He smites, it is an unfeeling tree.[2]

It is also noticeable that the region in which the miracles of the Old Testament chiefly move, is that of external nature; they are the dividing of the sea (Exod. xiv. 21), furnaces which have lost their power to consume (Dan. iii.), wild-beasts which have laid aside their inborn fierceness in whole (Dan. vi. 22), or in part (1 Kin. xiii. 24, 28), and the like. In the New it is mainly the sphere of man's life in which it moves. And consistently with this, the earlier miracles have oftentimes a colossal character. Thus it is with the miracles of Egypt, the miracles of Babylon: they are miracles eminently of strength; for under the influence of the great nature-worships of those lands, all religion had assumed a colossal grandeur in its outward manifestations. Compared with our Lord's works, wrought in the days of his flesh, those were the whirlwind and the fire, and his as the still small voice which followed. In that old time God was teaching his people, He was teaching also the nations with whom his people were brought wonderfully into contact, that He who had entered into covenant with one among all the nations, was not one god among many, the god of the hills, or the god of the plains (1 Kin. xx. 23) ; but that the God of Israel was the Lord of the whole earth, who wielded all its elements at his will.

But Israel at the time of the Incarnation had thoroughly learned that lesson, much else as it had still to learn; and the whole civilized world had practically outgrown polytheism. And thus the works of our Lord, though they bear not on their front the imposing character which did those of old, yet contain higher

---

[2] From this point of view we should explain our Saviour's rebuke to the sons of Zebedee, when they wanted to call down fire from heaven on a village of the Samaritans, "*as Elias did*" (Luke ix. 54) ; to repeat, that is, an Old Testament miracle.

and deeper truths. They are eminently miracles of the Incarnation, of the Son of God who had taken our flesh, and who, having taken, would heal it. Miracles of nature assume now altogether a subordinate place. They still survive, for this region of nature must still be claimed as part of Christ's dominion. But man, and not nature, is now the main subject of these mighty powers; and thus it comes to pass that, with less of outward pomp, less to startle and amaze, the new have a far deeper inward significance than the old.

2. THE MIRACLES OF THE APOCRYPHAL GOSPELS

The apocryphal gospels are instructive in that they show us what manner of gospels were the result, when men drew from their own fancy, and devised Christs of their own. Here the glory of the true comes out into strongest light by its comparison with the false. In nothing, perhaps, are these apocryphal gospels more worthy of note, than in the difference between the main features of their miracles and of those of the Canonical Gospels. Thus in the canonical, the miracle is indeed essential, but, at the same time, ever subordinated to the doctrine which it confirms. The miracles ever lead us off from themselves to their Author; they derive their worth from Him, not contrariwise He from them. They are parts of a vast organic whole, of which every part is in vital coherence with all the others. It is altogether otherwise with these apocryphal narratives. To say that the miracles occupy in them the foremost place would very inadequately express the facts of the case. They are everything. Some of these so-called histories are nothing else but a string of these; which stand wholly disconnected from the ministry of Christ. They are all miracles of the Infancy, — of that time whereof the canonical history is at pains to tell us that during it no miracle was wrought, the miracle in Cana of Galilee being his first (John ii. 11).

They are never *signs,* but at the best wonders and portents. Every higher purpose and aim is absent from them altogether. It is never felt that the writer is writing out of any higher motive than to excite and feed a childish love of the marvellous, never that he could say, "These are written, that ye might believe that Jesus is the Christ, the Son of God; and that believing ye might have life through his name" (John xx. 31). Indeed, so far from having a *religious,* they are often wanting in an *ethical* element. The Lord Jesus appears in them as a wayward, capricious, passionate child; to be feared indeed, seeing that He is furnished with such formidable powers of doing mischief, of avenging every wrong or accidental injury which He meets, every offence which He may take. Indeed Joseph is reported to say to Mary, "Whosoever sets himself against Him perishes."

It may be well to cite a few examples in proof, however unpleasantly some of them may jar on the Christian ear. Thus some children refuse to play with Him, hiding themselves from Him; He pursues and turns them into kids. Another child by accident runs against Him, and throws Him down; whereupon He, being exasperated, exclaims, "As thou hast made Me to fall, so shalt thou fall and not rise"; at the same hour the child fell down and expired. Such is the image which the authors of these books give us of the holy child Jesus. Even the miracles which are not of this revolting character are childish tricks, like the tricks of a conjurer, never solemn acts of power and love. He and some other children make birds and animals of clay; while each is boasting the superiority of his work, Jesus says, "I will cause those which I have made to go"; — which they do, the animals leaping and the birds flying, and at his bidding returning, and eating and drinking from his hand. While yet an infant at his mother's breast, He bids a palm-tree to stoop that she may pluck the dates; it obeys, and only returns to its position at his command. And as the miracles which He does, so those that are done in his honour, are idle or monstrous; the ox and the ass worshipping Him, a new-born infant in the crib, may serve for an example.

In all these, as will be observed, the idea of *redemptive* acts is wanting altogether; they are none of them the outward clothing of the inward facts of man's redemption. I would not of course imply that miracles of healing and of grace are *altogether* absent from these books; but only that they do not present to us any clear and consistent image of a Saviour full of grace and power, but an image rather, continually distorted and defaced by lines of passion and caprice, of impatience, peevishness, and anger. The most striking, perhaps, of the miracles respecting the child Jesus, is that of the falling down of the idols of Egypt at his presence in the land; for it has in it something of a deeper significance, as a symbol and prophecy of the overthrow of the idol worship of the world by Him who was now coming into the world. Again, the lions and the leopards gathering harmlessly around Him as He passed through the desert on the way to Egypt, is not alien to the true spirit of the Gospel, and has its analogy in the words of St. Mark, that He "was with the wild beasts" (i. 13) — a hint to us that in Him, the new head of the race, the second Adam, the Paradisaical state was given back (Gen. i. 28; Ps. viii. 6-8). But with a very few such partial exceptions as these, the apocryphal gospels are a barren and dreary waste of wonders without object or aim; and only instructive as making us strongly to feel, more strongly than otherwise we might have felt, how needful are other factors besides power for the producing of a true miracle; that wisdom and love must be there also; that where men conceive of power as its chiefest element, they give us only a hateful mockery of the divine.

3. THE LATER, OR ECCLESIASTICAL, MIRACLES

A few words must of necessity find place concerning the permanent miraculous gifts which have been challanged for the

Church as her rightful heritage, alike by some who have gloried
in their presumed presence, and by others who have lamented
their absence. It is not my belief that she has this gift of working
miracles, nor yet that she was intended to have it.

At first, as a strong presumption against the intended continu-
ance of these powers in the Church, may be taken the analogies
derived from the earlier history of God's dealings with his
people. We do not find the miracles sown broadcast over the
whole Old Testament history. In fact there are but two great
outbursts of these; the first at the establishing of the kingdom
under Moses and Joshua, when, as at once is evident, they could
not have been wanting; the second in the time of Elijah and
Elisha; that also a time of the utmost need, when, the Levitical
priesthood being abolished, and the faithful only a scattered
few among the ten tribes, it was a question whether the court-
religion which the apostate kings of Israel had set up, should
not quite overbear the true worship of Jehovah. There is in all
this an entire absence of prodigality in the employment of
miracles; they are ultimate resources, reserved for the great
needs of God's kingdom, not its every-day incidents. How unlike
this moderation to the wasteful expenditure of miracles in the
legends of the Middle Ages! There no perplexity can occur
so trifling that a miracle will not be brought in to solve it;
there almost no saint, certainly no distinguished one, is without
his *nimbus* of miracles around his head; they are adorned with
these in rivalry with one another, in rivalry with Christ Himself. That remarkable acknowledgment, "John did no miracle"
(John x. 41) finds no parallel in the records of their lives.

We must add to this the declarations of Scripture, on the
object of miracles, that they are for the confirming the word
by signs following, for authenticating a message as being from
heaven — that signs are for the unbelieving (1 Cor. xiv. 22).
What do they then in a Christendom? Signs are not for the

positively unbelieving, since, as we have seen, they will exercise no power over such as harden themselves against the truth; these will resist or evade them as surely as they will resist or evade every other witness of God's presence in the world; — but for the unbelieving who hitherto have been such by no fault of their own, for them to whom the truth is now coming for the first time. And if not always even for them now, — as they exist, for instance, in a heathen land, — we may sufficiently account for this by the fact that the Church of Christ, with its immense and evident superiorities of all kinds over everything with which it is brought in contact, and some portions of which superiority every man must recognize, is itself now the great witness and proof of the truth which it delivers. The truth, therefore, has no longer need to vindicate itself by an appeal to something else.

And then further, all that we might ourselves beforehand presume from the analogy of external things leads us to the same conclusions. We find all beginning to be wonderful — to be under laws different from, and higher than, those which regulate ulterior progress. Thus the powers evermore at work for the upholding of the natural world would have been manifestly insufficient for its first creation; there were other which must have presided at its birth, but which now, having done their work, have fallen back, and left it to follow the laws of its ordinary development. It is only according to the analogies of that which thus everywhere surrounds us, to presume that it was even so with the beginnings of the spiritual creation — the Christian Church. It is unquestionably so with the beginnings of that new creation in any single heart. In the regeneration, the strongest tendencies of the old nature are overborne; the impossible has become possible; by a mighty wonder-stroke of grace the polarity in the man is shifted. Shall we count it strange, then, that the coming in of a new order, not into a single heart, but into the entire world, should have been wonderful? It would have been inexplicable if it had been otherwise.

But this new order, having not only declared but constituted itself, henceforth submits itself in outward things, and for the present time, to those laws. All its true glory, which is its inward, it retains; but these powers, which are not the gift — for Christ Himself is the gift — but the signs of the gift, it foregoes. "Miracles," says Fuller, "are the swaddling clothes of the infant Churches"; and, we may add, not the garments of the full grown. They were as the proclamation that the king was mounting his throne; who, however, is not proclaimed every day, but only at his accession; when he sits acknowledged on his throne, the proclamation ceases. That the Church *has had* these wonders, — of this it preserves a record and attestation in the Scriptures of truth. The miracles recorded there live for the Church; they are as much present witnesses for Christ to us now as to them who actually saw them with their eyes.

Moreover, a very large proportion of the later miracles bear inward marks of spuriousness. The miracles of Christ and his Apostles, being the miracles of that highest and latest dispensation under which we live, — we have a right to consider as normal, in their chief features at least, for all future miracles, if such were to continue in the Church. The details might be different; yet the later must not, in their inner spirit, be totally unlike the earlier, or they will carry the sentence of condemnation on their front. They must not, for instance, lead us back under the bondage of the senses, while those other were ever framed to release from that bondage. They must not be aimless and objectless, fantastic freaks of power, while those had every one of them a meaning and distinct ethical aim, — were manifestations of his glory, that men might be drawn to the glory itself. They must not be ludicrous and grotesque, saintly jests, while those were evermore reverent and solemn and awful. And lastly,

they must not be seals and witnesses to aught which the conscience, enlightened by the Word and Spirit of God, — where-
unto is the ultimate appeal, and which stands above the miracle,
and not beneath it, — protests against as untrue (the innumerable Roman miracles which attest transubstantiation), or as error
largely mingling with the truth (the miracles which go to uphold
the whole Roman system), those other having set their seal only
to the absolutely true. Miracles with these marks upon them
we are bound by all which we hold most sacred, by all which
the Word of God has taught us, to reject and to refuse. It is
for the reader, tolerably acquainted with the Church-history of
the Middle Ages, to judge how many of its miracles will, if
these tests be acknowledged and applied, at once fall away, and,
failing to fulfil these primary conditions, will have no right even
to be considered any further.

Very interesting is it to observe how the men who in some
sort fell in with the prevailing tendencies of their age, yet did
ever, in their higher moods, with truest Christian insight, witness
against those very tendencies by which they, with the rest of
their contemporaries, were more or less borne away. Thus was
it with regard to the over-valuing of miracles, the esteeming of
them as the only evidences of an exalted sanctity. Against this
an unbroken testimony in all ages of the Church was borne;
not, indeed, sufficient to arrest the progress of an error into
which the sense-bound generations of men only too naturally
fall, yet witnessing that the Church herself was ever conscious
that the holy life was in the sight of God of higher price than
the wonderful works — that love is the greatest miracle of all
— that to overcome the world, this is the greatest manifestation
of the power of Christ in his servants.

Few points present greater difficulties than the attempt to fix
accurately the moment when these miraculous powers were withdrawn from the Church. This is difficult, because it is difficult

to say at what precise moment the Church was no longer in the act of *becoming,* but contemplated in the mind of God as actually *being;* when to the wisdom of God it appeared that He had adequately confirmed the word with signs following.

That this mighty tide of power should have ebbed only by degrees was what was to be looked for in that spiritual world which, like God's natural world, is free from all harsh and abrupt transitions. We can conceive the order of retrocession to have been in this way; that divine power which dwelt in all its fulness and intensity in Christ, was first divided among his Apostles, who, therefore, individually wrought fewer and smaller works than their Lord. It was again from them further subdivided among the ever-multiplying numbers of the Church, who, consequently, possessed not these gifts in the same intensity and plenitude as did the twelve. At the same time it must always be remembered that these receding gifts were ever helping to form that which should be their own substitute. If those wonders of a first creation have left us, yet they did not this till they could bequeath in their stead the standing wonder of a Church,[3] itself a wonder, and embracing manifold wonders in its bosom. For are not the laws of the spiritual world, as they are ever working in the midst of us, a continual wonder? What is the new birth in Baptism, and the communion of Christ's body and blood in the Holy Eucharist, and the life of God in the soul, and a kingdom of heaven in the world, what are these but every one of them wonders? wonders in this like the wonders of ordinary nature, as distinguished from those which accompany a new in-coming of power, that they are under a law which we can anticipate; that they conform to an absolute order, and one the course of which we can understand; — but not therefore the less divine.

---

[3] Augustine (*De Civ. Dei,* xxii. 8): "Whoso now demands prodigies, in order that he may believe, is himself a great prodigy, in that he believes not though the whole world believes."

While then it does not greatly concern us to know *when* this power was withdrawn, what does vitally concern us is, that we suffer not these carnal desires after miracles, as though they were certainly saints who had them, and they but imperfect Christians who were without them, as though the Church were inadequately furnished and spiritually impoverished which could not show them, to rise up in our hearts. It is little which we ourselves have known of the miracles of grace, when *they* seem to us poor and pale, when only the miracles of power have any attraction in our eyes.

CHAPTER V.

The Assaults on the Miracles

1. THE JEWISH

A RIGID monotheistic religion like the Jewish left but one way of escape from the authority of miracles which once were acknowledged to be such, and not set aside as mere collusions and sleights of hand. There remained nothing to say, but that which the adversaries of the Lord constantly *did* say, namely, that the works which He wrought were wrought by power from beneath: "This fellow doth not cast out devils but by Beelzebub, the prince of the devils" (Matt. xii. 24; cf. Mark iii. 22-27; Luke xi. 15-22). We have our Lord's own answer to the deep malignity of this assertion; his appeal, namely, to the whole tenor of his doctrine, and of the miracles wherewith He confirmed that doctrine — whether they were not altogether for the overthrowing of the kingdom of evil, — whether a lending by Satan of such power to Him would not be wholly inconceivable, being merely and altogether suicidal.

The furthering upon his part of such an assault against his own kingdom as, if successful, must overturn it altogether, is quite inconceivable. He who came, as all his words and his deeds testified, to "destroy the works of the devil," could not have come armed with *his* power, and helped onward by his aid. He appeals to every man's conscience, whether the doctrine to which they bear witness, and which bears witness to them, be from above, or from beneath: and if from above, then the power with which He accomplished them could not have been lent Him from beneath, since the kingdom of lies would never so contradict itself, as seriously to help forward the establishment of the kingdom of truth.

There is, indeed, at first sight a difficulty in the argument which our Saviour draws from the oneness of the kingdom of Satan. Hell is as much in arms against itself as against heaven; neither does our Lord deny that *in respect of itself* that kingdom is infinite anarchy, contradiction, division, and hate: only He asserts that *in relation to the kingdom of heaven* it is at one; there is one life in it and one soul in opposition to that. Just as a nation or kingdom may embrace within itself infinite parties, divisions, discords, jealousies, and heart-burnings; yet, if it is to subsist as a nation at all, it must not, *as regards other nations,* have lost its sense of unity; when it does so, of necessity it falls to pieces and perishes.

This accusation brought against the miracles of Christ, that they were done by the power of an evil magic, the heathen also sometimes used; but evidently having borrowed this weapon from the armoury of Jewish gainsayers. The heathen, however, had a method more truly their own of evading the force of the Christian miracles, which is now to consider.

2. THE HEATHEN (CELSUS, HIEROCLES, PORPHYRY)

A religion like the Jewish, which, besides God and the Angels in direct and immediate subordination to Him, left no spirits conceivable but those in rebellion against Him, the absolutely and entirely evil, this left no choice, when once the miracle was adjudged not to be from God, save to ascribe it to Satan. But it was otherwise in the heathen world, and with the "gods many" of polytheism. So long as these lived in the minds and thoughts of men, the argument from the miracles was easily evaded. For what at the utmost did they prove in respect of their author? What but this, that *a* god, it might be one of the higher, or it might be one of the middle powers, was with him? Wherefore should they yield exclusive allegiance to Him that wrought these works? The gods had spoken often by others also, had equipped them with powers equal to or greater than those claimed by his disciples for Jesus; yet no man therefore demanded for them that they should be recognized as absolute lords of the destinies of men. Æsculapius performed wonderful cures; Apollonius went about the world healing the sick, expelling demons, raising the dead; yet no man built upon these wonders a superstructure so immense as that which the Christians built upon the wonders of Christ.

Thus Celsus, as we learn from more than one passage in Origen's reply, adduces now the mythic personages of antiquity, now the magicians of a later date; though apparently with no very distinct purpose in his mind, but only with the feeling that somehow or other he can play them off against the divine Author of our religion, and defeat his claims to an allegiance of men such as excluded every other. Hierocles, governor of Bithynia, a chief instigator of the cruelties under Diocletian, followed in the same line. Having recounted various miracles wrought, as he affirms, by Apollonius, he proceeds thus: "Yet do we not account him who has done such things for a god, only for a man beloved of the gods: while the Christians, on the contrary, on the ground of a few insignificant wonder-works, proclaim their Jesus for a God."

This Apollonius, whose historical existence there seems no reason to call in question, was probably born about the time of the birth of Christ, and lived as far as into the reign of Nerva, A. D. 97. Save two or three isolated notices of an earlier date, the only record which we have of him is a *Life,* written by Philostratus, a rhetorician of the second century, and professing to be founded on contemporary documents, yet everywhere betraying its unhistoric character. It was composed indeed, as seems to me perfectly clear, with an eye to the life of our Lord; the parallels are too remarkable to have been the results of chance.

The arguments drawn from these parallels, so far as they were adduced in good faith and in earnest, have, of course, perished with the perishing of polytheism from the minds of men. Other miracles can no longer be played off against Christ's miracles; the choice which remains now is between these and none.

3. THE PANTHEISTIC (SPINOZA)

These two classes of assailants of the Scripture miracles, the Jewish and the heathen, allowed the miracles themselves to stand unquestioned as facts, but either challenged the source from which they came; or denied the consequences drawn from them by the Church. Not so the pantheistic deniers of the miracles, who assailed them not as being of the devil, not as insufficient proofs of Christ's claims of absolute lordship; but cut at their very root, denying that any miracle was possible, since it was contrary to the idea of God. For these opponents of the truth Spinoza may be said to bear the word. That objection is indeed only the necessary consequence of his philosophical system. The idea of freedom, as regards God, is saved; since, however, he affirms Him immanent in nature and not transcending it, this is only because He has Himself chosen these laws of nature as the one unchangeable manner of his working, and constituted them in his wisdom so elastic, that they shall prove, under all circumstances and in every need, the *adequate* organs and servants of his will. He is not bound to nature otherwise than by that, his own will. Still, however, Spinoza does affirm such a necessity. The *natura naturans* must unfold itself in the *natura naturata,* and thus excludes the possibility of any revelation, whereof the very essence is that it is a new beginning, a new unfolding by God of Himself to man, and especially excludes the miracle, which is itself at once the accompaniment, and itself a constituent part, of a revelation.

Let me here observe, that to deny that miracles can find a *fitting* place in God's moral and spiritual government of the world is one thing; to deny that they can find a *possible* place, that there is any room for them there, is another. The denial of their fitness, where honestly meant, involves no necessary assault on the essential attributes of God. With the denial of the *possibility* of miracles it is otherwise. In this denial there is in fact a withdrawal from Him of all which constitutes Him more than the animating principle of the world. He is no longer a God of freedom, a living God, above nature and independent of nature. Shut up and confined within this strait-waistcoat of nature, He is less favoured than some of the meanest of his creatures.

It would profit little to enter in detail on the especial charges which Spinoza brings against the miracle, as lowering, and un- worthy of, the idea of God. They are but the application to a particular point of the same charges which he brings against all revelation, namely, that to conceive any such is to dishonour, and cast a slight upon, God's great original revelation of Himself in nature and in man. With the miracle in particular he finds fault, as a bringing in of disorder into that creation, of which the only idea worthy of God is that of an unchangeable order. It is a making of God to contradict Himself, for the law which was violated by the miracle is as much God's law as the miracle which violated it. The answer to this objection has been already anticipated: the miracle is not a discord in nature, but the coming in of a higher harmony; not disorder, but instead of the order of earth, the order of heaven.

When, further, he imputes to the miracle that it rests on a false assumption of the position which man occupies in the uni- verse, flatters the notion that nature is to serve him, not he to bow to nature, it cannot be denied that it does rest on this assumption. But this were only a charge which would tell *against* it, supposing that true, which, so far from being truth, is indeed his first great falsehood of all, namely, that God is first a God *of nature,* and only a God *of men* as they find their place in the order of nature. But if, rather, man is "the crown of things," the end and object of all, if he be indeed the vicegerent of the Highest, the image of God, the first-fruits of his creatures, this world and all that belongs to it being but a school for the training of men, only having a worth and meaning when contemplated as such, then that the lower should serve, and, where need is, give way to the interests of the highest, were only beforehand to be expected.

Here, as is so often the case, something behind the miracle, something earlier in men's view of the relations between God and his creatures, has already determined whether they should accept or reject it, and this, long before they have arrived at the consideration of this specific matter.

4. The Sceptical (Hume)

Spinoza rested his objection to the miracles on the ground that the everlasting laws of the universe left no room for such; therefore, the form which the question in debate assumed in his hands was this, Are miracles (objectively) *possible?* Hume started his objection in altogether a different shape, namely, in this, Are miracles (subjectively) *credible?* He is a *doubter* of the possibility of arriving at any absolute truth. To this question Hume's answer is in the negative; or rather, in the true spirit of that philosophy which leaves everything in uncertainty, "It is always more probable that a miracle is false than true." Every miracle, he goes on to say, *is* a case of conflicting evidence. In its favour is the evidence of the attesting witnesses; against it the testimony of all experience which has gone before, and which witnesses for an unbroken order of nature. When we come to balance these against one another, the only case in which the evidence for the miracle could be admitted as prevailing would be that *in which the falseness or error of the attesting witnesses would be a greater miracle than the miracle which they affirm.* But no such case can occur. The evidence against a miracle having taken place is as complete as can be conceived. Even were the evidence in its favour as complete, it would only be proof against proof, and absolute suspension of judgment would be the wise man's part. But the evidence in favour of the miracle never makes claim to any such completeness. It is always more likely that the attesting witnesses were deceived, or were willing to deceive, than that the miracle took place. For, however many they may be, they must always be few compared with the multitudes who attest a fact which excludes their fact, namely, the uninterrupted succession of a natural order in the world; and those few, moreover, submitted to divers warping influences, from which the others, nature's witnesses, are altogether free. Therefore there is no case in which the evidence for any one miracle is able to outweigh the *a priori* evidence which is against all miracles. The argument, it will be seen, is sceptical throughout. Hume does not, like Spinoza, absolutely deny the possibility of a miracle; all he denies is that we can ever be convinced of one.

Here again, as on a former occasion, so long as we abide in the region of nature, miraculous and improbable, miraculous and incredible, may be admitted as convertible terms. But once lift up the whole discussion into a higher region, once acknowledge something higher than nature, a kingdom of God, and men the intended denizens of it, and the whole argument loses its strength and the force of its conclusions.

His argument is as that fabled giant, unconquerable so long as it is permitted to rest upon the earth out of which it sprang; but easily destroyed when once it is lifted into a higher world. It is not, as Hume would fain have us to believe, solely an intellectual question; but it is in fact the moral condition of men which will ultimately determine whether they will believe the Scripture miracles or not; this, and not the exact balance of argument on the one side or the other, which will cause this scale or that to kick the beam.

5. The Miracles Only Relatively Miraculous (Schleiermacher)

Another scheme for getting rid of the miraculous element in the miracle has been this: These works, it is said, were *relative* miracles, — miracles, in other words, for those in regard of whom they were first done, — as when a savage believes that a telescope has the power of bringing the far off instantaneously near, — but no miracles in themselves, being but in fact the anticipation of discoveries in the kingdom of nature, the works of one who, having penetrated deeper into her mysteries than those around him, could therefore wield powers which were unknown, and bring about results which were inexplicable, to them. It must be evident to the least thoughtful, that, however it may be sought to disguise the fact, the miracle does thus become no miracle and the doer of it can no longer be recognized as commanding nature in a way specifically different from other men, but only as one who has a clearer or earlier insight than others into her laws and the springs of her power. We have indeed here nothing else but a decently veiled denial of the miracle altogether. For thus it has no longer an eternal significance. With each enlargement of men's knowledge of nature a star in his crown of glory is extinguished, till at length it fades altogether into the light of common day, nay, rather declares that it was never more than a deceitful and meteor fire at the best.

Schleiermacher endeavors so to guard this view as that it shall appear an entire denial of the miracles, to dress it out and prevent its nakedness from appearing; but he does not, in fact, lift himself above it. Christ, he says, had not merely this deeper acquaintance with nature than any other that ever lived, but stands in a more inward connexion with nature. He is able to evoke, as from her hidden recesses and her most inward sanctuary, powers which none other could; although still powers which lay in her already. These facts, which seem exceptional, were deeply laid in the first constitution of the law; and now, at the turning-point of the world's history, by the providence of God, who had arranged all things from the beginning for the glory of his Son, did at his bidding emerge. Yet, single and without analogy as these "wonders of preformation" (for so one has called them) were, they belonged to the law as truly as when the aloe flowers, or is said to flower, once in a hundred years, it does this according to the law of its being. For ninety and nine years it would have seemed to men not to be the nature of the plant to flower, yet the flowering of the hundredth year is only the unfolding of a germ latent, so to say, in the heart of the plant from the beginning.

We see in this scheme that attempt to reconcile and atone between revelation and science, which was a main purpose of all Schleiermacher's writings. Yet is it impossible to accept the reconciliation which he offers; as it is really made, however skilfully the sacrifice may be concealed, altogether at the expense of the miracle — which, in fact, is no miracle, if it lay in nature already, if it was only the evoking of forces latent within, not a new thing, not the bringing in of the novel powers of a higher world; if the mysterious processes and powers by which those works were brought about, had been only undiscovered hitherto, and not undiscoverable, by the efforts of human inquiry.

Augustine has been sometimes quoted, but altogether unjustly, as favouring this scheme of the relatively miraculous. It is quite true that, when arguing with the heathen, he does demand why they refuse to give credence to the Scripture miracles, when they

believe so much that is inexplicable by any laws which their
experience supplied; that he instances some real, some also
entirely fabulous, phenomena of the natural world to which he
and they gave credence alike. But. it is not herein his meaning
to draw down the miracles to a level with natural appearances,
hitherto unexplained, but capable of and waiting their explanation. He did not merge the miracles in nature, but drew up a
portion of nature into the region of the miraculous. However
greatly as a natural philosopher he may have been here at fault,
yet all extenuating of the miracle was far from him; indeed he
ever refers it to the omnipotence of God as to its ultimate ground.

When he affirms that much *seems* to be against nature, but
nothing truly is, this may sound at first like the same statement
of the miraculous being such merely in relation to certain persons
and certain stages of our knowledge of this material world.
But it is only in sound that it is similar. Nature is for him but
the outward expression of the will of God; and all which he
affirms is, that God never can be contrary to God; that there
can be no conflict and collision of his wills; that whatever
comes in is as true an order, the result of as real a law, as
that which gives place to it; which must needs be, since it
has come in according to the will of God, which will is itself
the highest order, and law, and harmony.[1]

6. THE RATIONALISTIC (PAULUS)

The rise of rationalism may be looked at as an escape from
the conclusions of mere Deists concerning Christ's Person and
his Word, upon the part of some, who had indeed abandoned
the true faith of the Church concerning its Head, yet were not
prepared to give up the last lingering vestiges of their respect

---

[1] In the writings of Augustine (*Serm*. ccxlii 1) it is seen that he had perfectly seized
the essential property of a miracle, and distinguished it broadly from the relatively
miraculous, is plain from innumerable passages. Thus (*De Civ. Dei*, x. 16): "Miracles...
I speak not of those progidies which happen from time to time from natural causes,
occult indeed, yet constituted and arranged by divine providence, such monstrous births
of animals, and unusual appearances in heaven and earth."

for Holy Scripture and for Him of whom Scripture testified. What if it could be shown that Christ never professed to do any miracles, nor the sacred historians to record any? That it was only the lovers of, and cravers after, the marvellous, who had found any miracles there; — the books themselves having been intended to record merely natural events? Were not this an escape from the whole difficulty? The *divine,* it is true, in these narratives would disappear; but the *human* would be vindicated; the good faith, the honesty, the entire credibility of the Scripture historians, would remain unimpeached. And in Christ Himself there would be still that to which they could look up with reverence and love; they could still believe in Him as the truthful founder of a religion which they shrank from the thought of renouncing altogether. No longer being, as the Church declared Him, the worker of wonders, He would still abide for them, the highest pattern of goodness which the world hitherto had seen.

Their attempt was certainly a bold one. To suffer the sacred text to stand, and yet to find no miracles in it, did appear a hopeless task. For this, it must be always remembered, altogether distinguishes this system from later mythic theories, that it *does* accept the New Testament as historic throughout; it does appeal to the word of Scripture as the ground and proof of its assertions; its great assertion being that the Evangelists did not intend to relate miracles, but ordinary facts of everyday experience, works done by Jesus, now of friendship and humanity, now of medical skill, or other actions which from one cause or other seemed to them of sufficient significance to be worth recording. Thus Christ, they said, did not heal an impotent man at Bethesda, but only detected an impostor; He did not change water into wine at Cana, but brought in a new supply of wine when that of the house was exhausted; He did not walk on the sea, but on the shore; He did not raise Lazarus from the dead, but guessed from the description of his disease that he was only in a swoon, and happily found it as He had guessed.

This scheme, which many had already tried here and there, but which first appeared full blown and consistently carried through in the *Commentary* of Dr. Paulus, published in 1800, did not long survive in its first vigour. Every scholar, nay, every man who believed that language had any laws, was its natural enemy, for it stood only by the violation of all these laws. Even the very advance of unbelief was fatal to it, for in it there was a slight lingering respect to the Word of God. When men arose who did not shrink from the other alternative, who had no desire to hold by that Word at all, then there was nothing to hinder them from at once coming back to the common-sense view of the subject, namely that the Evangelists did at any rate *intend* to record supernatural events.

This scheme of interpretation, thus assailed from so many sides, and itself merely artificial, did not long hold its ground. And now, even in the land of its birth, it has entirely perished; on the one side a deeper faith, on the other a more rampant unbelief, have encroached on, and in the end wholly swallowed up, the territory which for a while is sought to occupy as its own.

7. The Historico-Critical (Woolston, Strauss)

The latest assault upon the miracles may not unfitly be termed the historico-critical. It declares that the records of them are so full of contradictions, psychological and other improbabilities, discrepancies between the account of one Evangelist and another, that upon close handling they crumble to pieces, and are unable to maintain their ground as history. Among the English Deists of the last century, Woolston especially addressed himself in this way to the undermining the historic credit of these narratives. When, in that great controversy which was raging in the early part of the last century, the defenders of revealed religion entrenched themselves behind the miracles, as defences from which they could never be driven, as irrefragable proofs of the divine origin of Christianity, Woolston undertook, by the engines of allegorical interpretation, to dislodge them from these also, and with this view published his notorious *Letters on the Miracles*. It is his manner in these to take certain miracles which Christ did, or which were wrought in relation to Him, two or three in a letter; he then seeks to show that, understood in their literal sense, they are stuffed so full with extravagances, contradictions, absurdities, that no reasonable man can suppose Christ actually to have wrought them; while as little could the Evangelists, as honest men, men who had the credit of their Lord at heart, have intended to record them as actually wrought, or desired us to receive them as other than allegories, spiritual truths clothed in the garb of historic events. The enormous difference between himself and those early Church writers, to whom he appeals, and whose views he professes to be only re-asserting, is this: they said, This history, being real, has also a deeper ideal sense; he upon the contrary, Since it is impossible that this history can be real, therefore it must have a spiritual significance. They build upon the establishment of the historic sense, he upon its ruins.

I shall not (as it is not needful) offend the Christian reader by the reproduction of any of his coarser ribaldry, which has sufficient cleverness to have proved mischievous enough; but will show by a single example the manner in which he seeks to detect weak points in the Scripture narratives. He is dealing with the miracle of the man sick of the palsy, who was let through the broken roof of the house where Jesus was, and thereupon healed (Mark ii. 1-12). But how, he demands, should there have been such a crowd to hear Jesus preach at Capernaum, where He was so well known, and so little admired? And then, if there was that crowd, what need of such urgent haste; it was but waiting an hour or two, and the multitude would have dispersed; "I should have thought their faith might have worked patience." Why did not Jesus tell the people to make way? Would they not have done so readily, since a miracle was the very thing they wanted to see? How should the pulleys, ropes, and ladder have been at hand to haul the sick man up? How strange that they should have had hatchets and other tools ready to hand, to break through the spars and rafters of the roof; and stranger still, that the good man of the house should have endured, without a remonstrance, his property to be so injured! How did those below escape without hurt from the falling tiles and plaster? And if there was a door in the roof, as some, to mitigate the difficulty, tell us, why did not Jesus go up to the roof, and there speak the healing word, and so spare all this trouble and damage and danger?

But enough;—it is evident that this style of objection could be infinitely multiplied. It is after this taking to pieces of the narrative, this triumphant showing, as he affirms, that it cannot stand in the letter, that Woolston proceeds, as a sort of salve, to say it may very well stand in its spirit, as an allegory and symbol of something else; and that so, and so only, it was intended. Thus what he offers by way of this higher meaning in the present case is as follows: By this poor man's palsy is signified "a dissoluteness of morals and unsteadiness of faith and principles, which is the condition of mankind at present, who want Jesus' help for the cure of it." The four bearers are the four Evangelists, "on whose faith and doctrine mankind is to be carried unto Christ." The house to the top of which he is to be carried is "the intellectual edifice of the world, otherwise called Wisdom's house." But "to the sublime sense of the Scriptures, called the top of the house, is man to be taken; he is not to abide in the low and literal sense of them." Then if he dare to "open the house of wisdom, he will presently be admitted to the presence and knowledge of Jesus."

Not very different is Strauss's own method of proceeding. He starts from the philosophic ground of Spinoza, that the miracle is impossible, since the laws of nature are the only and the necessary laws of God and of his manifestation; the strait waistcoat from which He cannot escape; and he then proceeds to the critical examination of the evangelical miracles in detail; but of course in each case to the trial of that which has been already implicitly tried and condemned. Thus, if he is ever at a loss, if any of the miracles give him trouble, he immediately falls back on his philosophic ground, and exclaims, "But if we admit it was thus, then we should have a miracle here; and we have started from this as our first principle, namely, that such is inconceivable." This mockery in every case he repeats, trying, one by one in particular, those which have all been condemned by him beforehand in the gross.

While Woolston professed to consider the miracles as the conscious clothing of spiritual truth, allegories devised artificially, and, so to speak, in cold blood, for the setting forth of the truths of the kingdom, Strauss gives them a freer birth and a somewhat nobler origin. They are the halo of glory with which the infant Church gradually and without any purposes of fraud clothed its Founder and Head. All that men had ever craved and longed for—deliverance from physical evil, dominion over the hostile powers of nature, victory over death itself,—they lent in larger abundance, in unrestrained fulness, to Him whom they felt greater than all. The Church in fact made or evolved its Christ, and not Christ his Church.

Here, as so often, we find the longings and cravings of men after a redemption, in the widest sense of that word, made to throw suspicion upon Him in whom these longings and cravings are affirmed to have been satisfied. But if we believe a divine life stirring at the root of our humanity, the depth and universality of such longings is a proof rather that they were meant some day to find their satisfaction, and not always to be mere hopes and dreams. And if so, in whom, save in Him whom we preach and believe—in whom, that is, but in Christ? What other beside Him could, with the slightest show of reason, be put forward as a fulfiller of the world's hopes, as realizer of the world's dreams?

CHAPTER VI.

The Apologetic Worth of the Miracles

A MOST interesting question remains. What place in the marshalling and presenting the evidences of Revelation should be allotted to the miracles? what service can they render here? The circumstances have been already noticed which hindered them from taking a very prominent place in the early apologies for the faith.[1] The Christian miracles had not as yet sufficiently extricated themselves from the multitude of false miracles, nor was Christ sufficiently discerned and distinguished from the various wonder-workers of his own and of past ages; and thus, even if men had admitted his miracles to be true and godlike, they would have been hardly nearer to the acknowledging of Christianity as the one faith, or to the accepting of Christ as "the way, the truth, and the life."

A far more prominent position has been assigned them in later times, especially during the last two centuries; and the tone and temper of modern theology abundantly explain the greater, sometimes the undue, because the exclusive, prominence, which in this period they have assumed.

Now this, which caused so much to be thrust greatly out of sight, as generally the deeper mysteries of our faith, which brought about a slight of the inner arguments for the truth of Revelation, caused the argument from the miracles to assume a disproportionate importance. A value too exclusive was set on

---

[1] Thus, in the *Apologies* of Justin Martyr, they are scarcely made use of at all. It is otherwise indeed with Arnobius, who (*Adv. Gen.* i. 42) lays much stress on them. Speaking of the truth of Christianity and of Christ's mission, he says, "There is no greater proof than the credibility of the acts done by Him, than the credibility of his works of power," and then appeals through ten eloquent chapters to his miracles. Augustine too is strong on their apologetic worth: thus in his *Confessions:* "Miracles lead us to faith, and are mainly wrought for the sake of unbelievers."

them; they were rent away from the truths for which they witnessed, and which witnessed for them,—only too much like seals torn off from the document which at once *they* rendered valid, and which in return gave importance to them. And thus, in this unnatural isolation, separated from Christ's person and doctrine, the whole burden of proof was laid on them. *They* were the apology for Christianity, the reason men should give for the faith which was in them.

It is not hard to see the motives which led to this. Men wanted an *absolute* demonstration of the Christian faith,—one which, objectively, should be equally good for every man: they desired to bring the matter to the same sort of proof as exists for a problem in mathematics or a proposition in logic. Yet the state of mind which made men so anxious to find for themselves, or to furnish for others, proofs of this nature, was not altogether a healthy one. It was plain that *their* faith had become very much an external historic one, who thus eagerly looked round for outward evidences, and found a value only in such; instead of turning in upon themselves as well, for evidence that they had "not followed cunningly devised fables," and saying, "We *know* the things which we believe—they are to us truer than aught else can be, for we have the witness of the Spirit for their truth. We have proved these things to be true, for they have come to us in demonstration of the Spirit and in power." In place of such an appeal to those mighty influences which Christ's words and works exercise on every heart that receives them, to their transforming, transfiguring power, to the miracles of grace which are the heritage of every one who has believed to salvation, instead of urging on the gainsayers in the very language of the Lord, "If any man will do his will, he shall know of the doctrine whether it be of God" (John vii. 17), this all as vague and mystical (instead of being seen to be, as it truly was, the most sure and certain of all) was thrown into the background. Men were afraid to trust themselves and their cause to evidences like these, and would know of no other statement of the case than this barren and hungry one:—Christianity is a divine revelation, and this the miracles which accompanied its first promulgation prove.

What we first find fault with here is the wilful abandonment of such large regions of proof, which the Christian Apologist ought triumphantly to have occupied as his own—the whole region, mainly and chiefly, of the inner spiritual life; the foregoing of any appeal to the mysterious powers of regeneration and renewal, which are ever found to follow upon a true affiance on Him who is the Giver of this faith, and who has pledged Himself to these very results in those who rightly receive it.

To these proofs he might at least have ventured an appeal, when seeking not to convince an unbeliever, but, as would be often his aim, to carry one that already believed round the whole circle of the defences of his position, to make him aware of the relative strength of each, to give him a scientific insight into the grounds on which his faith rested. Here, at any rate, the appeal to what he had himself known and tasted of the powers of the world to come, might well have found room. For, to use the words of Coleridge, "Is not a true, efficient conviction of a moral truth, is not *the creating of a new heart,* which collects the energies of a man's whole being in the focus of the conscience, the one essential miracle, the same and of the same evidence to the ignorant and to the learned, which no superior skill can counterfeit, human or demoniacal; is it not emphatically that leading of the Father, without which no man can come to Christ; is it not that implication of doctrine in the miracle, and of miracle in the doctrine, which is the bridge of communication between the senses and the soul;—that predisposing warmth which renders the understanding susceptible of the specific impressions from the history, and from all other outward seals of testimony?" And even were the argument with one who had never submitted himself to these blessed powers, and to whose experience therefore no like appeal could be made, yet even for him there is the outward utterance of this inward truth, in that which he could not deny, save as he denied or was ignorant of everything, which would make him one to be argued with at all,—the standing miracle, I mean, of a Christendom "commensurate and almost synonymous with the civilized world," —the mighty changes which this religion of Christ has wrought in the earth,—the divine fruits which it everywhere has borne, —the new creation which it has everywhere brought about,— the manner in which it has taken its place in the world, not as a forcible intruder, but finding all that world's preëstablished harmonies ready to greet and welcome it, to give it play and room,—philosophy, and art, and science practically confessing that only under it could they attain their highest perfection, that in something they had all been dwarfed and stunted and incomplete till it came. Little as it wears of the glory which it ought, yet it wears enough to proclaim that its origin has been more than mundane. Surely from a Christendom, even such as it shows itself now, it is fair to argue back to a Christ such as the Church receives, as the only adequate cause. It is an oak which from no other acorn could have unfolded itself into so tall and stately a tree.

It is true that in this there is an abandoning of the attempt to put the proof of Christianity into the same form as that of a proposition in an exact science. There is no more the claim made of giving to it that kind of certainty. But this, which may seem at first sight a loss, is indeed a gain; for the argument for all which as Christians we believe, is in very truth not logical and single, but moral and cumulative; and the endeavour to substitute a formal proof, where the deepest necessities of the soul demand a moral, is one of the most grievous shocks which

the moral sense can receive, as it is also a most fruitful source
of unbelief. Few in whose hands books of Evidences constructed
on this scheme have fallen, but must painfully remember the
shock which they suffered from their acquaintance with these—
how it took them, it may be, no little time to recover the healthy
tone of their minds, and the confidence of their faith; and how,
only by falling back upon what they themselves had felt and
known of the living power of Christ's words and doctrine in their
own hearts, could they escape from the injurious influences, the
seeds of doubt and misgiving, which these books had now, for
the first time perhaps, sown in their minds. They must remember
how they asked themselves, in deep inner trouble of soul: "Are
these indeed the grounds, and the only grounds, the sole founda-
tions on which the whole superstructure of my spiritual life
reposes? Is this all that I have to answer? Are these, and no more,
the reasons of the faith that is in me?" And then, if at any moment there arose a suspicion that some link in this chain of outward proof was wanting, or was too weak to bear all the weight
which was laid upon it,—and men will be continually tempted
to try the strength of that to which they have trusted all,—
there was nothing to fall back upon, with which to scatter and
put to flight suspicions and misgivings such as these. And that
such should arise, at least in many minds, is inevitable; for how
many points, as we have seen, are there at which a suspicion
may intrude. Is a miracle possible? Is a miracle provable? Were
the witnesses of these miracles competent? Did they not too
lightly admit a supernatural cause, when there were adequate
natural ones which they failed to note? These works may have
been good for the eye-witnesses, but what are they for me?
Does a miracle, admitting it to be a real one, authenticate the
teaching of Him who has wrought it And these doubts and
questionings might be multiplied without number. Happy the
man, and he only happy, who, if the outworks of his faith are
at any time thus assailed, can betake himself to an impregnable

inner citadel, from whence in due time to issue forth and repossess even those exterior defences, who can fall back on those inner grounds of belief, in which there can be no mistake, the testimony of the Spirit, which is above and better than all.[2]

And as it is thus with him, who sincerely desiring to believe, is only unwillingly disturbed with doubts and suggestions, which he would give worlds to be rid of for ever, so not less the expectation that by arguments thrown into strict syllogistic forms there is any compelling to the faith one who does not wish to believe, is absurd, and an expectation which all experience contradicts. All that he is, and all that he is determined to be, has pledged him to an opposite conclusion. Rather than believe that a miracle has taken place, a miracle from the upper world, and connected with precepts of holiness, to which precepts he is resolved to yield no obedience, he will take refuge in any the most monstrous supposition of fraud, or ignorance, or folly, or collusion. If no such solution presents itself, he will wait for such, rather than accept the miracle, with the hated adjunct of the truth which it confirms. In what different ways the same miracle of Christ wrought upon different spectators! He raised a man from the dead; here was the same outward fact for all; but how diverse the effects!—some believed, and some went and told the Pharisees (John xi. 45, 46). Heavenly voices were heard,—and some said it thundered, so dull and inarticulate had those sounds become to them, while others knew that they were voices wherein was the witness of the Father to his own Son (John xii. 28-30).

Are then, it may be asked, the miracles to occupy no place at all in the array of proofs for the certainty of the things which we have believed? So far from this, a most important place. Our loss would be irreparable, if they were absent from our sacred history, if we could not point to them there. It is

---

[2] See the admirable words of Calvin, *Instit.* i. 7, §§ 4, 5, on the Holy Scripture as ultimately its own proof.

not too much to say that this absence would be fatal. There are indeed two miracles, that of the Incarnation and that of the Resurrection, round which the whole scheme of redemption revolves, and without which it would cease to be a redemptive scheme at all. But we are speaking here not of miracles whereof Christ was the subject, but of those which he wrought; and of them too we affirm that they belong to the very idea of a Redeemer, which would remain altogether incomplete without them. They are not, what Lessing would have them, a part of the scaffolding of Revelation; which, as such a scaffolding, yielded a temporary service; but which, now that the building is finished and stands complete without them, retain no further significance; and cannot be considered binding on any man's faith. They are rather a constitutive element of the revelation of God in Christ. We could not conceive of Him as not doing such works; and those to whom we presented Him as Lord and Saviour might very well answer, "Strange, that One should come to deliver all other men from the bondage of nature which was crushing them, and should yet Himself have been subject to its heaviest laws,—Himself 'Wonderful' (Isai. ix. 6), and yet his appearance accompanied by no corresponding wonders in nature, —claiming to be the Life, and yet Himself helpless in the encounter with death; however much He may have promised in word, never realizing any part of his promises in deed; giving nothing in hand, no first-fruits of power, no pledges of greater things to come." They would have a right to ask, "Why did He give no signs that He came to connect the visible with the invisible world? why did He nothing to break the yoke of custom and experience, nothing to show men that the constitution which He professed to reveal has a true foundation?"[3] And who would not own that they had reason here, that a Saviour who so bore Himself during his earthly life, and his actual daily encounter

---

[3] Maurice, *The Kingdom of Christ*, vol. ii. p. 264.

with evil, would bring into most serious question his right to a Saviour's name? that He must needs show Himself, if He were to meet the wants of men, mighty not only in word but in work? that claiming more than a man's authority He should display more than a man's power?[4]

When we find fault with the use often made of these works, it is only because they have been forcibly severed from the whole complex of Christ's life and doctrine, and presented to the contemplation of men apart from these; because, while on his head are "many crowns" (Rev. xix. 12), one only has been singled out in proof that He is King of kings and Lord of lords. The miracles have been spoken of as though they borrowed nothing from the truths which they confirmed, but those truths everything from the miracles by which they were confirmed; when, indeed, the true relation is one of mutual interdependence, the miracles proving the doctrines, and the doctrines approving the miracles, and both held together for us in a blessed unity, in the person of Him who spake the words and did the works, and through the impress of highest holiness and of absolute truth and goodness, which that person leaves stamped on our souls;—so that it may be more truly said that we believe the miracles for Christ's sake, than Christ for the miracles' sake. Neither when we thus affirm that the miracles prove the doctrine, and the doctrine the miracles, are we arguing in a circle: rather we are receiving the sum total of the impression which this divine revelation is intended to make on us, instead of taking an impression only partial and one-sided.

---

[4] It was the fatal weakness of Mahomet, and from many utterances of his it is plain that he constantly felt it to be such, that he could show no miracles with which to attest his mission as divine. It is true that in a measure he won acceptance for himself and for his teaching without them; but he did this by throwing the sword, where Christ had thrown the cross, into the scale.

MIRACLES

CHAPTER I.

The Changing of the Water Into Wine

JOHN ii. 1-11.

THIS *beginning of miracles* is as truly an introduction to all other miracles which Christ wrought, as the parable of the Sower to all other parables which He spoke (Mark iv. 13). No other miracle has so much of prophecy in it; no other, therefore, would have inaugurated so fitly the whole future work of the Son of God. For that work might be characterised throughout as an ennobling of the common, and a transmuting of the mean; a turning of the water of earth into the wine of heaven.

And the third day there was a marriage in Cana of Galilee—on the third day, no doubt, after that on which Philip and Nathanael (i. 43) had attached themselves to Him. *And the mother of Jesus was there.* The absolute silence of Scripture leaves hardly a doubt that Joseph was dead before Christ's open ministry began. He is last expressly mentioned on occasion of the Lord's visit as a child to the Temple (Luke ii. 41); which, however, he must for a certain period have overlived (ver. 51). *And both Jesus was called, and his disciples, to the marriage.* These, invited with their Master, and, no doubt, mainly to do honour to their Master, are probably not the Twelve, but those five only whose calling has just before been recorded, Andrew and Peter, Philip and Nathanael (Bartholomew?), and the fifth, probably the Evangelist himself; who will thus have been an eye-witness of the miracle which he records. Him, as was seen long ago, we may with tolerable confidence recognize in the second but unnamed disciple, whom the Baptist detached from himself, that he might attach him to the Lord (John i. 35, 40). It is in St. John's favourite manner to preserve an incognito of this kind

63

(cf. xiii. 23; xviii. 15; xix. 26, 35), drawing away all attention from himself the teller, and fixing it on the events which he is telling.

None need wonder to find the Lord of life at this festival; for he came to sanctify all human life,—to consecrate its times of joy, as its times of sorrow; the former, as all experience teaches, needing above all such a consecration as only his presence, bodily or spiritual, can give. He was there, and by his presence there struck the key-note to the whole tenor of his future ministry. He should not be as another Baptist, a wilderness preacher, withdrawing himself from the common paths of men. His should be at once a harder and a higher task, to mingle with and purify the daily life of men, to bring out the glory of which was everywhere hidden there.[1] How precious is his witness here against an indolent and cowardly readiness to give up to the world, or to the devil, aught which, in itself innocent, is capable of being drawn up into the higher world of holiness, even as it is in danger of sinking down and coming under the law of the flesh and of the world! Nor is it without its significance, that this should have been *a marriage,* which He "adorned and beautified with his presence and first miracle that He wrought." No human relation is the type of so deep a spiritual mystery (cf. iii. 29; Matt. ix. 15; xxii. 1-14; xxv. 10; Rev. xix. 7; xxi. 2, 9; xxii. 17; 2 Cor. xi. 2), so worthy therefore of the highest honour. He foresaw too that, despite of this, some hereafter should arise in his Church who would despise marriage (1 Tim. iv. 3), or, if not despise, yet fail to give the Christian family all its dignity and honour. These should find no countenance from Him.[2]

---

[1] Augustine, or another under his name (*Serm.* xcii. *Appendix*): "He who took upon Him to wear our flesh did not scorn the conversation of men; nor did He despise the worldly institutions which He had come to correct. He was present at a marriage to sanction the bonds of concord."

[2] What a contrast does his presence here offer to the manner in which even a St. Cyprian yields up these very marriage festivals as occasions where purity must suffer; so that his counsel is, not to dispute them with the world, to vindicate them anew for holiness and for God, but only to avoid them altogether (*De Hab. Virg.* 3).

And when they wanted wine, — or, which is a better rendering
(R.V.), *when the wine failed,* — *the mother of Jesus saith unto
him, They have no wine.* His and his disciples' presence, un-
looked for perhaps, as of those just arrived from a journey, may
have increased beyond expectation the number of the guests; and
so the provision made for their entertainment have fallen short.
The Mother of Jesus from one reason or another, did not account it unseemly to interfere with, and in some sort to guide,
the festal arrangements.[3] Perhaps she was near of kin to the
bridegroom or the bride; at all events she was concerned at the
embarrassments of that humble household, and would willingly
have removed them. Yet what exactly she expected from her
divine Son, when she thus brought their need before Him, is
not so easy to determine. Something it is clear she did expect;
and this, like the message of the sisters of Bethany, "He whom
Thou lovest is sick" (John xi. 3), must be regarded as an implicit prayer. She could not, from anterior displays of his power
and grace (for see ver. 11), have now been emboldened to look
for further manifestations of the same. Some indeed take not so
absolutely the denial of all miracles preceding, but with this
limitation understood:—this was the first of his mighty works
wherein He *showed forth* his glory; other such works He may
have performed already in the inner circle of his family, and
thus have led them to expect more open displays of his grace and
power. But, without evading thus the Evangelist's plain declaration, we may well understand how she, who had kept and
pondered in her heart all the tokens and prophetic intimations
of the coming glory of her Son (Luke ii. 19, 51), should believe that in Him powers were latent, which, however He had
restrained them until now, He could and would put forth,
whenever a fit time had arrived. This is more probable than that
she had no definite purpose in these words; but only turned

---

[3] Lightfoot (*Harmony*, in loc.; cf. Greswell, *Dissert*, vol. ii. p. 120) supposes it
a marriage in the house of Mary (John xix. 25), wife of Cleophas.

to Him now, as having ever found Him a wise counsellor in least things as in greatest.

But whatever may have been the motives of her interference, it promises at first no good result. *Jesus saith unto her, Woman, what have I to do with thee? mine hour is not yet come.* Roman Catholic expositors have been very anxious to rid this answer of every shadow of rebuke or blame. Entire treatises have been written with this single purpose. Now it is quite true that in the address *Woman* there is nothing of indignity or harshness, though there may be the sound of such to an English ear. In his tenderest words to his mother from the cross, He employs the same address, "*Woman*, behold thy son" (John xix. 26). Indeed the compellation cannot fail to have something solemn in it, wherever the dignity of woman is felt. But it is otherwise with the words following, *What have I to do with thee?* All expositors of the early Church have found in them more or less of reproof and repulse; the Roman Catholics themselves admit the *appearance* of such; only they deny the reality. He so replied, they say, to teach *us*, not *her*, that higher respects than those of flesh and blood moved Him to the selecting of that occasion for the first putting forth of his divine power.[4] Most certainly it was to teach this; but to teach it first to her, who from her wondrous position as the "blessed among women" was more than any other, in danger of forgetting it; and in her to teach it to us all. "She had not yet," says Chrysostom, "that opinion of Him, which she ought, but because she bare Him, counted that, after the manner of other mothers, she might in all things command *Him*, whom it more became her to reverence and worship as her Lord." The true parallel to this passage, and that throwing most light on it, is Matt. xii. 46-50.

---

[4] Maldonatus: "He assumed the appearance of blaming his mother, when He blamed her very little, in order that He might show that not out of regard to man, or to the ties of blood, did He work the miracle, but out of pure charity, and for the manifestation of his nature."

Yet, with all this, any severity which this answer may seem to carry with it in the reading was mitigated, as we cannot doubt, in the manner of its speaking. For when she *saith unto the servants, Whatsoever he saith unto you, do it,* it is evident she read, and, as the sequel shows, rightly read, a "Yes" latent in his "No." Luther bids us here to imitate her faith, who, nothing daunted by the semblance of a refusal, reads between the lines of this refusal a better answer to her prayer; is confident that even the infirmity which clave to it shall not defeat it altogether; is so confident of this, as to indicate not obscurely the very manner of its granting. And yet this confidence of hers in his new interposition, following so close as it does on that announcement of his, *Mine hour is not yet come,* is not without its difficulty. If they were not interpreted by the event, these words might seem to defer not for some briefest interval the manifestation of his glory, but to postpone it altogether to some remote period of his ministry. Indeed, his *hour* is generally, most of all in the language of St. John, the hour of his passion, or of his departure from the world (vii. 30; viii. 20; xii. 23, 27; xiii. 1; xvii. 1). Here, however, and perhaps at vii. 6, it indicates a time close at hand. So she rightly understood it. Not till the wine was wholly exhausted would his *hour* have arrived. All other help must fail, before the *hour* of the great Helper will have struck.[5] Then will be time to act, when by the entire failure of the wine, manifest to all, the miracle shall be above all suspicion; else, in Augustine's words, He might seem rather to *mingle* elements than to *change* them.

Very beautiful is the facility with which our Lord yields Himself to the supply, not of the absolute wants merely, but of the superfluities, of others; yet this, as I must believe, not so much for the guests' sake, as for that of the bridal pair, whose marriage

---

[5] Calvin puts it well: "He signifies that his inaction up to this point has not proceeded from heedlessness or sloth. At the same time He indicates that the matter shall be his care when the opportunity comes. On the one hand He blames his mother for her unseasonable haste, on the other He gives her hope of the miracle."

feast, by the unlooked-for short-coming of the wine, was in danger of being exposed to mockery and scorn. We may contrast this his readiness to aid others with his stern refusal to minister by the same almighty power to his own extremest necessities. He who turned water into wine might have made bread out of stones (Matt. iv. 4) ; but spreading a table for others, He is content to hunger and to thirst Himself.

The conditions under which the miracle was accomplished are all such as exclude every suspicion of collusion. *And there were set there six waterpots of stone, after the manner of the purifying of the Jews, containing two or three firkins apiece.*[6] *Jesus saith unto them, Fill the waterpots with water. And they filled them up to the brim.* They were vessels for *water,* not for *wine;* thus none could insinuate that probably some sediment of wine remained in them, which, lending a flavour to water poured on it, formed thus a thinnest kind of wine; as every suggestion of the kind is excluded by the praise which the ruler of the feast bestows upon the new supply (ver. 10). The circumstance of these vessels being at hand is accounted for. They were there by no premeditated plan, but in accordance with the customs and traditionary observances of the Jews in the matter of washing (Matt. xv. 2; xxiii. 25; Mark vii. 2-4; Luke xi. 38) ; for this seems more probable than that this *purifying* has reference to any distinctly commanded legal observances. The quantity, too, which these vessels contained, was enormous; not such as might have been brought in unobserved, but *two or three firkins apiece.* And the vessels were empty; those therefore who on that bidding had filled them, as they knew, with water, became themselves by this act of theirs witnesses to the reality of the miracle. But for this it might only have appeared, as in fact

---

[6] Westcott quotes from Clarke's *Travels,* vol. ii. p. 445, a remarkable illustration. He writes: "Walking among these ruins [at Cana] we saw large massy stone waterpots, not preserved or exhibited as relics, but lying about, disregarded by the present inhabitants. From their appearance and the number of them, it was quite evident that the practice of keeping water in large stone pots holding from eighteen to twenty-seven gallons, was once common in the country."

it did only appear to the ruler of the feast, that the wine came from some unexpected quarter; he *knew not whence it was; but the servants which drew the water,*—not, that is, the water now made wine, but who *had drawn* the simple element on which the Lord put forth his transmuting powers—*knew.*

And he saith unto them. Draw out now, and bear unto the governor of the feast. It has been debated whether this *governor* was himself one of the guests, set either by general consent or by the selection of the host over the banquet; or a chief attendant, charged with ordering the course of the entertainment, and overlooking the ministrations of the inferior servants. The analogy of Greek and Roman usages points him out as himself a guest, invested with this office for the time; and a passage in the Apocrypha shows that the custom of selecting such a master of the revels was in use among the Jews. Indeed the freedom of remonstrance which he allows himself with the bridegroom seems decisive of his position, that it is not that of an underling, but an equal. It was for him to taste and distribute the wine; to him, therefore, the Lord commanded that this should be first brought, even in this little matter allowing and honouring the established order and usage of society, and giving to every man his due.

And they bare it, water now no more, but wine. Like other acts of creation, or, more strictly, of *becoming,* this of the water becoming wine is withdrawn from sight. That which is poured into the jars as water is drawn out as wine; but the actual process of the change we toil in vain to conceive: And yet in truth it is in no way stranger, save in the rapidity with which it is effected, than that which is every day going forward among us; but to which use and custom have so dulled our eyes, that commonly we do not marvel at it at all; and, because we can call it by its name, suppose that we have discovered its secret, or rather that there is no secret in it to discover. He who each

year prepares the wine in the grape, causing it to absorb, and
swell with, the moisture of earth and heaven, to transmute this
into nobler juices of its own, did now concentrate all those
slower processes into a single moment, and accomplish in an
instant what usually He takes many months to accomplish. This
analogy does not help us to understand what the Lord at this
time did, but yet brings before us that in it He was working in
the line of (*above,* indeed, but not *across,* or counter to) his
more ordinary operations, the unnoticed miracles of everyday
nature. That which this had peculiarly its own, which took it
out from the order of nature, was the power and will by which
all the intervening steps of these tardier processes were over-
leaped, their methods superseded, and the result attained in an
instant.

*When the ruler of the feast had tasted the water that was
made wine, and knew not whence it was: (but the servants
which drew the water knew;) the governor of the feast called
the bridegroom,*—called, that is, to him, and with something
of a festive exclamation, not unsuitable to the season, exclaimed:
*Every man at the beginning doth set forth good wine; and when
men have well drunk, then that which is worse: but thou hast
kept the good wine until now.* Many interpreters have been very
anxious to rescue the word, which we have rendered *well drunk,*
and the R. V. *drunk freely,* from implying aught of excess;[7] lest
it might appear that we had here one of those unseemly revels
which too often disgraced a marriage, — with all the difficulties
of Christ's sanctioning by his presence so great an abuse of God's
gifts, and, stranger still, ministering by his divine power to a still
larger excess. But there is no need to deal thus anxiously with
the word. We may be quite sure there was no such excess here;
for to this the Lord would as little have given allowance by his
presence, as He would have helped it forward by a special

_____
[7] Cf. *Gen.* xliii. 34, LXX, where the same word occurs; and still more to the
point, Ps. xxxvii. 9.

wonder-work of his own. *The ruler of the feast* does but refer to a common practice. There is no special reference to the guests present, but only to the corrupt customs and fashions too common in the world.

Of a piece with this is *their* unworthy objection, to whom the miracle is incredible, seeing that, even if the Lord did not minister to an excess already commenced, still by the creation of "so large and perilous a quantity of wine" (for the quantity was enormous[8]), He would have put temptation in men's way. With the same justice every good gift of God which is open to any possible abuse, every plenteous return of the field, every large abundance of the vineyard, might be accused of being a temptation put in men's way; and so in some sort it is (cf. Luke xii. 16), a proving of men's temperance and moderation in the midst of abundance. For man is not to be perfected by exemption *from* temptation, but rather by victory *in* temptation; and the only temperance which has any value, which indeed deserves the name, has its source not in the scanty supply, but in the strong self-restraint. That this gift should be large, was what we might have looked for. He, a King, gave as became a king.

But the governor of the feast, who only meant to describe a sordid economy of this world, gave utterance to a deeper truth than he meant. Such at any rate may be most fitly superinduced upon his words; nothing less than the whole difference between the order of Christ's giving and of the world's. The world does indeed give its best and choicest, its *good wine,* first, but has only poorer substitutes at the last. *When men have well drunk,* when their spiritual palate is blunted, when they have lost the discernment between moral good and evil, then it palms on them that which is worse; what it would not have dared to offer at the first,—coarser pleasures, viler enjoyments, the drink

---

[8] Each of these six vessels did in round numbers hold some twenty gallons or more.

of a more deadly wine. Those who worship the world must confess at last that it is best represented by that great image which Nebuchadnezzar beheld in his dream (Dan. ii. 31); the head showing as fine gold, but the material growing ever baser, till it finishes with the iron and clay at the last.

But it is otherwise with the guests of Christ, the heavenly bridegroom. He ever reserves for them whom *He* has bidden, *the good wine* unto the last. In the words of the most eloquent of our divines, "The world presents us with fair language, promising hopes, convenient fortunes, pompous honours, and these are the outside of the bowl; but when it is swallowed, these dissolve in an instant, and there remains bitterness and the malignity of coloquintida. Every sin smiles in the first address, and carries light in the face, and honey in the lip; but when we *have well drunk,* then comes *that which is worse,* a whip with six strings, fears and terrors of conscience, and shame and displeasure, and a caitiff disposition, and diffidence in the day of death. But when after the manner of purifying of the Christians, we fill our waterpots with water, watering our couch with our tears, and moistening our cheeks with the perpetual distillations of repentance, then Christ turns our water into wine, first penitents and then communicants — first waters of sorrow and then the wine of the chalice; . . . for Jesus keeps the best wine to the last, not only because of the direct reservations of the highest joys till the nearer approaches of glory, but also because our relishes are higher after a long fruition than at the first essays, such being the nature of grace, that it increases in relish as it does in fruition, every part of grace being new duty and new reward."[9]

This beginning of miracles did Jesus in Cana of Galilee. The Evangelist expressly and pointedly excludes from historic credit the miracles of the Infancy, which are found in such rank

---

[9] Jeremy Taylor, *Life of Christ.*

abundance in nearly all the apocryphal Gospels; for, of course, he does not mean that this was the first miracle which Jesus wrought in Cana, but that this miracle in Cana was the first which He wrought; and the Church has ever regarded these words as decisive on this point. The statement is important, and connects itself with one main purpose of St. John in his Gospel, namely, to repel and remove all unreal notions concerning the person of his Lord—notions which nothing would have helped more to uphold than those merely phantastic and capricious miracles which are ascribed to this Infancy.

Of none less or lower than the Son could it be affirmed that He *manifested forth his glory;* every lesser or lower would have manifested forth the glory of God. As God, as therefore Lord of glory (Jam. ii. 1), He rays forth light from Himself, and this effluence and effulgence is *his glory* (John i. 14; Matt. xvi. 27; Mark viii. 38). The Evangelist, as one cannot doubt, has Isai. xl. 5 — "and the glory of the Lord shall be revealed" — in his eye, claiming that in this act of Christ's those words were fulfilled. Of this "glory of the Lord" we hear continually in the Old Testament: thus Exod. xvi. 7; Ezek. i. 28; iii. 23; ix. 23; x. 18; xi. 23; xxxix. 21; xliii. 2. While He tabernacled as the Son of Man upon earth it was for the most part hidden. The veil of flesh which He had consented to wear concealed it from the sight of men. But now, in this work of grace and power, it burst through the covering which concealed it, revealing itself to the eyes of his disciples; they "beheld his glory, the glory as of the only begotten of the Father." *And his disciples believed on him* (cf. xvi. 30, 31). The work, besides its more immediate purpose, had this further result; it confirmed, strengthened, exalted their faith, who, already believing in Him, were thus the more capable of receiving an increase of faith — of being lifted from faith to faith, advanced from faith in an earthly teacher to faith in a heavenly Lord[10] (1 Kin. xvii. 24).

This first miracle of the New Covenant has its inner mystical meaning. The first miracle of Moses was a turning of water into blood (Exod. vii. 20); and this had its fitness; for the law, which came by Moses, was a ministration of death, and working wrath (2 Cor. iii. 6-9). But the first miracle of Christ was a turning of water into wine, this too a meet inauguration of all which should follow, for his was a ministration of life; He came, the dispenser of that true wine which makes glad the heart of man (Ps. civ. 15). This prophetic aspect of the miracle we must by no means miss. He who turned now the water into wine, should turn in like manner the poorer dispensation, the thin and watery elements of the Jewish religion (Heb. vii. 18), into richer and nobler, into the gladdening wine of a higher faith. Nor less do we behold symbolized here, that whole work which the Son of God is evermore accomplishing in the world, — ennobling all that He touches, making saints out of sinners, angels out of men, and in the end heaven out of earth, a new paradise of God out of the old wilderness of the world. For the prophecy of the world's regeneration, of the day in which his disciples shall drink of the fruit of the vine new in his kingdom, is here. In this humble supper we have the rudiments of the glorious festival, at the arrival of which his *hour* shall have indeed come, who is Himself the true Bridegroom, even as his Church is the Bride.

---

[10] This is plainly the true explanation (in the words of Ammonius, "They received an increase of their faith in Him," of Grotius, "They are said to have believed on Him as believing more firmly").

CHAPTER II

The Healing of the Nobleman's Son

JOHN iv. 46-54.

S*O Jesus came again into Cana of Galilee, where he made the water wine.* It is altogether in St. John's manner thus to identify a place or person by some single circumstance which has made them memorable in the Church for ever; thus compare vii. 50; xix. 39; again, i. 44; xii. 21; and again, xiii. 23, 25; xxi. 20. *And there was a certain nobleman, whose son was sick at Capernaum* — possibly, as by some has been supposed,[1] Chuza, "Herod's steward," whose wife, remarkably enough, appears among the holy women that ministered to the Lord of their substance (Luke viii. 3). Only some mighty and marvellous work of this kind would have drawn a steward of Herod's, with his family, into the Gospel net. Others have suggested Manaen, the foster-brother of Herod (Acts xiii. 1). But all this is merest guesswork. What we know of him is this, that whether one of these, or some other not elsewhere named in Scripture, *when he heard that Jesus was come out of Judaea into Galilee, he went unto him, and besought him that he would come down, and heal his son: for he was at the point of death.* From a certain severity which speaks out in our Lord's reply, *Except ye see signs and wonders, ye will not believe,* we conclude that this petitioner was one *driven* to Jesus by the strong constraint of an outward need, a need which no other but He could supply (Isai. xxvi. 16), rather than one *drawn* by the inner necessities and desires of his soul. Sharing in the carnal temper of the Jews in general (for the plural, *ye will not believe,* is meant to include many in a common condemnation), he had (hitherto,

---

[1] Lightfoot, Chemnitz, and others.

at least) no organ for perceiving the glory of Christ as it shone forth in his person and in his teaching. *Signs and wonders* might compel him to a belief, but nothing else; how unlike in this to those Samaritans whom the Lord had just quitted, and who, without a miracle, had "believed because of his word" (John iv. 41). But "the Jews require a sign" (1 Cor. i. 22), and this one, in the poverty of his present faith, straitened and limited the power of the Lord. The Healer must *come down,* if his son is to be cured. The nobleman cannot raise himself to the height of those words of the Psalmist, "He *sent* his word, and He healed them."

And yet, if there be rebuke in the Lord's answer, there is encouragement as well; an implied promise of a miracle, even while the man is blamed, that nothing less than a miracle would induce him to put his trust in the Lord of life. And so he accepts it; for reading no repulse in this word of a seeming, and indeed of a real, severity, he only urges his suit the more earnestly, *Sir, come down ere my child,* or *my little child die.* He still, it is true, links the help which he seeks to the bodily presence of the Lord; he is still far off from the faith and humility of another, who said, "Lord, I am not worthy that thou shouldest come under my roof: but speak the word only, and my servant shall be healed" (Matt. viii. 8). Much less does he dream of a power that could raise the dead: Christ might heal his sick; he has no thought of Him as one who could raise his dead. A faith so weak must be strengthened, and can only be strengthened through being proved. Such a gracious purpose of at once proving and strengthening we trace in the Lord's dealings with the man which follow. He does not come down with him, as had been asked; but sends the suppliant away with a mere word of assurance that it shall fare well with his child: *Go thy way; thy son liveth* (cf. Matt. viii. 13; Mark vii. 29). And the father is content with that assurance; he *believed the*

word that Jesus had spoken unto him, and he went his way,
expecting to find that it should be done according to that word.
The miracle, one might say, was a double one — on the body
of the absent child, on the heart of the present father; one cured
of his sickness, the other of his unbelief.

A comparison of the Lord's dealings with this nobleman and
with the centurion of the other Gospels is instructive (Matt. viii.
5-13; Luke vii 1-10). Assuredly He has not men's persons in
admiration who comes not, but only *sends,* to the son of this
nobleman (cf. 2 Kin. v. 10, 11), Himself visiting the servant
of that centurion. And there is more in the matter than this.
Here, being entreated to come, He does not; but sends his
healing word; there, being asked to speak at a distance that
word of healing, He rather proposes Himself to come; for here,
as Chrysostom explains it well, a narrow and poor faith is en-
larged and deepened, there a strong faith is crowned and
rewarded. By not going He increases this nobleman's faith; by
offering to go He brings out and honours that centurion's
humility.

*And as he was now going down, his servants met him, and
told him, saying, Thy son liveth.* Though faith had not struck
its roots quickly in his soul, it would appear to have struck them
strongly at last. His confidence in Christ's word was so entire,
that he proceeded leisurely homewards. It was not till the next
day that he approached his house, though a journey from one
city to the other need not have occupied many hours. *Then
enquired he of them the hour when he began to amend,* to be
a little better; for at the height of his faith the father had
looked only for a slow and gradual amendment. *And they said
unto him, Yesterday at the seventh hour the fever left him.* It was
not merely, they would imply, that at the hour they name there
was a turning-point in the disorder, and the violence of the
fever abated; but it *left him* altogether; as in the case of Simon's

wife's mother, who, at Christ's word, "immediately arose and ministered unto them" (Luke iv. 39). *So the father knew that it was at the same hour, in the which Jesus said unto him, Thy son liveth:*[2] *and himself believed, and his whole house.* This he did for all the benefits which the Lord had bestowed on him, accepting another and crowning benefit, even the cup of salvation; and not he alone; for his conversion drew after it that of all who belonged to him; for by consequences such as these God brings us to a consciousness of the manner in which not merely the great community of mankind, but each smaller community, a nation, or as in this case a family, is united and bound together under its federal head, shares in the good or in the evil which is his (cf. Acts xvi. 15, 34;xviii.).

But did he not believe already? Whether we understand that faith was first born in him now, or, being born already, received now a notable increase, it is plain in either case that the Lord by those words of his, *Except ye see signs and wonders, ye will not believe,* could not have intended to cast any slight on miracles, as a mean whereby men may be brought to the truth; or, having been brought, are more strongly established in the same.

One question before leaving this miracle claims a brief discussion, namely, whether this is the same history as that of the servant of the centurion (Matt. viii. 5; Luke vii. 2); here repeated with only immaterial variations. There is nothing to warrant it, almost nothing to render it plausible. Not merely the external circumstances are widely different; but more decisive still, the inner kernel and heart of the two narratives is different. That centurion is an example of a strong faith, this nobleman of a weak faith; that centurion counts that if Jesus will but speak the word, his servant will be healed; while this nobleman is

---

[2] A beautiful remark of Bengel's: "The more carefully the divine works and benefits are considered, the more nourishment faith acquires."

so earnest that the Lord should come down, because in heart
he limits his power, and counts that nothing but his actual
presence will avail to help his sick; that other is praised, this
rebuked of the Lord. So striking are these differences, that
Augustine[3] compares, but for the purpose of contrasting, the
faith of that centurion, and the unbelief of this nobleman.
Against all this, the points of likeness, and suggesting identity,
are slight and superficial; as the near death of the sufferer, the
healing at a distance and by a word, and the returning and finding the sick well. Assuredly it is nothing strange that two
miracles should have such circumstances as these in common.

---

[3] *In Ev. Joh. tract* xvi.: "See the distinction: the ruler desired the Lord to come
down to his house; the centurion declared himself to be unworthy. The latter was
answered, 'I will come and heal him'; the former, 'Go, thy son liveth.' There He
promised his presence, here He healed by a word. Yet the man here had insisted upon
his presence, while the other had declared himself unworthy of it. Here is a ceding to
loftiness, there a conceding to lowliness of mind."

CHAPTER III.

The First Miraculous Draught of Fishes

LUKE v. 1-11.

THERE have been in all times those who have deemed themselves bound to distinguish the incident here narrated from
that recorded in St. Matthew (iv. 18) and St. Mark (i. 16-20).

Some difficulties, yet not very serious ones, in bringing the
two accounts to a perfect agreement, every one will readily
admit. But surely the taking refuge at once and as often as such
meet us, in the assumption that events closely resembling one
another, with only slight variations, happened to the same people
two or three times over, is a very questionable way of escape
from embarrassments of this kind; will hardly satisfy one who
honestly asks himself whether he would admit it in dealing with
any other records. In the extreme unlikelihood that events should
thus repeat themselves a far more real difficulty is created, than
any which it is in this way hoped to evade. Let us only keep
in mind the various aspects, various yet all true, in which the
same incident will present itself from different points of view
to different witnesses; the very few points in a complex circumstance which any narrative whatever can seize, least of all a
written one, which in its very nature is limited; and we shall
not wonder that two or three relators have brought out different
moments, divers but not diverse, of one and the same event.
Rather we shall be grateful to that providence of God, which
thus sets us oftentimes not merely in the position of one looker-
on, but of many; which allows us to regard the acts of Christ,
every side of which is significant, from many sides; to hear of
his discourses not merely so much as one disciple took in and

81

carried away, but also that which sank especially deep into the heart and memory of another.

But when we compare John i. 40-42, does it not appear that three out of these four, Andrew and Peter certainly, and most probably John himself (ver. 35), had been already called? No doubt they had then, on the banks of Jordan, been brought into a transient fellowship with their future Lord; but, after that momentary contact, had returned to their ordinary occupations, and only at this later period attached themselves finally and fully to Him, henceforth following Him withersoever He went.[1] This miracle most probably it was, as indeed seems intimated at ver. 8, which stirred the very depths of their hearts, giving them such new insights into the glory of Christ's person, as prepared them to yield themselves without reserve to his service. Everything here bears evidence that not now for the first time He and they have met. So far from their betraying no previous familiarity with the Lord, as some have affirmed, Peter, calling Him *Master,* and saying, *Nevertheless at thy word, I will let down the net,* implies that he had already received impressions of his power, and of the authority which went with his words. Moreover, the *two* callings, a first and on this a second, are quite in the manner of that divine Teacher, who would hasten nothing, who was content to leave spiritual processes to advance as do natural; who could bide his time, and did not expect the full corn in the ear on the same day that He had cast the seed into the furrow. On that former occasion He sowed the seed of his word in the hearts of Andrew and Peter; which having done, He left it to germinate; till now returning He found it ready to bear the ripe fruits of faith. Not that we need therefore presume such gradual processes *in all.* But as some statues are cast in a mould and at an instant, others only little by little hewn and shaped and

---

[1] It is often said that the other was, "a summons to knowledge and acquaintance, or to faith, this to apostleship." See the remarks of Scultetus, *Crit Sac.* vol. vi. p. 1956.

polished, as their several material, metal or stone, demands the
one process or the other, so are there, to use a memorable expression of Donne's *"fusile Apostles"* like St. Paul, whom one
and the same lightning-flash from heaven at once melts and
moulds; and others who by a more patient process, here a little
and there a little, are shaped and polished into that perfect
image, to which the Lord, the great master-sculptor, will have
them finally attain.

*And it came to pass, that, as the people pressed upon him
to hear the word of God, he stood by the lake of Gennesaret;*
by that lake whose shores had been long ago designated by the
prophet Isaiah as a chief scene of the beneficent activity of
Messiah (Isai. ix. 1, 2); and, as He stood, He *saw two ships
standing by the lake: but the fishermen were gone out of them,
and were washing their nets. And he entered into one of the
ships, which was Simon's, and prayed him that he would thrust
out a little from the land. And he sat down, and taught the
people out of the ship. Now when he had left speaking, he said
unto Simon, Launch out into the deep, and let down your nets
for a draught.* This He says, designing Himself, the meanwhile,
to take the fishermen in *his* net. For He, who by the foolish
things of the world would confound the wise, and by the weak
things of the world would confound the strong,[2] who meant,
as Augustine has it, to draw emperors to Himself by fishermen,
and not fishermen by emperors, lest his Church should even seem
to stand in the wisdom and power of men rather than of God
— He saw in these simple fishermen of the Galilaean lake the
aptest instruments of his work.[3] *And Simon answering said unto
him, Master, we have toiled all the night, and have taken nothing;* but, with the beginnings of no weak faith already working

[2] Compare the call of the prophet Amos: "I was no prophet, neither was I a
prophet's son, but I was an herdman, and a gatherer of sycomore fruit; and the Lord
took me as I followed the flock, and the Lord said unto me, Go, prophesy unto my
people Israel" (vii. 14, 15; cf. 1 Kin. xix. 19).
[3] See Augustine, *Serm.* ccclxxxi.

within him, he adds, *nevertheless at thy word I will let down the net* — for these are not the words of one despairing of the issue; who, himself expecting nothing, would yet, to satisfy the Master, and to prove to Him the fruitlessness of further efforts, comply with his desire. And this act of faith is abundantly rewarded; *And when they had this done, they inclosed a great multitude of fishes,* so many indeed, that *their net brake,* or better, *their net was breaking. And they beckoned unto their partners, which were in the other ship, that they should come and help them.*

It was not merely that Christ by his omniscience *knew* that now there were fishes in that spot. Rather we behold in Him here the Lord of nature, able, by the secret yet mighty magic of his will, to guide and draw the unconscious creatures, and make them minister to the higher interests of his kingdom; we recognize in Him the ideal man, the second Adam, in whom are fulfilled the words of the Psalmist: "Thou madest him to have dominion over the works of thy hands; thou hast put all things under his feet, . . . the fowl of the air, *and the fish of the sea, and whatsoever passeth through the paths of the seas"* (Ps. viii. 6, 8). Yet since the power by which He drew them then is the same that guides evermore their periodic migrations, which, *marvellous* as it is, we yet cannot call *miraculous,* there is plainly something that differences this miracle, with another of like kind (John xxi 6), and that of the stater in the fish's mouth (Matt. xvii. 27), from Christ's other miracles; — in that these three are not comings in of a new and hitherto unwonted power into the region of nature; but *coincidences, divinely brought about,* between words of Christ and facts in that natural world. An immense haul of fishes, or a piece of money in the mouth of one, are in themselves no miracles; but the miracle lies in the falling in of these with a word of Christ's, which has pledged itself to this coincidence beforehand. The natural is lifted up into the domain of the miraculous by the manner in which it is timed, and the ends which it is made to serve.

And they came, and filled both the ships, so that they began to sink. It was a moment of fear, not indeed because their ships were thus overloaded and sinking; but rather that now this sign revealed to them something in the Lord which before they had not apprehended, and which filled them with astonishment and awe. Peter, as so often, is spokesman for all. He, while drawing the multitude of fishes into his net, has himself fallen into the net of Christ. He can no longer, in the deep apprehension of his own unholiness, endure a Holy One so near. *When Simon Peter saw it, he fell down at Jesus' knees, saying, Depart from me; for I am a sinful man, O Lord. For he was astonished, and all that were with him, at the draught of the fishes which they had taken.* At moments like these the deepest things that are in the heart come forth to the light. And the deepest thing in man's heart under the law is this sense of God's holiness as something bringing death and destruction to the unholy creature. "Let not God speak with us, lest we die"; this was the voice of the people to Moses, as "they removed and stood afar off" (Exod. xx. 18, 19). Below this is the utterly profane state, in which there is no contradiction felt between the holy and the unholy, between God and the sinner. Above it is the state of grace; in which all the contradiction is felt, God is still a consuming fire, yet not any more for the sinner, but only for the sin. It is still felt, felt far more strongly than ever, how profound a gulf separates between sinful man and a holy God; but felt no less than this gulf has been bridged over, that the two can meet, that in One who shares with both they have already met.

It would indeed have fared ill with Peter, had Christ taken him at his word, and departed from *him,* as He departed from others who made the same request Matt. viii. 34; ix. 1; cf. Job

xxii. 17) ; but who made it in quite a different spirit from his.
If Peter *be* this *sinful man,* the more is the need that Christ
should be near him; and this He implicitly announces to him
that He will be. And first He reassures him with that comfort-
able *Fear not,* that assurance that He is not come to destroy,
but to save. And that Peter may have less cause to fear, Christ
announces to him the mission and the task which He has for
him in store: *From henceforth thou shalt catch men;* or, as it is
in St. Mark, "I will make you to become fishers of men." In
these words is the inauguration of Peter, and with him of his
fellows, to the work of their apostleship. Such an inauguration,
not formal, nor always in its outward accidents the same, — on
the contrary, in these accidents displaying an infinite richness
and variety, such as reign alike in the kingdoms of nature and of
grace, — is seldom absent, when God calls any man to a great
work in his kingdom. But infinitely various in outer circumstances, in essence it is always one and the same.

The Lord clothes his promise in the language of that art
which was familiar to Peter; the fishermen is to *catch* men, as
David, taken from among the sheep-folds, was to *feed* them
(Ps. lxxviii. 71, 72). There is here a double magnifying of
Peter's future occupation as compared with his past. It is *men,*
and not poor fishes, which henceforth he shall take; and he
shall take them *for life,* and not, as he had hitherto taken his
meaner prey, only for death.

It is not for nothing that the promise here clothes itself in
language drawn from the occupation of the fisher, rather, for
example, than in that borrowed from the nearly allied pursuits
of the hunter. The fisher more often takes his prey alive; he
draws it *to* him, does not drive it *from* him;[4] and draws all
which he has taken to one another; even as the Church brings

---

[4] Spanheim (*Dub. Evang.* vol. iii. p. 350): "Those whom the Lord called he
would not have to be hunters, but fishers, not men who drive their prey from them,
but who gather it in."

together the divided hearts, the fathers to the children, gathers
into one fellowship the scattered tribes of men. Again, the
work of the fisher is one of art and skill, not of force and
violence.[5] There is now a captivity which is blessed, blessed
because it is deliverance from a freedom which is full of woe,
—a "being made free from sin and becoming servants to God."

*And when they had brought their ships to land, they forsook
all, and followed him,* or, as St. Mark has it, with one of those
small but never insignificant additions in which he is so rich,
*they left their father Zebedee in the ship with the hired servants,
and went after him.* But what, some ask, was that *all* which
they forsook, that they should afterwards magnify it so much,
saying, "Behold, *we have forsaken all,* and followed thee: what
shall we have therefore" (Matt. xix. 27)? Whatever it was, it
was their *all,* and therefore, though no more than a few poor
boats and nets, it was much; for love to a miserable hovel may
hold one with bands as hard to break as those which bind another
to a sumptuous palace; seeing it is the worldly affection which
holds, and not the world; and the essence of the renunciation
lies not in the more or less which is renounced, but in the spirit
wherein the renunciation is carried out. These Apostles might
have left little when they left their *possessions;* but they left
much, and had a right to feel that they had left much, when
they left their *desires.*

---

[5] So Ovid (*Halieut.*): "Our labour rests in skill": cf. 2 Cor. xii. 16: "Being crafty,
I caught you with guile."

CHAPTER IV.

The Stilling of the Tempest

IT WAS evening, the evening, probably, of that day on which the Lord had spoken all those parables recorded in Matt. xiii. (cf. Mark iv. 35), when, seeing great multitudes about Him still, *He gave commandment to depart unto the other side* of the lake, to the more retired region of Peraea. *And when they had sent away the multitude,* which, however, was not effected without three memorable sayings to three who formed part of it (Matt. viii. 19-22; cf. Luke ix. 57-62), *they took him even as he was* (that is, with no preparation for a voyage), *in the ship.* But before the voyage was accomplished, *behold, there arose a great tempest in the sea.* A sudden and violent squall, such as these small inland seas, surrounded with mountain gorges, are notoriously exposed to, descended on the bosom of the lake. The danger was ever growing more urgent, until *the waves beat into the ship, so that it was now full.* The Master, weary and worn out with the toils of the day, continued sleeping still: He was, as St. Mark alone records for us, *in the hinder part of the ship, asleep on a pillow.* In Him we behold here the exact reverse of Jonah (Jon. i. 5, 6); the fugitive prophet asleep in the midst of a like danger out of a dead conscience, the Saviour out of a pure conscience — Jonah by his presence making the danger, Jesus yielding a pledge and assurance of deliverance from it.[1]

But the disciples understood not this. They may have hesitated long before they ventured to arouse Him; yet at last the

---

[1] Jerome: "Of this miracle we read the type in Jonah, when amid the peril of the others he himself is composed, sleeps, and is awakened, and, by his command, and the sacrament of his suffering, delivers those who awake him."

extremity of the peril overcame their hesitation, and they did so, not without exlamations of haste and terror; as is evidenced by the double *Master, Master* of St. Luke. This double compellation always marks a special earnestness on the part of the speaker. In St. Mark, the disciples rouse their Lord with words almost of rebuke, as if He were unmindful at once of their safety and of his own: *Master, carest thou not that we perish?* for in this their *we* they included no doubt their beloved Lord as well as themselves. *And he saith unto them, Why are ye fearful, O ye of little faith?* — from St. Matthew it would appear, first chiding their want of faith, and then pacifying the storm; though the other Evangelists make the rebuke addressed to them not to have preceded, but to have followed, the allaying of the winds and waves. Probably it did both: He spoke first to his disciples, calming their agitation with a word; and then, having quieted the tumult of the outward elements, He again turned to them, and more deliberately rebuked their lack of faith in Him[2]. *Of little faith,* according to St. Matthew He calls them; St. Mark's, *How is it ye have no faith?* must be modified and explained by the milder rebuke which the other Evangelists record. They were not wholly *without* faith; for, believing in the midst of their unbelief, they turned to Christ in their fear. They had faith, but it was not at hand, as the Lord's question, *Where is your faith?* (Luke viii 25) sufficiently implies. They had it, as the weapon which a soldier has, but cannot lay hold of at the moment when he needs it the most. Their sin lay not in seeking help of Him; for this indeed became them well; but in the *excess* of the terror which they displayed: *Why are ye so fearful?*[3] in their counting it possible that the ship which bore their Lord could ever perish.

---

[2] Theophylact: "Having first calmed the storm of their souls, He then lays that of the sea also."

[3] Calvin: "By this particle [so] He signifies that they were beyond measure afraid; . . . hence it is plain that not every kind of fear is contrary to faith. For if we fear nothing the sluggish carelessness of the flesh creeps upon us."

Then he arose, and rebuked the winds and the sea; and there was a great calm. We must not miss the force of that word *rebuked,* preserved by all three Evangelists; and as little the direct address to the furious elements, *Peace, be still,* which St. Mark only records. There is here a distinct tracing up of all the discords and disharmonies in the outward world to their source in a person; even as this person can be no other than Satan, the author of all disorders alike in the natural and in the spiritual world. The Lord elsewhere *rebukes a fever* (Luke iv. 39), where the same remarks will hold good. Nor is this rebuke unheard or unheeded; for not "willingly" was the creature thus made "subject to vanity" (Rom. viii. 20). Constituted as man's handmaid at the first, it is only reluctantly, and submitting to an alien force, that nature rises up against him, and becomes the instrument of his hurt and harm. In the hour of her wildest uproar, she knew the voice of Him who was her rightful Lord, gladly returned to her allegiance to Him, and in this to her place of proper service to that race of which He had become the Head, and whose lost prerogatives He was reclaiming and reasserting once more. And to effect all this, his *word* alone was sufficient; He needed not, as the greatest of his servants had needed, an instrument of power, apart from Himself, with which to do his mighty work; not the rod of Moses (Exod. xiv. 16, 21, 22), and as little the mantle of Elijah (2 Kin. ii. 14); but at his word only *the wind ceased, and there was a great calm.*

The Evangelists proceed to describe the moral effect which this signal wonder exercised on the minds of those that were in the ship; — it may be, also on those that were in the *other little ships,* which St. Mark has noted as sailing in their company: *The men marvelled, saying, What manner of man is this, that even the winds and the sea obey him?* We see here, no doubt, the chief ethical purpose to which, in the providence of

God who ordered all things for the glory of his Son, this miracle was intended to serve. It was to lead his disciples into thoughts ever higher and more awful of that Lord whom they served, more and more to teach them that in nearness to Him was safety and deliverance from every danger. The danger which exercised, should likewise strengthen, their faith, — who indeed had need of a mighty faith, since God, in St. Chrysostom's words, had chosen them to be the athletes of the universe.

We shall do no wrong to the literal truth of this and other of Christ's miracles, by recognizing the character at once symbolic and prophetic, which many of them also bear, and this among the number. The sea is evermore in Scripture the symbol of the restless and sinful world (Dan. vii. 2, 3; Rev. xiii. 1; Isai. lvii. 20). As Noah and his family, the kernel of the whole humanity, were once contained in the Ark tossed on the waters of the deluge, so the kernel of the new humanity, of the new creation, Christ and his Apostles, in this little ship. And the Church of Christ has evermore resembled this tempested bark, the waves of the world raging horribly around it, yet never prevailing to overwhelm it, — and this because Christ is in it (Ps. xlvi. 1-3; xciii. 3, 4) ; who roused by the cry of his servants, rebukes these winds and these waters, and delivers his own from their distress.

CHAPTER V.

The Demoniacs in the Country of the Gadarenes

MATT. viii. 28-34; MARK v. 1-20; LUKE viii. 26-39.

THE consideration of this, the most important, and, in many respects, the most perplexing of all the cures of demoniacs recorded in the New Testament, will demand some prefatory remarks on the general subject of the demoniacs of Scripture.

It is, of course, easy enough to cut short the whole inquiry by saying these demoniacs were persons whom we at this day should call insane — epileptic, maniac, melancholic. There was no doubt a substratum of disease, which in many cases helped to lay open the sufferer to the worse evil, and upon which this was superinduced. But the scheme which confounds these cases with those of disease, and, in fact, identifies the two, does not exhaust the matter and this for more reasons than one.

And first, our Lord Himself uses language which is not reconcilable with any such explanation. He everywhere speaks of demoniacs not as persons merely of disordered intellects, but as subjects and thralls of an alien spiritual might; He addresses the evil spirit as distinct from the man; "Hold thy peace, and come out of him" (Mark i. 25).

Besides this, the phenomena themselves are such as no hypothesis of the kind avails to explain. For that madness was not the constituent element in the demoniac state is clear, since not only are we without the slightest ground for supposing that the Jews would have considered all maniacs, epileptic or melancholic persons, to be under the power of evil spirits; but we have distinct evidence that the same malady they did in some cases attribute to an evil spirit, and in others not; thus showing that

93

the malady and possession were not identical in their eyes, and that the assumption of the latter was not a mere popular explanation for the presence of the former. Thus, on one occasion they bring to the Lord one dumb (Matt. ix. 32), on another one dumb and blind (xii. 22), and in both instances the dumbness is traced up to an evil spirit. Yet it is plain that they did not consider all dumbness as having this root; for in the history given by St. Mark (vii. 32) of another deaf and dumb, the subject of Christ's healing power, it is the evident intention of the Evangelist to describe one labouring only under a natural defect; with no least desire to trace the source of his malady to any demoniacal influence. Whatever may have been the symptoms which enabled those about the sufferers to make these distinctions, the fact itself of their so discriminating between cases of the very same malady, proves decisively that there were not certain diseases which, without more ado, they traced up directly to Satan; but that they did designate by this name of possession, a condition which, while it was very often a condition of disease, was also always a condition of much more than disease.

This being so, the question which presents itself is this, namely, what peculiar form of Satanic operation does the Scripture intend, when it speaks of men as possessed, or having devils? Is their evil ethical, or is it merely physical? *Merely* physical it certainly is not. Doubtless the suffering of the demoniac often was great; yet we should err, if we saw in him, as in the victims of ghastly and horrible diseases, *only* another example of the mighty woe which Satan has brought in upon our race. Nor yet, on the other hand, is his evil purely ethical; we have in him something else than merely a signal sinner, a foremost servant of the devil, who with heart and will and waking consciousness is doing his work; for this, whatever his antecedent guilt may have been, and often, I should imagine, it had been great, the demoniac evidently is not. But what in him strikes us the most is the strange confusion of the physical and the psychical, each intruding into the proper domain of the other. There is a breaking up of all the harmony of the lower, no less than of the higher life; the same discord and disorganization manifesting itself in both. Nor does the demoniac, like the wicked, stand only in near relation to the kingdom of Satan as a whole. It is with him as if of the malignant spirits of the pit. One had singled him out for its immediate prey; as when a lion or a leopard, not hunting in the mass a herd of flying antelopes, has fastened upon and is drinking out the life-blood of one.

But the awful question remains, How should any have sunken into this miserable condition, have been entangled so far in the bands of the devil, or of his ministers? We should find ourselves altogether upon a wrong track, did we conceive of the demoniacs as the worst of men, and their possession as the plague and penalty of a wickedness in which they had greatly exceeded others. Rather we must esteem the demoniac as one of the unhappiest, but not, of necessity, one of the guiltiest of our race. We all feel that Judas' possession, when Satan entered into him (John xiii. 27), was specifically different from that of one of the unhappy persons who were the subjects of Christ's healing power. The horror and deep anguish of a sinner at the contemplation of his sin may have helped on this overthrow of his spiritual life, — anguish which a more hardened sinner would have escaped, but escaped it only by being a worse and a more truly devilish man. We are not then to see in these cases of possession the deliberate giving in to the Satanic will, of an utterly lost soul, but, in many instances at least, the still recoverable wreck of what might once have been a noble spirit.

And, consistently with this, we find in the demoniac the sense of a bondage in which he does not acquiesce. His state is, in the most literal sense of the word, "a possession": another is ruling in the high places of his soul, and has cast down the rightful lord from his seat; and he knows this; and out of his consciousness of it there goes forth from him a cry for redemption, so soon as ever a glimpse of hope is afforded, an unlooked-for Redeemer draws near. This sense of misery, this yearning after deliverance, is that, in fact, which constituted these demoniacs subjects for Christ's healing power. Without it they would have been as little subjects of this as the devils, in whom evil has had its perfect work, in whom there is nothing for the divine grace to take hold of; — so that in their case, as in every other, faith was the condition of healing. There was in them a spark of higher life, not yet trodden out; which, indeed, so long as they were alone, was but light enough to reveal to them their proper darkness; and which none but the very Lord of life could have fanned again into a flame. But He who came "to destroy the works of the devil," as He showed Himself lord over purely physical evil, a healer of the diseases of men, and lord no less over purely spiritual evil, a deliverer of men from their sins, — manifested Himself also lord in these complex cases partaking of the nature of either, ruler also in this border land, where these two regions of evil touch one another, and run so strangely and inexplicably one into the other.

Yet while thus "men possessed with devils" is in no wise an expression equivalent to surpassingly wicked men, born of the serpent seed, of the devil's regeneration, and so become his children (Acts xiii. 10), — seeing that in such there is no cry for redemption, no desire after deliverance, it is more than probable that lavish sin, above all, indulgence in sensual lusts, superinducing, as it often would, a weakness of the nervous system, wherein is the especial band between body and soul, may have laid open these unhappy ones to the fearful incursions of the powers of darkness. They were greatly guilty, though not the guiltiest of all men. And this they felt, that by their own act they had given themselves over to this tyranny of the devil, a tyranny from which, as far as their horizon reached, they could see no hope of deliverance, — that to themselves they owed that this hellish might was no longer *without* them, which being resisted would flee from them; but a power which now they could not resist, and which would not flee.

One objection to this view of the matter may be urged, namely, that if possession be anything more than insanity in some of its different forms, how comes it to pass that there are no demoniacs now, that these have wholly disappeared from among us? But the assumption that there are none now, itself demands to be proved. It is not hard to perceive why there should be few by comparison. For in the first place, if there was anything that marked the period of the coming of Christ, and that immediately succeeding, it was the wreck and confusion of men's spiritual life. That whole period was "the hour and power of darkness," of a darkness which then, as just before the dawn of a new day, was the thickest. The world was again a chaos, and the creative words, "Let there be light," though just about to be spoken, were not uttered yet.

Moreover we cannot doubt that the might of hell has been greatly broken by the coming of the Son of God in the flesh; and with this a restraint set on the grosser manifestations of its power; "I beheld Satan as lightning fall from heaven" (Luke x. 18; cf. Rev. xx. 2). His rage and violence are continually hemmed in and hindered by the preaching of the Word and ministration of the Sacraments.

It may well be a question moreover, if an Apostle, or one gifted with Apostolic discernment of spirits, were to enter into a madhouse now, he might not recognize some of the sufferers there as "possessed." Certainly in many cases of mania and epilepsy there is a condition very analogous to that of the demoniacs. The fact that the sufferer, and commonly those around him, may apprehend it differently, is not of the essence of the matter; they will but reflect in this the popular impression of their time. Thus, no doubt, the Jews unreasonably multiplied the number of the possessed, including among cases of possession many slighter forms of disharmony in the inner life. But the case immediately before us is one in which no question can exist, since the great Physician of souls Himself declares it one of a veritable possession, and treats it as such; and to this we will address ourselves now.

The connexion is very striking in which this miracle stands with that other which went immediately before. Our Lord has just shown Himself as the pacifier of the tumults and the discords in the outward world; He has spoken peace to the winds and to the waves, and hushed the war of elements with a word. And Christ will accomplish here a yet mightier work than that which He accomplished there; He will prove Himself here also the Prince of Peace, the restorer of the lost harmonies; He will speak, and at his potent word this madder strife, this blinder rage which is in the heart of man, will allay itself, and here also there shall be a great calm.

In seeking to combine the accounts given us of this memorable healing, a difficulty meets us at the outset, this namely, that St. Matthew speaks of two demoniacs, while St. Mark and St. Luke only of one. However we may account for it, one, it is evident, did fall into the background; and, therefore, following the later Evangelists, I shall speak in the main as they do, of the one demoniac who met the Lord as He came out of the ship.

The picture of the miserable man is fearful. He *had his dwelling among the tombs,* that is, in places unclean because of the dead men's bones which were there (Num. xix. 11, 16; Matt. xxiii. 27; Luke xi. 44). To those who did not therefore shun them, these tombs of the Jews afforded ample shelter (Isai. lxv.

4), being either natural caves, or recesses artificially hewn out of the rock. Many such tombs may still be found in the immediate neighborhood of Gadara.[1] This man was possessed of that extraordinary muscular strength which maniacs so often put forth (cf. Acts xix. 16), and thus *no man could bind him, no, not with chains,* or more correctly, *no not with a chain;* so St. Mark v. 3. St. Matthew alone relates how he had made the way impassable for travellers; St. Luke alone that he was without clothing (cf. 1 Sam. xix. 24; Dan. iv. 33), which, however, is assumed in St. Mark's statement that after he was healed he was found *clothed, and in his right mind,* sitting at Jesus' feet. Yet with all this, he was not so utterly lost, but that from time to time there woke up in him a sense of his misery, and of the frightful bondage under which he had come; although this could express itself only in his cries, and in a blind rage against himself as the true author of his woe; *always, night and day, he was in the mountains, and in the tombs, crying, and cutting himself with stones.*[2]

This man with his companion starting from their dwelling-place in the tombs, rushed down to encounter, it may have been with hostile violence, the intruders who had dared to set foot on their domain. Or possibly they were at once drawn to Christ by the secret instinctive feeling that He was their helper, and repelled from Him by the sense of the awful gulf that divided them from Him, the Holy One of God. At any rate, if it *was* with purposes of violence, ere the man reached Him his mind was changed; *for he had commanded the unclean spirit to come*

---

[1] See Burckhardt, and, for the whole scenery of this miracle, Stanley, *Sinai and Palestine*, p. 372. "The most interesting remains of this miracle, Stanley, *Sinai and the Bible*, s. v., "are its tombs, which dot the cliff for a considerable distance round the city. They are excavated in the limestone rock, and consist of chambers of various dimensions, some more than twenty feet square, with recesses in the sides for bodies. The doors are slabs of stone, a few being ornamented with panels; some of them still remain in their places. The present inhabitants of Um Keis [the old Gadara] are all troglodytes, 'dwelling in tombs,' like the poor maniacs of old."

[2] Prichard, describing a case of raving mania: "He habitually wounded his hands, wrists, and arms, with needles and pins; . . . the blood sometimes flowed copiously, dropping from his elbows when his arms were bare."

out of the man (Luke viii. 29), and the unclean spirit had recognized one that had a right to command; against whom force
would avail nothing; and, like others on similar occasions, sought
by a strong adjuration to avert his coming doom. He *ran and
worshipped him, and cried with a loud voice, and said, What
have I to do with thee, Jesus, thou Son of the most high God?*
(cf. Luke iv. 34, 41; Acts xvi. 17). *I adjure thee by God, that
thou torment me not.* Herein the true devilish spirit speaks out,
which counts it a torment not to be suffered to torment others.
In St. Matthew they say, *Art thou come hither to torment us
before the time?* so that, by their own confession, a time is
coming when there shall be an entire victory of the kingdom
of light over that of darkness (Rev. xx. 10). All Scripture agrees
with this, that the judgment of the angels is yet to come (1 Cor.
vi. 3); they are "reserved in everlasting chains under darkness
unto the judgment of the great day" (Jude 6); and what the
unclean spirits deprecate here, is the bringing in, by anticipation,
of that final doom.

The first bidding of Christ is not immediately obeyed; — the
unclean spirits remonstrate, do not at once abandon their prey.
No doubt He could have compelled them to this, had He pleased;
but the man might have perished in the process (cf. Mark ix.
26). Even that first bidding had induced a terrible paroxysm.
It was then of Christ's own will, of the Physician wise and tender
as He was strong, to proceed step by step. And, first, He demands
of him his name, — some say, to magnify the greatness of the
deliverance and the Deliverer, by showing, through the answer,
the power and malignity of the foe that should be overcome.
But, more probably, the question was addressed *to the man.* It
should calm him, by bringing him to recollection that he was a
person, having once been apart from, and not even now inex-
tricably bound up with, those spiritual wickednesses which had
dominion over him. But if so meant, either the evil spirit

snatches at the answer and replies for himself, or the unhappy man, instead of recurring to his true name, that which should remind him of what he was before h.e fell under this thraldom, declares his sense of the utter ruin of his whole moral and spiritual being. In his reply, *My name is Legion: for we are many*, truth and error are fearfully blended. Not on one side only, but on every side, the walls of his spirit have been broken down. They who dominate his life are "lords many." When it is said of Mary Magdalene, that out of her had gone *seven* devils (Luke viii. 2), something of the same truth is expressed, — that her spiritual life was laid waste, not on one side only, but on many (cf. Matt. xii. 45).

And then again, with that interchange of persons which was continually going forward, the unclean spirit, or rather the man become now his organ, speaks out anew, entreating not to be sent into *the deep,* or as it would be better *the abyss* (Luke viii 31), or, clothing his petition in the form of a notion which belonged to the man whom he possessed, *that he would not send them away out of the country* (Mark v. 10). The request is in both cases the same; for, according to Jewish notions, certain countries being assigned to evil as well as to good spirits, whose limits they were unable to overpass, to be sent out of their own country, no other being open to them, implied being sent into *the abyss,* or bottomless pit, since that remains for them alone.

Hereupon follows a circumstance which has ever proved one of the chief stumbling-blocks offered by the Evangelical history. The devils, if they must leave their more welcome habitation, the heart of man, yet entreat, in their inextinguishable desire of harming, or out of those mysterious affinities which continually reveal themselves between the demoniacal and the bestial, to be allowed to enter into the swine; — of which a large herd, — *about two thousand,* — were feeding on the neighbouring cliffs. But to the evil all things turn to evil. The wicked, Satan (Job

i. 11) and his ministers, are sometimes heard, and the very granting of their petitions issues in their worst confusion and loss (Num. xxii. 20; Ps. lxxviii. 29, 31). So is it now: the prayer of these evil spirits was heard; but only to their ruin. They are allowed to enter into the swine; but the destruction of the whole herd follows.[3]

The first cavil which has been raised here is this — What right had the Lord to inflict this loss on the owners of the swine? It might be sufficient to answer to this, that Christ did not send the devils into the swine; He merely drove them out from the man; all beyond this was merely permissive.[4] But supposing that He had done so, a man is of more value than many swine; this would have been motive enough for allowing them to perish. It may have been necessary for the permanent healing of the man that he should have this outward evidence and testimony that the hellish powers which held him in bondage for so long had quitted their hold.

But setting aside all apologies, on what ground, it may be asked, is this which the Lord here wrought, made more the subject of cavil than any other loss inflicted upon men by Him from whom all things come, and who therefore can give or take away according to the good pleasure of his will? Oftentimes his taking away is in a higher sense a giving; a withdrawing of the meaner thing, to make receptive of the better. Thus might it well have been intended here, however the sin of these Gadarenes hindered the gracious design.

But the narrative is charged with contradictions and absurdities. The unclean spirits ask permission to enter into the swine; yet no sooner have they thus done than they defeat their own

---

[3] For the exact spot which was the scene of this catastrophe see Konrad Furrer, *Die Bedeutung der Bibl. Geographie*, p. 19. "These creatures," says Dr. Thompson (*The Land and the Book*, p. 378), "still abound at this place, and in a state as wild and fierce as though they were still possessed."

[4] Augustine: "The devils were driven out and permitted to go into the swine"; and Aquinas: "But that the swine were driven into the sea was no work of the divine miracle, but was the work of the devils by divine permission."

purpose. It is nowhere, however, said that they *drove* the swine down the steep place into the sea. It is just as easy, and much more natural, to suppose that against *their* will the swine, when they found themselves seized by this new and strange power, rushed themselves in wild and panic fear to their destruction. But in either case, whether they thus destroyed themselves, or were impelled by the foul spirits, there reveals itself here the very essence and truest character of evil, which evermore outwits and defeats itself; which, stupid, blind, self-contradicting, and suicidal, can only destroy, and will involve itself in the common ruin rather than not destroy. And what, if in the fierce hatred of these foul spirits of darkness against the Prince of light and life, they may have been willing to bring any harm on themselves, if only they might so bring on Him the ill-will of men, and thus traverse and hinder his blessed work? And this, no doubt, they did effectually here; for it was fear of further losses, and alienation from Christ on account of those by his presence already entailed upon them, which moved the people of the country to urge Him that He would leave their coasts.

But the point of most real difficulty is the *entering* of the devils into the swine, — the working, that is, of the spiritual life on the bestial, which seems altogether irreceptive of it, and to possess no organs through which it could operate. I will only suggest that perhaps we make to ourselves a difficulty here, too easily assuming that the lower animal world is wholly shut up in itself, and incapable of receiving impressions from that which is above it. The assumption is one unwarranted by deeper investigations, which lead rather to an opposite conclusion, — not to a breaking down of the boundaries between the two worlds, but to the showing in what wonderful ways the lower is receptive of impressions from the higher, both for good and for evil. Nor does this working of the spiritual on the physical life stand

isolated in this single passage of Scripture, but we are taught
the same lesson throughout (Gen. iii. 17; Rom. viii. 22).

There are two stages of feeling in regard of their divine
Visitor which the people of the country of the Gadarenes pass
through; the second of these much less favourable than the first.
When attention is called to this point, they are evident enough,
both in the third Gospel and still more so in the second. In the
last we read how *they that fed the swine fled, and told it in the
city, and in the country. And they went out to see what it was
that was done,* and seeing the healed man, *they were afraid.* The
first impression which the miracle and the sight of the restored
demoniac make upon them is one of fear; but this fear was a
very common accompaniment of the strange and mighty works
which Jesus did, and as an introduction to better things by no
means in itself to be deprecated. Presently, however, the story
of what had befallen the possessed is told over again, by the
eye-witnesses of it, *and also concerning the swine* — this last
apparently for the first time. But with this knowledge of the
means by which the man was healed, the whole attitude of the
people to his Healer is altered. *They began to pray him* — so
they had not prayed Him before — *to depart out of their coasts.*
This was their time of trial. It should now be seen whether the
kingdom of heaven was first in their esteem; whether they would
hold all else as cheap by comparison. Under this trial they failed.
It was nothing to them that a man, probably a fellow-citizen,
was delivered from that terrible bondage, that they saw him
sitting at the feet of Jesus (Luke x. 39; Acts xxii. 3), *clothed,
and in his right mind.* The breach in their worldly estate alone
occupied their thoughts. For spiritual blessings brought near
to them they cared nothing at all; and *they were afraid,* being
ignorant what next might follow. They felt the presence of
God's Holy One intolerable to them; that to them, remaining
in their sins, it could only bring mischiefs, of which they had

made the first experience already. And having no desire to be delivered from their sins, they entreated Him to go. And *their* prayer also was heard (Ps. lxxviii. 29-31) ; for God sometimes hears his enemies in anger (Num. xxii, 20), even as He refuses to hear his friends in love (2 Cor. xii. 8, 9).

But the healed would fain have accompanied his Healer: and *when he was come into the ship, prayed him that he might be with him.* Was it that he feared, as Theophylact supposes, lest in the absence of his Deliverer the spirits of the pit should resume their dominion over him, and nowhere felt safe but in immediate nearness to Him? — or did he only desire, out of the depth of his gratitude, henceforth to be a follower of Him to whom he owed this mighty deliverance? Whatever was his motive, the Lord had other purposes with him. He was Himself quitting those who had shown themselves so unworthy of his presence; but He would not leave Himself without a witness among them. The man, so wonderfully delivered from the worst bondage of the Evil One, should be to them a standing monument of God's grace and power, an evidence that He would have delivered them, and was willing to heal them still, from all the diseases of their souls: *Jesus suffered him not, but saith unto him, Go home to thy friends, and tell them how great things the Lord hath done for thee, and hath had compassion on thee.* And the man did so, and not without effect: *he departed, and began to publish in Decapolis how great things Jesus had done for him: and all men did marvel.*[5]

Yet this command that he should go and declare the great things done for him, may very well have found its further motive in the special moral condition of the man. Only by a

---

[5] Augustine (*Quaest. Evang.* ii. 13): "That by this every man may understand that after the remission of his sins he must return to a good conscience, and must serve the Gospel for the sake of the salvation of others also, that so at last he may rest with Christ; and this, lest, in the too hasty desire to be already with Christ, he may neglect the ministry of preaching appointed for the redemption of his brother." He makes in the same place this whole account an historico-prophetic delineation of the exorcizing, so to speak, of the heathen world of its foul superstitions and devilish idolatries.

reference to this moral condition are we able to account for
the apparently contradictory injunctions which the Lord laid
on those whom He had healed: — some being forbidden to say
anything of God's goodness to them (Matt. viii. 4; Luke viii.
56), — this one commanded to publish everywhere the mercy
which he had received. We may very well suppose that where
there was danger of all deeper impressions being scattered and
lost through a garrulous repetition of the outward circumstances
of the healing, silence was enjoined, that so there might be an
inward brooding over the gracious and wondrous dealings of
the Lord. But where, on the contrary, there was a temperament
over-inclined to melancholy, sunken and shut up in itself, a
sufferer needing to be drawn out from self, and into healthy
communion with his kind, — as was evidently the case with
such a solitary melancholic sufferer as is here before us, — there
the command was, that the man should go and tell to others
the great things which God had done for him, and by the very
act of this telling maintain the healthy condition of his own
soul.

CHAPTER VI

The Raising of Jairus' Daughter

MATT ix. 18, 19, 23-26; MARK v. 22, 24, 35-43; LUKE viii. 41, 42, 49-56.

THIS miracle is by St. Mark and St. Luke made immediately to follow our Lord's return from that eastern side of the lake, which He had quitted when the inhabitants, guiltily at strife with their own good, had besought Him to depart out of their coasts (Matt. viii. 34). By St. Matthew other events, the curing of the paralytic, his own calling, and some discourses with the Pharisees, are inserted between. Yet of these only the latter (ix. 10-17) the best harmonists find really to have here their proper place. *While he spake these things unto them, behold, there came a certain ruler, and worshipped him.* The two later Evangelists record his name *Jairus,* and more accurately define his office; he was *one of the rulers of the synagogue.* The synagogue, we can hardly doubt was that of Capernaum, where now Jesus was (Matt. ix. 1). It is a remarkable token of the honour in which the Lord was at this time held by some who stood high among the rulers of the people, that one of these should come worshipping, doing, that is, reverent homage to Him, and seeking from Him so mighty a boon as that which this one sought at his hands. For he comes to Him, saying, *My daughter is even now dead: but come and lay thy hand upon her, and she shall live.* Thus St. Matthew; but the other Evangelists with an important variation: *My little daughter lieth at the point of death* (Mark v. 23): *He had one only daughter, about twelve years of age, and she lay a dying* (Luke viii. 42). This, which the after history shows to have been more exactly the fact, is not hard to reconcile with the statement in St. Matthew. When the father left his child, she was at the latest gasp; he knew that

107

life was ebbing so fast when he quitted her side, that she could scarcely be living still;[1] and yet, having no certain notices of her death, he was perplexed whether to speak of her as departed or not, and thus at one moment would express himself in one language, at the next in another. Strange that a circumstance like this, so drawn from the life, so testifying to the reality of the things recorded, should be urged by some as a contradiction between one Gospel and another!

That Lord upon whose ear the tidings of woe might never fall in vain, at once *arose, and followed him, and so did his disciples.* The crowd which had been listening to his teaching followed also, curious and eager to see what the Lord would do or would fail to do. The miracle of the healing of the woman with an issue of blood took place upon the way, and is entirely separable from this history, though not without its moral bearing upon it; for the delay of which her act was the occasion must have sorely tried the agonized father. But we detect no signs of impatience on his part, and this no doubt was laid to his account. While the Lord was yet speaking to the woman, *there came from the ruler of the synagogue's house certain which said, Thy daughter is dead: why troublest thou the Master any further?* St. Luke mentions but one, probably the especial bearer of the message, whom others went along with. They who, perhaps, had faith enough to believe that He could fan the last expiring spark of life into a flame, had not the stronger faith to anticipate the harder thing, that He could rekindle that spark of life, after it had been quenched altogether. Perhaps the father's hope would have perished too, and no room have been left for this miracle, faith, the necessary condition, being wanting, if a gracious Lord had not seen the danger, and prevented his unbelief. *As soon as Jesus heard the word that was spoken,*

---

[1] Bengel: "This he said at a guess." Augustine (*De Cons. Evang.* ii. 28): "For such was his despair that his desire was rather that she should be brought to life, since he did not think it possible she should be found alive, who was dying when he left her."

he saith unto the ruler of the synagogue, Be not afraid, only believe. There is something very gracious in that *as soon.* The Lord spake upon the instant, not leaving any time for a thought of unbelief to insinuate itself into the father's mind, such as might have altogether stood in the way of a cure, but preoccupying him at once with words of encouragement and hope.

And now He takes with Him three of his Apostles, Peter and James and John, the same three who were allowed, on more than one later occasion, to be witnesses of things withdrawn from the others. We read here for the first time of such an election within the election; and the fact of such now finding place would mark, that this was a new era in the life of the Lord. The work on which He was entering now was so strange and so mysterious that none but these, the flower and crown of the apostolic band, were its fitting witnesses. The parents were present for reasons altogether different. With those, and these, and none other, *He cometh to the house of the ruler of the synagogue, and seeth the tumult, and them that wept and wailed greatly,* as St. Mark, or *the minstrels and the people making a noise,* as St. Matthew, has it. There, as everywhere else, He appears calming and pacifying: *He saith unto them, Why make ye this ado, and weep? the damsel is not dead, but sleepeth. And they laughed him to scorn;* St. Luke alone adds the important words, *knowing that she was dead,* which to my mind are quite decisive as to what the *intention* of the sacred writer was — namely, to record a quickening from the dead, and not the recovery from a swoon.

Some have considered his words, common to all the Evangelists, *The maid is not dead, but sleepeth,* so explicit, as to leave them no choice but to refuse to number this among the actual raisings from the dead. They account it only a raising from a death-like swoon; though possibly a swoon from which the maiden would never have been recalled but for that life-giving touch and voice. Had this, however, been the case, Christ might have bidden the father to dismiss his fear, for *He*, who knew all, knew that there was yet life in the child. But that *Be not afraid, only believe,* is an evident summoning him to a trust in the almightiness of Him, to whose help he had appealed. Then too Christ uses exactly the same language concerning Lazarus, "Our friend Lazarus sleepeth" (John xi. 11), which He uses about this maiden; and we know that He spoke there not of a death-like swoon, but of death. As Lazarus did but sleep, because Jesus was about to "awake him out of sleep," so was this maiden only sleeping because her awakening in like manner was so near.[2] Besides this, to speak of death as a sleep, is an image common to all languages and nations. Nor is it hard to perceive why the Lord should use this language here. First, for the father's sake. The words are for the establishing of his trembling faith; they are a saying over again, *Be not afraid, only believe.* He, the Lord of life, takes away that word of fear, *She is dead,* and substitutes that milder word which contains the pledge of an awakening, *She sleepeth.*

He expelled from the house the crowd of turbulent mourners; and this for two reasons. Their presence, in the first place, was inappropriate and superfluous there; death was so soon to give place to returning life, that it did not deserve the name. But more than this, the boisterous and tumultuous grief gave no promise of the tone and temper of spirit, which became the witnesses of so holy and awful a mystery to say nothing of the scornful spirit with which they had received the assurance, that the child should presently revive. Such scorners shall not witness the holy act: the pearls should not be cast before them.

The house was now solitary and still. Two souls, believing and hoping, stand like funeral tapers beside the couch of the

---

[2] Fritzsche: "Hold not the damsel dead, but think her to be asleep, since she will soon return to life." Godet still better: "Jesus means that in the order of things over which he rules, death is no longer death, but takes the character of a monumentary slumber."

dead maiden — the father and the mother. The Church is represented in the three chief of its Apostles. Hereupon the solemn awakening finds place, and this without an effort on his part who is absolute Lord of the quick and the dead. *He took the damsel* — she was no more than a child, being *of the age of twelve years* (Mark v. 42) — *by the hand* (cf. Acts ix. 41), *and called, saying, Maid arise.* St. Mark preserves for us, having probably received from the lips of Peter, the very words which the Lord spake in the very language wherein He uttered them, *Talitha, Cumi.* And at that word, and at the touch of that hand, *her spirit came again, and she arose straightway* (Luke viii. 56), *and walked* (Mark v. 42). Hereupon, at once to strengthen that life which was come back to her, and to prove that she was indeed no ghost, but had returned to the realities of a mortal existence (cf. Luke xxiv. 41; John xxi. 5; Acts x. 41), and as marking the absolute calm of his own spirit, which took in the least as the greatest, *He commanded to give her meat.* The parents in that ecstatic moment might easily have forgotten it.

We have here again the somewhat perplexing charge addressed to the parents, namely *that they should tell no man what was done* (Matt ix. 30; Mark v. 43; Luke viii. 56). There is no such prohibition recorded by St. Matthew as laid upon them, while yet his statement leaves us no choice but to conclude that either having received this charge they gave no heed to it, or that such heed as they gave had profited nothing, for he tells us how *the fame hereof went abroad into all that land.* I call this charge perplexing, for the number of those who knew that the child had been dead and had been brought back to life, and who must have associated this fact with Christ's presence, was so large that it seems idle to have given them an injunction which certainly they would not observe. We may best, I think, understand this prohibition as an expression on our Lord's part of his desire to check that moral agitation of men's spirits which a dwelling on his miracles might so easily have occasioned, and which might at this period of his ministry have proved so serious a hindrance to it.

St. Mark does not fail to record, as is his manner, the profound impression which this miracle made on the beholders; *they were astonished with a great astonishment* (cf. i. 27; ii. 12; iv. 41; vi. 51; vii. 37). St. Luke records the same, but with a slighter emphasis, and dwelling only on the astonishment of the parents.

These miracles of raising from the dead, whereof this is the first, have always been regarded as the mightiest outcomings of the power of Christ; and with justice. The line between health and sickness is not definitely fixed; the transition from this to that is frequent. In like manner storms alternate with calms; and Christ's word which stilled the tempest, did but effect in a moment what the very conditions of nature must have effected in the end. Even the transmutation from water to wine, and the multiplication of bread, are not without their analogies in nature, however remote; and thus too is it with most of the other miracles. But between death and life a gulf lies which no fact furnished by our experience can help us even in imagination to bridge. It is nothing wonderful, therefore, that miracles of this class are signs more spoken against than any other among all the mighty works of the Lord.

The present will be a fitting moment to say something on the relations in which the three miracles of this transcendent character stand to one another; for they are not exactly the same miracle repeated three times over, but may be contemplated as each a more marvellous outcoming of the great power of Christ than the preceding. We shall at once recognize in the quickening of him that had been four days dead (John xi. 17), a still mightier wonder than in the raising of the young man who was borne out to his burial (Luke vii. 12) ; whose burial, according to Jewish custom, will have followed death by an interval, at most, of a single day; and again in *that* miracle a mightier outcoming of Christ's power than in the present, wherein life's flame, like some newly extinguished taper, was still more easily re-kindled, when thus brought in contact with Him who is the fountain-flame of all life. Immeasurably more stupendous than all these, will be the wonder of that hour, when all the dead of old, who will have lain, some of them for many thousand years, in the dust of death, shall be summoned from and shall leave their graves at the same quickening voice (John v. 28, 29).

CHAPTER VII.

The Healing of the Woman With An Issue of Blood

MATT. ix. 20-22; MARK v. 25-34; LUKE viii. 43-48.

IN ALL three reports which we have of this miracle, it is mixed up with that other of the raising of Jairus' daughter, and cuts that narrative in two. Such overflowing grace is in Him, the Prince of life, that as He is hastening to accomplish one work of grace and power, He accomplishes another, as by the way.

The Lord had consented to follow Jairus to his house, *and much people thronged him and pressed him,* curious, no doubt, to witness what the issue would be. But it was not so with all. Mingled with and confounded in that crowd was *a certain woman, which had an issue of blood twelve years, and had suffered many things of many physicians, and had spent all that she had, and was nothing bettered, but rather grew worse.* This woman, afflicted so long, who had suffered much from her disease, perhaps more from her physicians, all whose means had been exhausted in costly remedies and in the vain quest of some cure, *when she had heard of Jesus, came in the press behind, and touched his garment. For she said, If I may touch but his clothes, I shall be whole.* Her faith, who so argued, was most real; we have the Lord's own testimony to this (*Thy faith hath saved thee*); while yet her conception of the manner of the working of Christ's healing power was a material conception, and not unmingled with error. He healed, she must have supposed, by no power of his holy will, but rather by a certain magical influence and virtue which dwelt in Him, and emanated from Him. It is possible that she *touched the hem of his garment* (cf. Mark vi. 56), not merely as its uttermost part, that therefore which

115

she, timidly drawing near, could most easily reach, but as attrib-
uting a peculiar sanctity to it. For this hem, or blue fringe on the
borders of the garment, was put there by divine command, and
served to remind the Jewish wearer of the special relation to
God in which he stood (Num. xv. 37-40; Deut. xxii. 12). But
the faith of this woman, though thus imperfect in its form, was
yet in its essence most true. It therefore was the channel to her
of the blessing which she desired. No sooner had she touched
the hem of his robe than *straightway the fountain of her blood
was dried up; and she felt in her body that she was healed of
that plague.*

The boon which she had gotten she would fain carry away
in secret, if she might, but *Jesus, immediately knowing in himself that virtue had gone out of him, turned him about in the
press and said, Who touched my clothes?* The Evangelists employ language which in a measure falls in with the current of the
woman's thoughts; yet we cannot for an instant suppose that
healing power went forth from the Lord without the full consent
of his will.[1] For if power went forth from Him to heal, without
reference, on his part, to the spiritual condition of the person
that was its subject, the ethical, which is ever by far the most
important aspect of the miracle, would at once disappear. But
He who saw Nathaniel under the fig-tree (John i. 48), who
"needed not that any should testify of man, for He knew what
was in man" (John ii. 25), must have known of this woman
how sorely in her body she required his help, and how in her
spirit she possessed that faith which was the one channel of
communication between Him and any human need. Nor may
his question, *Who touched my clothes?* be urged as implying
that He was ignorant who had so done. That question was asked
with quite another purpose than this. Had she succeeded in
carrying away in secret that good which she had gotten, it would

---

[1] Chrysostom: "She received her health from a willing and not from an unwilling
healer, for He knew who it was that touched Him."

have failed to be at all that excellent gift to her which her Saviour intended that it should be. For this it was needful that she should be drawn from her hiding-place, and compelled to avouch both what she had sought, and what had found, of help and healing from Him. With as little force can it be urged that it would have been inconsistent with absolute truth for the Lord to profess ignorance. The same offence might be found with Elisha's "Whence comest thou, Gehazi?" (2 Kin. v. 25), when his heart went with his unfaithful servant all the way that he had gone; and even in the question of God Himself to Adam, "Where art thou?" (Gen. iii. 9). In every case there is a moral purpose in the question.

Out of that thronging multitude one only *touched* with the touch of faith. Others there may have had complaints as inveterate as hers; but such, though as near or nearer in body, yet lacked that faith which would have been the connecting link between Christ's power and their need; and thus they crowded upon Him, but did not *touch* Him, did not so touch that virtue went forth from Him on them. It is evermore thus in the Church of God. Many *throng* Christ;[2] his in name; near to Him outwardly; in actual contact with the sacraments and ordinances of his Church; yet not *touching* Him, because not drawing nigh in faith, not looking for, and therefore not obtaining, life and healing from Him, and through these.

The disciples, and Peter as their spokesman, wonder at the question. A certain sense of its unreason as it presents itself to them, marks their reply: *Thou seest the multitude thronging thee, and sayest thou, Who touched me?* He, however, reaffirms the fact, *Somebody hath touched me: for I perceive that virtue is gone out of me.* And now the woman, perceiving that any further attempts at concealment were useless, that to repeat the

---

[2] I cannot but think that the substitution of *crush* for *throng* here, as for instance it is done in the R. V., is a mistake, that *throng* with its slightly archaic air should have been suffered to remain.

denial which she probably had made with the rest, for *all denied* (Luke viii. 45), would profit her nothing; unable, too, to escape his searching glance, for *He looked round about to see her* (Mark v. 32), *came trembling,* fearing it may be his anger, for the touch of one afflicted as she was caused ceremonial uncleanness (Lev. xv. 19, 25) ; *and falling down before him, she declared unto him,* and this *before all the people for what cause she had touched him, and how she was healed immediately.* Olshausen traces very beautifully the grace which reigns in this miracle, and in the order of the circumstances of it. This woman would have borne away a maimed blessing, hardly a blessing at all, had she been suffered to bear it away in secret and unacknowledged, and without being brought into any personal communion with her Healer. Her divine Healer draws her from concealment; but even here, so far as possible, He spares her; for not before, but after she is healed, does He require the open confession from her lips. Waiting till the cure is accomplished, He helps her through the narrow way. Altogether spare her this painful passage He could not, for it pertained to her birth into the new life.

And now He dismisses her with words of gracious encouragement: *Daughter, be of good comfort* (cf. Matt. ix. 10) ; *thy faith hath made thee whole* (cf. Luke vii. 50; xvii. 19; xviii. 42).[3] Her faith had made her whole, and Christ's virtue had made her whole. Not otherwise we say that we are justified by faith, and justified by Christ; faith not being itself the blessing, but the organ by which the blessing is received. *Go in peace* (cf. 1 Sam. i. 17) ; this is not merely, "Go with a blessing," but "Enter into peace, as the element in which thy future life shall move"; — *and be whole of thy plague,* — which promise was at once fulfilled to her; for *the woman was made whole from that hour.*

---

[3] Godet: "Thy faith, and not as thou thinkest, the physical touch. Jesus thus refers to the moral order the power which she placed only in the material."

If we keep in mind how her uncleanness separated her off as one impure, we shall have here an exact picture of the sinner, drawing nigh to the throne of grace, but out of the sense of his impurity not "with boldness," rather with fear and trembling, hardly knowing what there he shall expect; but who is welcomed there, and all his carnal doubtings and questionings at once chidden and expelled, dismissed with the word of an abiding peace resting upon him.

CHAPTER VIII.

The Opening of the Eyes of Two Blind in the House

MATT. ix. 27-31.

WE have here a miracle which St. Matthew alone has recorded, being the first of those many healings of the blind related (Matt. xii. 22; xx. 30; xxi. 14; John ix.) or alluded to (Matt. xi. 5; Luke vii. 21) in the Gospels; each of them a literal fulfilment of that prophetic word of Isaiah concerning the days of Messiah: "Then the eyes of the blind shall be opened" (xxxv. 5). That they should be so many is nothing wonderful, whether we regard the fact from a natural or a spiritual point of view. Regarded naturally, their number need not surprise us, if we keep in mind how far more common a calamity is blindness in the East than with us. Regarded from a higher point of view, we need only remember how constantly sin is contemplated in Scripture as a moral blindness (Deut. xxviii. 29; Isai. lix. 10; Job xii. 25; Zeph. i. 17), and deliverance from sin as a removal of this blindness (Isai. xxix. 18; xlii. 18; xliii. 8; Ephes. v. 8; Matt xv. 14).

And when Jesus departed thence — from the house of Jairus, Jerome supposes; but too much stress must not be laid on the connexion in which St. Matthew sets the miracle, nor the conclusion certainly drawn that he intended to place it in such immediate relation of time and place — *two blind men followed him, crying, and saying, Thou Son of David, have mercy on us.* In that *Son of David* they recognize Him as the promised Messiah (Matt. xxi. 9; xxii. 42; cf. Ezek. xxxiv. 23, 34; Luke i. 32). But their faith must not stop short in this mere confession of Him; it must be further tried; and the Lord proceeds to try it. The Lord for a while seems to pay no regard to their cries. It is only *when he was come into the house,* and *the blind men came to him* there, so testifying the faith of their hearts, that He yields to them.[1] He must obtain too, a further confession from their own lips: *Believe ye that I am able to do this?* And it is only after they, by their *Yea, Lord,* have avouched that they had faith to be healed, that the blessing is made theirs. Then *touched he their eyes,* and that simple touch was enough. On other occasions He uses as conductors of his power, and helps to the faith of those who should be healed, some further means, — the clay mingled with spittle (John ix. 6, 7), or the moisture of his mouth alone (Mark viii. 23). We nowhere read of his opening the blind eyes simply by his word, though this of course lay equally within the range of his power. The words, *According to your faith be it unto you,* are instructive for the insight they give us into the relation of man's faith and God's gift. The faith, which in itself is nothing, is yet the organ for receiving everything. It is the conducting link between man's emptiness and God's fulness; and herein is all the value which it has.

And Jesus straitly charged them, saying, See that no man know it (cf. Mark i. 45; v. 43; Matt. xvii. 2). *But they, when they were departed, spread abroad his fame in all that country.* Roman Catholics applaud rather than condemn these men for not adhering strictly to Christ's command. The teachers in that Church of will-worship see in their disobedience the irrepressible overflowings of grateful hearts, which, as such, should be regarded not as a fault, but a merit. But of the interpreters of the Reformed Church, whose first principle is to take God's Word as absolute rule and law, and to worship Him not with self-advised services, but after the pattern which He has shown, all stand fast to this, that obedience is better than sacrifice, even though the sacrifice be intended for God's special honour (1 Sam.

---

[1] Calvin: "He wished to prove their faith by deed and words: for by keeping them in suspense, nay, by actually passing by as if He did not hear, He makes proof of their patience and of what root faith had taken in their hearts."

xv. 21). They see in this publishing of the miracle, despite of Christ's word to the contrary, a fault which remained a fault, even while they recognize it as one which only grateful hearts could have committed.[2]

---

[2] Farrar (*Life of Christ*, vol. i. p. 359) judges these busy babblers still more harshly than I have done; and has perhaps warrant sufficient for this greater severity.

CHAPTER IX.

The Healing of the Paralytic

MATT. ix. 1-8; MARK ii. 1-12; LUKE v. 17-26.

THE account of St. Luke would leave us altogether in ignorance *where* this miracle of healing took place. From St.
Matthew we learn that it was in *his own city*, Capernaum, as
from this description we should have justly concluded, even if
St. Mark had not named it by name; seeing that as Bethlehem
was the birth-place of Christ, and Nazareth his nursing-place, so
was Capernaum his ordinary dwelling-place (cf. Matt. xvii. 24)
from the time of his rejection by the Nazarenes (Luke iv. 30,
31).[1] *And it came to pass on a certain day, as he was teaching,
that there were Pharisees and doctors of the law sitting by, which
were come out of every town of Galilee, and Judea, and Jerusalem.* It may have been a conference which had brought together as listeners and spectators a multitude so vast that all
avenues of approach to the house were blocked up; *there was no
room to receive them, no, not so much as about the door;* and
thus for later comers no opportunity, by any ordinary means, of
near access to the Lord (cf. Matt. xii. 46, 47). Among these
were some *bringing one sick of the palsy.* Only St. Mark records
for us that he *was borne of four;* St. Luke with him relates the
novel method which these took to bring him within that circle
of healing: *When they could not come nigh unto him for the
press, they uncovered the roof where he was: and when they had
broken it up, they let down the bed wherein the sick of the
palsy lay.* They first ascended to the roof. This was not so
difficult, seeing that commonly there was a flight of steps on

---

[1] Chrysostom: "Bethlehem bare Him, Nazareth nurtured Him, Capernaum had
Him continuously as an inhabitant."

the outside of the house, by which access to the roof was obtained. A portion of the roof was removed, and so the bed on which the palsied man lay let down before the Lord.

He who never takes ill that faith which brings men to Him, but only the unbelief which keeps them from Him, is in nothing offended at this interruption; yea, rather beheld with an eye well pleased the boldness of this act of theirs: *Jesus seeing their faith said unto the sick of the palsy; Son, be of good cheer; thy sins be forgiven thee* or, as St. Luke has it, *Man, thy sins are forgiven thee.* Had we only the account of St. Matthew, we might be at a loss to understand wherein their special faith consisted, or why their faith, more than that of many others who brought their sick to Jesus (cf. Mark vi. 55, 56 vii. 32), should have been noted. From the other Evangelists we learn that it was a faith which overcame hindrances, and was not to be baffled by difficulties.[2] *Their faith* is not, as Jerome and Ambrose understand it, the faith of the bearers only. These must not be excluded; but unless the sick man had approved what they did, it would not have been done.

In what follows we have a beautiful example of the way in which the Giver of all good things gives *before* we ask, and *better* than we ask. This poor suppliant had as yet asked nothing; save in that earnest effort to struggle into the immediate neighbourhood of the Lord; and all that in this he dared to ask, certainly all that his friends and bearers sought for him, was that he might be healed of his palsy. Yet in him, no doubt, there was a deep feeling of the root out of which all sickness grows, namely, out of sin; perhaps in his own sickness he recognized the penalty of some especial sin whereof his conscience accused him. *Son, be of good cheer; thy sins be forgiven thee,* are words addressed to one burdened with a more intolerable weight than that of his bodily infirmities. Some utterance upon his part of

---

[2] Bengel: "Faith penetrates through all obstacles to come to Christ."

a penitent and contrite heart may very probably have called out those words. In other instances the forgiveness of sin *follows* the outward healing; for we may certainly presume that such a forgiveness was the portion of the thankful Samaritan (Luke xvii. 19), of the impotent man, first healed, and then warned to sin no more (John v. 14) ; but here the remission of sin takes the precedence: nor is it hard to perceive the reason. In the sufferer's own conviction there existed so close a connexion between his sin and his sickness, that the bodily healing would have been scarcely intelligible to him, would have hardly brought home to him the sense of a benefit, unless in his conscience he had been also set free; perhaps he was incapable even of receiving the benefit, till the message of peace had been spoken to his spirit.

The absolving words are no mere desire that so it might be, but *declaratory* that the man's sins *were* forgiven. God's justification of a sinner is not merely a word spoken *about* him, but a word spoken *to* him and *in* him; not an act of God's *immanent* in Himself, but *transitive* upon the sinner. The murmurers and cavillers also understood rightly of this forgiveness of sins, that it is a *divine* prerogative; that no one can forgive sin save him against whom all sin is committed, that is, God; and out of this conviction, most true in itself, but most false in their present application of it, *certain of the scribes sitting there* said within themselves, *Why doth this man thus speak blasphemies?* (cf. Luke vii. 49; John x. 33). *Who can forgive sins but God only?*

Olshausen bids us note here the profound insight into the relations between God and the creature, involved in the scriptural use of the word "blasphemy"; a use of which profane antiquity knew nothing. With it 'to blaspheme' meant only to speak evil of a person (a use not foreign to Scripture, 1 Cor. iv. 13; Tit. iii. 2; 2 Pet. ii. 2; Jud. 8), and then, to speak something of an evil omen. The monotheistic religion alone included in blasphemy not merely words of cursing and outrage against the name of God, but all snatchings on the part of the creature at honours which of right belonged only to the Creator (Matt. xxvi. 65; John x. 36).[3] Had He who in his own name declared, *Thy sins be forgiven thee,* been less than the only-begotten Son of the Father and sharer in all prerogatives of the Godhead, He would indeed have spoken blasphemies, as they supposed. Believing Him only a man, they were right in saying He blasphemed. Their sin was not in this, but in that self-chosen blindness of theirs, which would not allow them to recognize any glory in Him higher than man's; in the pride and the obstinacy which led them, having arrived at a foregone conclusion as to what kind of Saviour they would have, wilfully to close their eyes to all in their own Scriptures which set Him forth as other than they had themselves resolved He should be.

The Lord is said to have *perceived in his spirit that they so reasoned within themselves.* His soul was human, but his *spirit* was divine; and by this divine faculty He perceived the unspoken counsels and meditations of their hearts[4] (John vi. 61). They should be doubly convinced; and first by the proof that the thoughts and meditations of all hearts were open and manifest to Him, while yet it is God only who searches into these. (1 Sam. xvi. 7; 1 Kin. viii. 39; 1 Chron. xxviii. 9; 2 Chron. vi. 30; Jer. xvii. 10; Ezek. xi 5; Prov. xv. 11; Acts i. 24.) *Why reason ye these things in your hearts?* And on this first conviction there follows a second: *Whether is it easier to say to the sick of the palsy, Thy sins be forgiven thee; or to say, Arise, and take up thy bed, and walk?* He indicates to them here the exact line of their hard and unrighteous thoughts about Him. Something of this sort they were murmuring within themselves. "Any

---

[3] Bengel: "It is blasphemy, 1, when things unworthy of God are ascribed to Him; 2, when things worthy of God are denied to Him; 3, when things which belong to God are ascribed to those to whom they are not due."

[4] Grotius: "Not as the prophets, by inspiration, but by his own spirit."

pretender may go about the world, saying to this man and that, *Thy sins be forgiven thee.* But what proof is there that this word of his, spoken on earth, is ratified in heaven?" And our Lord's answer, meeting this evil thought of theirs, is in fact this: "I will therefore put Myself to a decisive proof. I will speak a word, I will claim a power, which if I claim falsely, I shall be convicted upon the instant as an impostor and a deceiver. *But that ye may know that the Son of man hath power on earth to forgive sins, (he saith to the sick of the palsy), I say unto thee, Arise, and take up thy bed, and go thy way into thine house.* By the effects, as they follow or do not follow, you may judge whether I have a right to say to him, *Thy sins be forgiven thee.*"

In our Lord's argument it must be carefully noted that He does not ask, "Which is easier, to forgive sins, or to raise a sick man by a word?" but, "Which is easier, to claim this power, or to claim that; *to say,* Thy sins be forgiven thee, or *to say,* Arise and walk?" And he then proceeds: "That is easier, and I will now prove my right to say it, by saying with effect and with an outward consequence setting its seal to my truth, the harder word, *Rise up and walk.* By doing that which is submitted to the eyes of men, I will attest my right and power to do that which, in its very nature, lies outside of the region of visible proofs. From this which I will now do openly and before you all, you may conclude that it is no 'robbery' (Phil. ii. 6) upon my part, no snatching at what is not mine, to claim also the power of forgiving men their sins."

In *power on earth* there lies a tacit antithesis to power in heaven. "This power is not exercised, as you deem, only by God *in heaven;* but also by the Son of man *on earth.* You rightly assert that it is only exercised by Him whose proper dwelling is in the heavens; but He, who in the person of the Son of man, has descended also upon earth, has brought down this power with Him here. On earth also is One who can speak and it is done." It at first surprises that as *Son of Man* He claims this power; for this of forgiving sins being a *divine* attribute, we might expect that He would now call Himself by his better name, since only as Son *of God* such prerogative was his. Unless the two natures had been indissolubly knit together in a single person, no such language could have been used; yet *Son of man* being the standing title whereby the Lord was well pleased to designate Himself, asserting as it did that He was at once one with humanity, and the crown of humanity, it is simpler to regard the term here as merely equivalent to Messiah, without attempting to extort any dogmatic conclusions from it. All which our Lord explicitly claimed for Himself in those great discourses recorded in John v. 17-23; x. 30-38, He implicitly claims here.

And now this word of his is confirmed and sealed by a sign following. The man did not refuse to answer this appeal: *And immediately he arose, took up the bed* (cf. John v. 8; Acts ix. 34), *and went forth before them all;* the couch which was before the sign of his sickness being now the sign of his cure; and they who just before barred and blocked up his path, now making way for him, and allowing free egress from the assembly (cf. Mark x. 48, 49).

Of the effects of this miracle on the Pharisees nothing is told us; probably there was nothing good to tell. But the people, less hardened against the truth, *marvelled,* so we read in St. Matthew, but better, *were afraid;*[5] or as St. Mark has it, *they were all amazed* (cf. Matt. xii. 23; Mark i. 27; v. 42; vi. 51; vii. 37), *and glorified God, saying, We never saw it on this fashion* (cf. Matt. xv. 31; John xi. 45, 46). The miracle had done its office. The beholders marvelled and their marvel found

---

[5] Arnobius (*Con. Gen.* i. 45), speaking generally of Christ's healings, but with manifest allusion to this: "Men carried home their beds, who but a little before had been borne on the shoulders of others." Bengel: "The bed had borne the man, now the man was bearing the bed."

utterance in the ascription of glory to God, *who had given such power unto men.* We need not suppose that they very accurately explained to themselves, or could have explained to others their feeling of holy exultation. They dimly understood, but they mightily felt, that the *Son of Man* possessed these powers as the true Head and Representative of the race, that therefore gifts to Him were a rightful subject of rejoicing for every member of the family of man.

CHAPTER X.

The Cleansing of the Leper

MATT. viii. 1-4; MARK i. 40-45; LUKE v. 12-16.

WE shall ill understand this miracle without something first said concerning leprosy in general, and the meaning of the uncleanness attached to it in the Levitical law. It will be necessary to correct a mistake. I refer to the mistaken assumption that leprosy was catching from one person to another; and that lepers were so carefully secluded from their fellow-men, lest they might communicate the poison of the disease to others; as, in like manner, that the torn garment, the covered lip, the cry "Unclean, unclean" (Lev. xiii. 45), were warnings to all that they should keep aloof, lest unawares touching a leper, or drawing into too great a nearness, they should become partakers of his disease. Nearly all who have looked closest into the matter agree that the sickness was incommunicable by ordinary contact from one person to another.

All the notices in the Old Testament, as well as in other Jewish books, confirm the statement that we have here something very much higher than a mere sanitary regulation. Thus, where the law of Moses was not observed, no such exclusion necessarily found place; Naaman the leper commanded the armies of Syria (2 Kin. v. 1). And even where the law of Moses was in force, the stranger and the sojourner were expressly exempted from the ordinances relating to leprosy. How, moreover, should the Levitical priests, had the disease been this creeping infection, have themselves escaped it, obliged as they were by their very office to submit the leper to actual handling and closest examination?

The ordinances concerning leprosy had another and far deeper significance. It is clear that the same principle which made all having to do with death, as mourning (Lev. xxi. 1,; Ezek. xliv. 25) ; a grave (Luke xi. 44; Matt. xxiii. 27), a corpse, the bones of a dead man (Ezek. xxxix. 12-15; 2 Kin. xxiii. 20), the occasions of a ceremonial uncleanness, inasmuch as all these were signs and consequences of sin, might consistently with this have made every sickness an occasion of uncleanness, each of these being also death beginning, partial death — echoes in the body of that terrible reality, sin in the soul. But instead of this, in a gracious sparing of man, and not driving things to the uttermost, God took but one sickness in which to testify that evil was not from Him, could not dwell with Him. He linked this teaching but with one; by his laws concerning it to train men into a sense of a clinging impurity, which needed a Pure and a Purifier to overcome and expel, and which nothing short of his taking of our flesh could drive out.

And fearful was that disease, round which this solemn teaching revolved. Leprosy was nothing short of a living death, a corrupting of all the humours, a poisoning of the very springs, of life; a dissolution little by little of the whole body, so that one limb after another actually decayed and fell away. The disease, moreover, was incurable by the art and skill of man; not that the leper might not return to health; for, however rare such cases might be, they are contemplated as possible in the Levitical law. But then the leprosy left the man, not in obedience to any skill of the physician, but purely and merely through the good will and mercy of God.

The leper, thus fearfully bearing about in the body the outward and visible tokens of sin in the soul, was treated throughout as a sinner, as one in whom sin had reached its climax, as *dead* in trespasses and sins. He was himself a dreadful parable of death. He bore about him the emblems of death (Lev. xiii.

45) ; the rent garments, mourning for himself as one dead; the head bare, as was their wont who were defiled by communion with the dead (Num. vi. 9; Ezek. xxiv. 17) ; and the lip covered (Ezek. xxiv. 17).[1] In the restoration, too, of a leper, precisely the same instruments of cleansing were in use, the cedar-wood, the hyssop, and scarlet, as were used for the cleansing of one defiled through a dead body, or aught pertaining to death; these same being never employed on any other occasion (cf. Num. xix. 6, 18, with Lev. xiv. 4-7). And leprosy being this sign and token of sin, and of sin reaching to and culminating in death, could not do otherwise than entail a total exclusion from the camp or city of God. God is not a God of the dead; He has no fellowship with death, for death is the correlative sin; but only of the living.

Nothing in all this in the least implied that the leper was a worse or guiltier man than his fellows. Being, indeed as it was, this symbol of sin, leprosy was often the punishment of sins committed against the divine government. Miriam, Gehazi, Uzziah are all cases in point. The Jews themselves called it "the finger of God," and emphatically "the stroke."

Seeing then that leprosy was this outward and visible sign of the innermost spiritual corruption, on no fitter shape of physical evil could the Lord of life show forth his power. He will thus prove Himself the conqueror of death in life; and He therefore fitly urges his victory over this most terrible form of physical evil as a convincing testimony of his Messiahship. Nor may we doubt that the terribleness of the infliction, the extreme suffering with which it was linked, the horror with which it must have filled the sufferer's mind, as he marked its slow but inevitable progress, to be arrested by no human hand, the ghastly hideousness of its unnatural whiteness (Num. xii. 10; Exod. iv. 6; 2 Kin. v. 27), must all have combined to draw out his pity,

---

[1] Spencer calls him well "a walking sepulchre"; and Calvin: "They were accounted dead whom leprosy inhibited from the sacred assembly."

in whom love went hand in hand with power, the Physician and Healer of the bodies as of the souls of men.

We address ourselves now to the first of these acts at once of healing and of cleansing whereof the Gospels keep a record. His discourse upon the Mount has scarcely ended, when this and other of his most memorable miracles are performed. He will thus set his seal to all that He has just been teaching, and vindicate his right to speak in the language of authority which He has there held[2] (Matt. vii. 29). As He was descending from the mountain, *behold, there came a leper and worshipped him;* he was one, in the language of St. Luke, *full of leprosy;* he was leprous from head to foot. This man had ventured, it may be, to linger on the outskirts of the listening crowd, and, undeterred by the severity of the closing sentences of Christ's discourse, came now to claim the blessings promised at its opening to the suffering and the mourning.

Such worship as he offered to the Lord was an act of profound reverence, but not of necessity a recognition of a divine character in Him to whom it was offered. Some vague sense of the Divinity which invested the Lord this sufferer may not have been without; even as the words in which he clothed his petition are the utterance of a faith at once so true and so humble, content, having declared its desire, to leave the granting or the withholding of this to a higher wisdom and love: *Lord, if thou wilt, thou canst make me clean.* There is no questioning here of power; nothing of unbelief. *And Jesus, moved with compassion,* as St. Mark alone records, *put forth his hand, and touched him,* ratifying and approving his utterance of faith, by granting his request in the very words wherein that request had been made: *I will; be thou clean. And immediately his leprosy was cleansed.* This touching of the unclean by Christ is noteworthy, drawing

---

[2] Jerome: "After preaching and teaching an occasion is rightly presented for signs, that the foregoing sermon might be fixed in the hearts of its hearers by means of miracles of power."

after it, as according to the ordinances of the Law it did, a ceremonial uncleanness. Another would have defiled *himself* by
touching the leper (Lev. xiii. 44-46) ; but He, Himself remaining undefiled, cleansed him whom He touched; for in Him
health overcame sickness, — and purity, defilement, — and life,
death.[3]

And Jesus saith unto him, See thou tell no man (cf. Matt. ix.
30; xii. 16, xvi. 20; xvii. 9; Mark iii. 12; v. 43; vii. 36;
viii. 26; ix. 9; Luke viii. 56; ix. 21). If the prohibition did not
find its motive in the inner moral condition of the man, its
more probable reason was, lest his own stiller ministry should
be hindered by the untimely concourse of multitudes, drawn to
Him in the hope of worldly benefits (as on this very occasion
actually did occur, Mark i. 45) ; or in the expectation of seeing
wonderful things; or it might be, lest the enmity of his foes
should be prematurely roused by the fame of his mighty deeds
(John xi. 46, 47). But, as has been observed already (see pp.
191, 192), the injunction to one that he should proclaim, to
another that he should conceal, the great things which God had
wrought for him, had far more probably a deeper motive, and
grounded itself on the different moral conditions of the persons
healed. Grotius and Bengel suggest very plausibly that this *See
thou tell no man* should be taken with this limitation — "till
thou hast fulfilled that which I enjoin thee, that is, to *go thy
way, shew thyself to the priest, and offer the gift that Moses
commanded, for a testimony unto them."* Till this was accomplished, he should hold his peace; lest, if a rumour of these
things went before him, the priests at Jerusalem, out of envy,
out of a desire to depreciate what the Lord had wrought, might
deny that the man had ever been a leper, or else that he was
now truly cleansed. We may thus account for the notice of St.
Mark, *he forthwith sent him away*, or, *put him forth;* He would

---

[3] He touched the leper, says Theophylact, "showing that his sacred flesh imparted
sanctification."

allow no lingering, but required him to hasten on his errand, lest a report of his cure should outrun him. We should understand the words, *"for a testimony against them* (cf. Mark vi. 11; Luke ix. 5); for a witness against their unbelief, who refuse to give credence to Me, even while I legitimate my claims by such mighty works as these; works to the reality of which they will have set their own seal, accepting thy gift, readmitting thee, as one truly cleansed, into the congregation"[4] (John v. 36; xv. 24). On the healed leper's neglect of this command to keep silence, for instead of so doing, *he went out, and began to publish it much, and to blaze abroad the matter.* (Mark i. 45), see what has been said already on a similar act of disobedience (page 125).

---

[4] Maldonatus: "That the priests might be without excuse if they believe not on Him, whose miracles they had proved."

CHAPTER XI.

The Healing of the Centurion's Servant

MATT. viii. 5-13; LUKE vii. 1-10.

THERE has been occasion already to denounce the error of confounding this miracle of healing with that of the nobleman's son, recorded by St. John (iv. 46). But while we may not seek forcibly to reduce to a single story two narratives which record events entirely different, there is matter enough in the two reports of this miracle, the one by St. Matthew, the other by St. Luke, on which the harmonist may exercise his skill. According to the first Evangelist, the centurion comes a petitioner in his own person for the boon which he desires; according to the third, he sends others as intercessors and mediators between himself and the Lord, with other differences which necessarily follow and flow from this. Doubtless the latter is the more strictly literal account of the circumstances, as they actually came to pass; St. Matthew, who is briefer, telling it as though the centurion did in his own person, what, in fact, he did by the intervention of others — an exchange of persons of which all historical narrative and all the language of our common life are full. A comparison of Mark x. 35 with Matt xx. 23 will furnish another example of the same.

And when Jesus was entered into Capernaum, there came unto him a centurion, beseeching him, and saying, Lord, my servant lieth at home grievously tormented. This centurion, probably one of the Roman garrison of Capernaum, was by birth a heathen; but was one of many who were at this time deeply feeling the emptiness and falsehood of all the polytheistic religions, and who had attached themselves by laxer or closer bonds, as proselytes of the gate, or proselytes of righteousness, to the congre-

139

gation of Israel and the worship of Jehovah, finding in Judaism
a satisfaction of some of the deepest needs of their souls, and a
promise of the satisfaction of all. He was one among the many
whom the providence of God had so wonderfully prepared in all
the great cities of the Greek and Roman world as a link of communication between Gentile and Jew, in contact with both —
holding to the first by their race, and to the last by their religion;
and who must have materially helped to the early spread of the
faith and to the ultimate coalescence of Gentile and Jew in one
Christian Church.

But with the higher matters which he had learned from his
intercourse with the people of the Covenant, he had learned
that there was a middle wall of partition between them and the
children of the stock of Abraham. And thus, as we learn from
St. Luke (vii. 3), he did not himself approach, but *when he
heard of Jesus, he sent unto him the elders of the Jews, beseeching him that he would come and heal his servant,* a servant who
was dear unto him,[1] but who now *was sick, and ready to die.*
The Jewish elders executed their commission with fidelity and
zeal, pleading for him as for one whose affection for the chosen
people, and active well-doing in their behalf, had merited this
return of favour: *They besought him instantly, saying, That he
was worthy for whom he should do this: for he loveth our
nation, and he hath built us a synagogue.* Nor did they plead
in vain. *Jesus went with them.*

But presently even this request seemed to the maker of it too
bold. *And when he was now not far from the house, the centurion sent friends to him, saying unto him, Lord, trouble not
thyself: for I am not worthy that thou shouldest enter under my*

---

[1] Calvin: "Luke in this way anticipates a doubt which might come over the minds
of his readers: for we know that slaves were not held in such value that their masters
would be as anxious as this about their lives, except in the case of those who had
won favour by unusual zeal, faithfulness, or other virtue. Luke, therefore, shows that
this was no common or paltry human chattel, but a faithful and rarely gifted slave
who enjoyed exceptional favour with his lord; hence such great anxiety for his life
and such zealous commendation."

roof. It was not merely that he, a heathen, might claim no near access to the King of Israel; but there was, no doubt, beneath this and mingling with this, a lively sense of his own personal unworthiness, of his unfitness for a close communion with a holy being. And thus, in Augustine's words, "counting himself unworthy that Christ should enter into his doors, he was counted worthy that Christ should enter into his heart." This centurion received *Him* in his heart, whom he did not receive in his house.[2]

But say in a word, and my servant shall be healed. He knows that Christ's *word,* without his actual presence, will be sufficient; there is that in his own experience which assures him as much; for, he adds, *I am a man under authority, having soldiers under me: and I say to this man, Go, and he goeth; and to another, Come, and he cometh; and to my servant, Do this, and he doeth it.* He contemplates the relation of Christ to the spiritual kingdom in an aspect as original as it is grand. The Lord presents Himself to him as the true Caesar and *Imperator,* the highest over the military hierarchy, not of earth, but of heaven (Col. i. 16). He would say, "With Angels and Spirits to obey thy word and run swiftly at thy command, Thou canst fulfil from a distance all the good pleasure of thy will. There is then no need that Thou shouldest come to my house; only commission one of these genii of healing, who will execute speedily the errand of grace and power on which Thou shalt send him."

In all this there was so wonderful a union of faith and humility, that it is nothing strange to read that the Lord Himself was filled with admiration: *When Jesus heard it, he marvelled, and said to them that followed, Verily I say unto you, I have not found so great faith, no, not in Israel.*[3] Where faith is, there will

---

[2]Augustine (*Serm.* lxxvii. 12): "He did not receive him into his house, but he had received him already into his heart. The more humble, the more capacious, and the more full. For the hills drive back the water, but the valleys are filled by it."

[3] Augustine: "I have not found in the olive that which I found in the wild olive. Therefore let the olive which exalts herself be broken off, and the humble wild olive be graffed in. Lo! here is he that graffs in, here is he that breaks off!" Cf. *In Joh. tract.* xvi. ad finem.

be the kingdom of God; so that this saying already contains a warning to his Jewish hearers, of the danger they are in of forfeiting blessings whereof others are showing themselves worthier than they. But the words which follow are far more explicit: *And I say unto you, That many shall come from the east and west,* that is, from the ends of the earth (Isai. xlv. 6; Mal. i. 11); *and shall sit down with Abraham, and Isaac, and Jacob, in the kingdom of heaven,* shall be partakers of the heavenly festival (Isai. xxv. 6; Luke xiv. 16; Rev. xix. 9, 17); *but the children of the kingdom shall be cast out into outer darkness: there shall be weeping and gnashing of teeth;* or, worse than this, *the weeping and gnashing of teeth;* that which is the allotted portion of these (Matt. viii. 42, 50; xxii. 13; xxiv. 51; xxv. 30). In other words, the kingdom should be taken from them, "and given to a nation bringing forth the fruits thereof" (Matt. xxi. 43); because of their unbelief, they, the natural branches of the olive tree, should be broken off, and the wild olive should be graffed in (Rom. xi. 17-24; Acts xiii. 46; xix. 9; xxviii. 28; Matt. iii. 9).

And Jesus said unto the centurion, or to him in his messengers, *Go thy way; and as thou hast believed, so be it done unto thee. And his servant was healed in the selfsame hour;* — not merely was there an abatement of the violence of the disease, but it left him altogether (John iv. 52, Matt. viii. 15). There is a certain difficulty in defining the exact character of the sickness from which he was thus graciously delivered. Of every form of palsy it could not be said that those taken by it are *grievously tormented,* or that they are *ready to die.* But paralysis with contraction of the muscles is accompanied with intense suffering, and, when united, as it much oftener is in the hot climates of the East and of Africa than among us, with tetanus, both *grievously torments,* and rapidly brings on dissolution.

CHAPTER XII.

The Demoniac in the Synagogue of Capernaum

MARK i. 23-27, LUKE iv. 33-36.

THE healing of this demoniac, the second miracle of the kind which the Evangelists record at any length, has its own features of interest. What distinguishes it the most is the testimony which the evil spirit bears to Christ, and *his* refusal to accept it; though this circumstance is not without its parallels elsewhere (Matt. viii. 29; Mark i. 34). This history stands in very instructive relation with another in the Acts (xvi. 16-18).

Our Lord was teaching, as was his wont upon a Sabbath (cf. Luke iv. 16; Acts xiii. 14, 15), in the synagogue of Capernaum; and the people now, as on other similar occasions (see Matt. vii. 29; Mark i. 22; xi. 18), *were astonished at his doctrine, for his word was with power.* It was ordained by the providence of his Heavenly Father, that the opportunity should here be offered Him for confirming his word with signs following. *There was in their synagogue a man with an unclean spirit;* or, as St. Luke describes it, *with the spirit of an unclean devil;* but not therefore excluded from the public worship of God; and this spirit felt at once the nearness of One who was stronger than all that kingdom whereto he belonged; of One whose mission it was to destroy the works of the devil. And with the instinct and consciousness of this danger which so nearly threatened his usurped dominion, he cried out, — not the man himself, but the evil spirit, — *saying, Let us alone; what have we to do with thee, thou Jesus of Nazareth? art thou come to destroy us?* (cf. Matt. viii. 29; 2 Pet. ii. 4; Jude 6). *I know thee who thou art, the Holy One of God.* "The devils believe and tremble." The unholy, which is resolved to be unholy still, understands well that

143

its death-knell has sounded, when *the Holy One of God* (cf. Ps. xvi. 10) has come to make war against it.

But what could have been the motive to this testimony thus born? It is strange that the evil spirit should, without compulsion, proclaim to the world the presence in its midst of the Holy One of God, of Him who should thus bring all the unholy to an end. It remains either, with Theophylact and Grotius, to understand this as the cry of abject and servile fear, that with fawning and flatteries would fain avert from itself the doom which with Christ's presence in the world must evidently be near; — to compare, as Jerome does, this exclamation to that of the fugitive slave, dreaming of nothing but stripes and torments when he encounters unawares his well-known lord, and now seeking by any means to deprecate his anger;[1] — or else to regard this testimony as intended only to injure in the world's estimation Him in whose favour it is rendered. There was hope that the truth itself might be brought into suspicion and discredit, thus receiving attestation from the spirit of lies; and these confessions of Jesus as the Christ may have been meant to traverse and mar his work, even as we see Mark iii. 22 following hard on Mark iii. 11. The fact that Christ would not allow this testimony, that He *rebuked him, saying, Hold thy peace, and come out of him*, goes some way to render this the preferable explanation.

But was his word in the present instance that word of power we might justly expect? Christ has bidden the evil spirit to hold his peace, and yet only after *he had torn him, and cried with a loud voice, he came out of him* (cf. Acts viii. 7). But in truth he *was* obedient to this command of silence; he did not *speak* any more, and that was what our Lord forbade; this loud cry was nothing but an inarticulate utterance of rage and pain.

---

[1] Grotius: "He wishes to soothe Jesus with his blandishments, since he has found how unequal he was in strife with him." Jerome (*Comm. in Matt.* ix.): "As if runaway slaves should after a long while see their master, and pray only to escape whipping."

Neither is there any contradiction between St. Luke, who reports that the evil spirit *hurt him not,* and St. Mark, who describes him as having *torn him.* He did him no permanent injury; St. Luke himself reporting that he cast him on the ground; with which the language of the second Evangelist, that he threw him into strong convulsions, in fact consents. We have at Mark ix. 26 (cf. Luke ix. 42) an analogous case, although there a paroxysm more violent still accompanies the going out of the unclean spirit; for what the devil cannot keep as his own, he will, if he can, destroy.

St. Mark never misses an opportunity of recording the profound impression which Christ's miracles made on those that witnessed them. *And they were all amazed, insomuch that they questioned among themselves, saying, What thing is this? what new doctrine is this? for with authority commandeth he even the unclean spirits, and they do obey him.*

CHAPTER XIII.

The Healing of Simon's Wife's Mother

MATT. viii. 14-17; MARK i. 29-31; LUKE iv. 38-40.

THIS miracle is by St. Mark and St. Luke linked immediately, and in a manner that marks historic connexion, with that which has just come under our notice. Thus St. Mark: *And forthwith, when they were come out of the synagogue, they entered into the house of Simon and Andrew.* In St. Luke it is only *Simon's house.* His stronger personality, as we may suppose, causes Andrew to fall into the background. *And when Jesus was come into Peter's house, he saw his wife's mother laid, and sick of a fever, — of a great fever,* as St. Luke informs us, the physician in all probability using this epithet in its technical sense, and not merely to express the intensity of the fever which had visited her. It is St. Luke also who alone mentions the intercession of some on her behalf; *they besought him for her;* though as much perhaps is implied in St. Mark's *anon they tell him of her.* Again it is to St. Luke that we owe the graphic touch, *he stood over her,* and the very noticeable phrase, *he rebuked the fever,* as on another occasion, *he rebuked the winds and the sea* (viii. 24). To the other Evangelists he leaves to record that *he touched her hand* (cf. Dan. x. 15; Rev. i. 17; Luke vii. 14; viii. 54), or *took her by the hand and lifted her up.* From that life-giving touch health and strength flowed into her wasted frame; *the fever left her,* and left her not in that state of extreme weakness and exhaustion which fever usually leaves behind, when in the ordinary course of things it has abated;[1] not

---

[1] Jerome (*Comm. in Matt.* in loc.) observes this: "Men are so constituted that after a fever the body grows more weary, and when convalescence begins the evils of sickness are more felt. But the health which is given by the Lord restores wholly and at once, and it was not enough that she should be healed, but, in order to show the intensity of her strength, it is added she arose and ministered unto them."

147

slowly convalescent; but cured so perfectly that *immediately she arose and ministered unto them* (cf. John iv. 52), — providing for those present what was necessary for their entertainment; — a pattern, it has been often observed, to all restored to spiritual health, that they should use this strength in ministering to Christ and to his people.

The fame of this miracle, following close upon another wrought on the same day, spread so rapidly, that *when the even was come, or when the sun did set,* as Mark has it, *they brought unto him many that were possessed with devils: and he cast out the spirits with his word, and healed all that were sick.* Not till the sun was setting or had actually set brought they their sick to Jesus. Hammond and Olshausen suggest, that they waited till the heat of the middle day, which these were ill able to bear, was past. Others assume that this day being a Sabbath (cf. Mark i. 21, 29, 32), they were unwilling to violate its sacred rest. Chrysostom on one occasion sees here more generally an evidence of the faith and eagerness of the people, who, even when the day was spent, still came streaming to Christ, and laying their sick before Him that they might be healed.

All this found place, as St. Matthew tells us, *that it might be fulfilled which was spoken by Esaias the prophet, saying, Himself took our infirmities, and bare our sicknesses.* Not a few have seized on this *that it might be fulfilled* as a proof that St. Matthew did not see any reference in the passage which he cites from Isaiah (liii. 4) to the vicarious and atoning work of the Christ; and even allowing that there was there a prophecy of Him as a remover of the world's woe, yet not as Himself coming under that woe that so He might remove it. Doubtless there is a difficulty, or difficulties rather, for there are two, about this citation — the first, why St. Matthew should bring it at all into connexion with the healing of the bodily diseases of men; and the second, how there should have been any more real ful-

filment of it herein, than in every other part of the earthly
ministry of Christ. The first of these difficulties is easily disposed
of. The connection is so intimate between sin and suffering,
death (and disease is death beginning) is so directly the consequence of sin, all the weight of woe which rests upon the world
is in one sense so distinctly penal, that the Messiah might be
regarded equally as in his proper work, as fulfilling the prophecies which went before concerning Him, whether He were removing the sin, or removing the sickness, sorrow, pain, which
are the results of the sin.

The other question is one of a more real embarrassment. In
what true sense could He be affirmed to bear the sicknesses, or
Himself to take the infirmities which He healed?

Not this day only, but every day of his earthly life was a
coming under, upon his part, those evils which He removed
from others. For that which is the law of all true helping,
namely, that the burden which you would lift, you must yourself
stoop to and come under (Gal. vi. 2), the grief which you
would console, you must yourself feel with, — was truest of all
in Him upon whom the help of all was laid.[2] Not in this single
aspect of his life, namely, that He was a healer of sicknesses,
were these words of the prophet fulfilled, but rather in the life
itself, which brought him in contact with the thousand forms
of want and woe, of discord in man's outward life, of discord
in man's inner being. Every one of these, as a real consequence
of sin, and at every moment contemplated by Him as such,
pressed with a living pang into the holy soul of the Lord (John
xi. 33, 35). St. Matthew quotes these words in reference to one
day of our Lord's work upon earth; but we only enter into their
full force when we recognize that, eminently true of that day,
— and here we may fitly urge its long and exhausting toils, —

---

[2] Hilary: "Absorbing into the suffering of his body the infirmities of human
weakness."

they were also true of all other days, and of all other aspects of that ministry which He came into the world to fulfil. He bore these sicknesses, inasmuch as He bore that mortal suffering life, in which alone He could bring them to an end, and finally swallow up death, and all that led to death, in victory.

CHAPTER XIV.

The Raising of the Widow's Son

LUKE vii. 11-16.

ST. LUKE is the only Evangelist who tells of more than one whom the Lord raised from the dead. St. Matthew and St. Mark tell us only of Jairus' daughter; St. John only of Lazarus. St. Luke, recording the first of these miracles in common with the two earlier Evangelists, has this one which is peculiarly his own. *And it came to pass the day after, that he went into a city called Nain; and many of his disciples went with him, and much people.* That healing of the centurion's servant at a distance and with a word was no doubt a great miracle; but *the day after* was to see a far mightier and more wonderful work even than this.

Now when he came nigh to the gate of the city, behold there was a dead man carried out, the only son of his mother, and she was a widow: and much people of the city was with her. It was thus ordained in the providence of God that the witnesses of this miracle should be many; the *much people* that were with the Lord, in addition to the *much people* which accompanied the funeral procession. The circumstance of his meeting this at *the gate of the city,* while being one of those coincidences which, seeming accidental, are yet deep laid in the councils of his providence, is at the same time a natural incident, and is accounted for by the fact that the Jews did not suffer to inter the dead among the living, but buried them without the walls of their cities. Even they who were touched with no such lively sense of human sorrows as was He who made all sorrows his own, might have been moved and doubtless were moved to compassion here. The bitterness of the mourning for an only son had passed into a

151

proverb; thus compare Jer. vi. 26: "Make thee mourning, as
for an only son, most bitter lamentation."

And when the Lord[1] *saw her, he had compassion on her, and
said unto her, Weep not.* How different this *Weep not,* from
the idle "Weep not," which so often proceeds from the lips of
earthly comforters, who, even while they thus speak, give no
sufficient reason why the mourner should cease from weeping.
But He who came down from heaven, one day to make good
that word, "God shall wipe away *all* tears from their eyes; and
there shall be no more death, neither sorrow, nor crying, neither
shall there be any more pain" (Rev. xxi. 4), shows now some
effectual glimpses and presages of his power. At the same time,
as Olshausen has observed, we must not suppose that compassion
for the mother was the *determining* motive for this mighty spiritual act on the part of Christ. The joy of the mother was indeed
the nearest consequence of the act, but not the final cause; —
that, though at present hidden, was, no doubt, the spiritual awakening of the young man for a higher life, through which alone
the joy of the mother could become true and abiding.

And he came and touched the bier. The intimation was
rightly interpreted by those for whom it was intended; *and
they that bare him stood still.* Then follows the word of power:
Young man, I say unto thee, Arise. It is spoken, as in every
instance, in his own name, — "I, who am the Prince of life,
who have the keys of death and the grave, bid thee to live."
And that word of his was potent in the kingdom of death;
he that was dead sat up, no need of other hands to raise him
now, *and began to speak.* Christ raises from the bier as easily
as another from the bed,[2] — herein putting a difference between
Himself and his own messengers and ministers; for they only
with prayer and effort (I Kin. xvii. 20-22; cf. Acts ix. 40), or

---

[1] Godet: "The phrase The Lord is hardly found in the Gospels except in Luke,
and as a rule only in the narratives peculiar to him": x. 1; xi. 39; xii. 42; xiii. 15;
xvii. 5, 6; xviii. 6; xxii. 31, 61.
[2] Augustine (*Serm.* xcviii. 2).

after a long and patient exercise of love (2 Kin. iv. 34), won
back his prey from the jaws of death; the absolute *fulness* of
power dwelling not in them, who were but as servants in the
house of another, and not as He, a Son in his own.

And he delivered him to his mother (cf. 1 Kin. xvii. 23;
2 Kin. iv. 36; Luke ix. 42). Faint prelude this of that which
He has in store; for not otherwise shall He once, when his
great "Arise" shall have awakened not one, but all the dead,
deliver as many as have fallen asleep in Him to their beloved,
for mutual recognition and for a special fellowship of joy. We
have the promise and pledge of this in the three quickenings of
the dead which prefigure that coming resurrection. *And there
came a fear on all:* for all tokens of God's immediate nearness
bring with them fear as their first result; and if afterwards joy,
yet not this to all (cf. Mark i. 27; v. 15; Luke v. 9) ; *and they
glorified God* (cf. Matt. ix. 8; Mark ii. 12), *saying, That a great
prophet is risen up among us; and, That God hath visited his
people.* This could be no ordinary prophet, they concluded rightly, since none but the very chief in the olden times, an Elijah or
an Elisha, had revived the dead. They glorified God, that with
the raising up of so great a prophet, *the* prophet that should
come (Deut. xviii. 15; Luke i. 68, 69; John i. 21, 46; iv. 25;
vi. 14; Acts iii. 22; vii. 37), He had brought the long and
dreary period to a close, during which all prophecy had been
silent. We may a little understand their delight, when they
found that God had still his ambassadors to men, that perhaps
the greatest of all these ambassadors was actually among them,
and the restoration of his people not far off.

The closing words *And this rumour of him went forth
throughout all Judaea, and throughout all the region round
about* constitute the link of connexion between what the Evangelist has just narrated and what he is about to narrate. The
report, he would say, of this miracle was so great that it

filled not Galilee alone, where it was wrought, but all Judaea, and the region beyond, reaching even to the dungeon at Machaerus where the Baptist lay a prisoner.

CHAPTER XV.

The Healing of the Impotent Man at Bethesda

JOHN v. 1-16.

THE ablest commentator in the Roman Catholic Church begins his observations on this miracle with the utterance of his hearty wish that St. John had added one word, and told us *at what feast of the Jews* it was wrought.[1] Certainly a vast amount of learned discussion would so have been spared; for this question has been much debated. We shall do well to stand here upon the ancient ways, and to take this feast which our Lord adorned with his presence and signalized with this great miracle, as *the* feast, that which was the mother of all other feasts, the passover.

Now there is at Jerusalem by the sheep market a pool, which is called in the Hebrew tongue Bethesda, having five porches. The true Bethesda Robinson thinks he finds, though on this he speaks with hestitation, in what now goes under the name of the Fountain of the Virgin, being the upper fountain of Siloam.

In these lay a great multitude of impotent folk, of blind, halt, withered. Our Version is slightly defective here. It leaves an impression that *impotent folk* is the genus, presently subdivided into the three species, *blind, halt, withered;* whereas, instead of three being thus subordinated to one, all four are coördinated with one another. We should read rather, *In these lay a great multitude of sick, blind, halt, withered.* The words which complete this third verse, *waiting for the moving of the water,* lie under a certain suspicion, as verse four has certainly no right to a place in the text. That fourth verse the most im-

---

[1] Maldonatus: "John would have saved us much trouble and disputation, had he added but a single word to show which feast of the Jews this was."

portant Greek and Latin copies are alike without, and most of
the early Versions. In other MSS. which retain this verse, the
obelus which hints suspicion, or the asterisk which marks rejection, is attached to it; while those in which it appears unquestioned belong mostly to a later recension of the text. And
the undoubted spuriousness of this fourth verse has spread a
certain amount of suspicion over the last clause of the verse
preceding; which yet has not the same amount of diplomatic
evidence against it, nay, in some sort seems almost necessary to
make the story intelligible. At first probably a marginal note,
expressing the popular notion of the Jewish Christians concerning the origin of the healing power which from time to time
these waters possessed, by degrees it assumed the shape in which
now we have it: for there are marks of growth about it, betraying themselves in a great variety of readings,—some copies
omitting one part, and some another of the verse: little by little,
it procured admission into the text. For the statement itself,
there is nothing in it which need perplex or offend, or which
might not have found place in St. John. It rests upon that religious view of the world, which in all nature sees something
beyond and behind nature, which everywhere recognizes a going
forth of the immediate power of God, invisible agencies of his,
whether personal or otherwise, accomplishing his will.[2] That
Angels should be the ministers of his will would be only according to the analogy of other Scripture (Heb. i. 7; Rev. vii.
2) ; while in the Angel *of the waters* (Rev. xvi. 5) we have a
remarkable point of contact with the statement of this verse; of
agreement between John the Seer and, supposing these words
are allowed to stand, John the Evangelist.

From among this suffering expectant multitude Christ singles
out one on whom to display his power;—one only, for He came

---

[2] Theophylact mentions a curious explanation of the virtues of this pool which
some in his time accepted: "It was generally supposed that the water received some
divine property from the mere washing in it of the entrails of the sacrificial victims."

not *now* to be the healer of men's bodies, save only as He could annex to this healing the truer healing of their souls and spirits. *And a certain man was there, which had an infirmity thirty and eight years.* These words, *thirty and eight*, express the duration not of his life, but of his infirmity; but without implying that he had waited for health from that pool during all that time; though yet his waiting there, as we learn from ver. 7, had been long. *When Jesus saw him lie, and knew that he had been now a long time in that case, he saith unto him, Wilt thou be made whole?* A superfluous question, it might seem; for who would not *be made whole,* if he might? His very presence at the place of healing attested his desire. But the question has its purpose. This poor man had been so often defeated of a cure that hope was dead or wellnigh dead within him, and the question is asked to awaken in him anew a yearning after the benefit which the Saviour was about to impart. Our Lord assisted him now to the faith, which He was about presently to demand of him.

The answer, *Sir, I have no man, when the water is troubled, to put me into the pool,* contains no direct reply, but an explanation why he had continued so long in his infirmity. He, himself helpless, and with no man to aid, could never be this first, always therefore missed the blessing; *while I am coming, another steppeth down before me.* But the long and weary years of baffled expectation are now to find an end: *Jesus saith unto him, Rise, take up thy bed, and walk.* This taking up of his bed shall serve as a testimony to all of the completeness of the cure (cf. Matt. ix. 6; Acts ix. 34). The man believed that word to be accompanied with power; made proof, and found that it was so: *immediately the man was made whole, and took up his bed, and walked.* This *bed,* as is hardly necessary to observe, is not our modern four-poster, but a poor pallet, which, rolled up, could very easily be moved from one spot to another. *And on the same day was the sabbath* — a significant addition, explaining all which follows.

The Jews therefore said unto him that was cured, It is the sabbath day. It is not lawful for thee to carry thy bed. By *the Jews* we understand here, as constantly in St. John, not the multitude, but the Sanhedrists, the spiritual heads of the nation (i. 19; vii. 1; ix. 22; xviii. 12, 14; cf. ver. 3; xx. 19). These find fault with the man, for had not Moses, or rather God by the mouth of Moses, said of the Sabbath, "In it thou shalt not do any work" (Exod. xx. 10), and still more to the point Jeremiah, "Take heed to yourselves, and bear no burden on the sabbath day" (xvii. 21). It was lawful to heal on the Sabbath day; it was lawful then to do whatever was immediately involved in, and directly followed on, the healing. And here lay ultimately the true controversy between Christ and his adversaries, namely, whether it was most consonant to the law of God to do good on that day or to leave it undone (Luke vi. 9). Starting from the unlawfulness of leaving good undone, Christ asserted that He was its true keeper, keeping it as God kept it, with the highest beneficent activity, which was identical with deepest rest, —and not, as they accused Him of being, its breaker. Already the pharisaical Jews had laid down such a multitude of prohibitions, and drawn so infinite a number of hair-splitting distinctions, that a plain and unlearned man could hardly know what was forbidden and what was permitted. This poor man did not concern himself with these subtle casuistries of theirs. It was enough for him that One with power to make him whole, One who had shown compassion to him, bade him to do what he was doing: *He answered them, He that made me whole, the same said unto me, Take up thy bed, and walk*[3]—surely the very model of an answer, when the world finds fault and is scandalized

---

[3] Augustine (*In Ev. Joh. tract. xvii.*): "Was I not to do his bidding from whom I had received health?"

with what a Christian is doing, contrary to its traditions, and to the rules which *it* has laid down!

After this greater offender they inquire now, as being the juster object of censure and of punishment: *Then asked they him, What man is that which said unto thee, Take up thy bed, and walk?* The malignity of the questioners reveals itself in the very shape which their question assumes. They do not take up the poor man's words on their more favourable side, which would also have been the more natural: nor ask, "What man is that which made thee whole?" But, probably themselves knowing perfectly well, or at least guessing, who his Healer was, they insinuate by the form of their question that *He* could not be from God who gave a command which they, the interpreters of God's law, esteemed so grievous an outrage against it. So will they weaken and undermine any influence which Christ may have obtained over this simple man—an influence already manifest in his finding the Lord's authority sufficient to justify him in the transgression of their commandment.

But the man could not point out his benefactor; *he that was healed wist not who it was: for Jesus had conveyed himself away, a multitude being in that place*—not to avoid ostentation and the applauses of the people; but this mention of the multitude shall explain the facility with which He withdrew.

Afterward Jesus findeth him in the temple (cf. ix. 35). We may accept it as a token for good that Jesus found him there rather than in any other place; returning thanks, as we may well believe, for the signal mercies so lately vouchsafed to him (cf. Isai. xxxviii. 22; Acts iii. 8; Luke xvii. 15). And He, who sought ever to connect with the healing of the body the better healing of the soul, suffers not this matter to conclude thus: but by a word of solemn warning, declares to the sufferer that all his past life lay open and manifest before Him; interprets to him the past judgment, bids him not provoke future and more terrible: *Behold, thou art made whole: sin no more, lest a worse thing come unto thee* — words which give us an awful glimpse of the severity of God's judgments even in this present time; for we must not restrict, as some have done, this *worse thing* to judgment beyond the grave: — *a worse thing* even in this life might befall him than those eight and thirty years of infirmity and pain. Let no man, however miserable, count that he has exhausted the power of God's wrath.

What the past sin of this sufferer had been we do not know, but the sufferer himself knew very well; his conscience interpreted the warning. This much, however, is plain to us; that Christ connected the man's suffering with his own particular sin; for, however He rebuked elsewhere men's uncharitable way of tracing such a connection. (Luke xiii. 2, 3; John ix. 3); yet He never meant thereby to deny that if much of judgment is deferred, much also is even now proceeding. However unwilling we may be to receive this, bringing as it does God so near, and making retribution so real and so prompt a thing, yet is it true notwithstanding. As some eagle, pierced with a shaft feathered from its own wing, so many a sufferer, even in this present time, sees and is compelled to acknowledge that his own sin fledged the arrow, which has pierced him and brought him down. And lest he should miss the connection, oftentimes he is punished, it may be is himself sinned against by his fellow-man, in the very kind wherein he himself has sinned against others (Judg. i. 6, 7; Gen. xlii. 21; Wisd. xi. 16; Ezek. xxxv. 6, 15; Jer. li. 49; Hab. ii. 8; Rev. xvi. 6). The deceiver is deceived, as was Jacob (Gen. xxvii. 19, 24; xxix. 23; xxxi. 7; xxxvii. 32); the violator of the sanctities of family life is himself wounded and outraged in his tenderest and dearest relations, as was David (2 Sam. xi. 4; xiii. 14; xvi. 22).

The man departed, and told the Jews that it was Jesus, which had made him whole. The man probably learned from the bystanders the name of his deliverer, and went and told it,—assuredly not, as some assume, in treachery, or to augment the envy already existing against Him, — but gratefully proclaiming aloud and to the rulers of his nation the physician who had healed him.[4] He may have counted, in the simplicity of his heart, that the name of Him, whose reputation, though not his person, he had already known, whom so many counted as a prophet, or even as the Messiah Himself, would be sufficient to stop the mouths of the gainsayers. Had he wrought in a baser spirit, he would not, as Chrysostom ingeniously observes, have gone and told them *that it was Jesus, which had made him whole,* but rather that it was Jesus, who had bidden him to carry his bed. Moreover, we may be quite sure that the Lord, who knew what was in man, would not have wasted his benefits on so mean and thankless a wretch as this man would have thus shown himself to be.

His word did not allay their displeasure, only provoked it the more. *And therefore did the Jews persecute Jesus, and sought to slay him, because he had done these things on the sabbath day.* Christ had in their eyes wilfully violated the Sabbath, and the penalty of this wilful violation was death (Num. xv. 32-36). But there was no such violation here; and He, returning good for evil, will fain raise them to the true point of view from which to contemplate the Sabbath, and his own relation to it as the Only-begotten of the Father. He is no more a breaker of the Sabbath than his Father is, when He upholds with an energy that knows no pause the work of his creation from hour to hour and from moment to moment: *My Father worketh hitherto, and I work;* Christ's work is but the reflex of his Father's work. Abstinence from an outward work is not essential to the observance of a Sabbath; it is only more or less the necessary condition

---

[4] Calvin: "Nothing was less in his mind than to excite ill-will against Christ; for he expected anything rather than that they should rage so vehemently against Christ. His mood was thus one of gratitude, since he wished that the honour justly due might result to his healer."

of this for beings so framed and constituted as ever to be in danger of losing the true collection and rest of the spirit in the multiplicity of earthly toil and business. Man indeed must cease from *his* work, if a higher work is to find place in him. He scatters himself in his work, and therefore must collect himself anew, and have seasons for so doing. But with Him who is one with the Father it is otherwise. In Him the deepest rest is not excluded by the highest activity; nay rather, in God, in the Son as in the Father, they are one and the same.

But so to defend what He has done only exasperates his adversaries the more. They have here not a Sabbath-breaker merely, but a blasphemer as well; for the Lord was here claiming divine attributes for Himself: *Therefore the Jews sought the more to kill him, because he not only had broken the sabbath, but said also that God was his Father, making himself equal with God* (Lev. xxiv. 16; John viii. 58, 59; x. 31; xix. 7). Strange, if the Unitarians are right, that He should have suffered them to continue in their terrible mistake, that He should not at once have taken this stumbling-block out of their way, and explained to them that they mistook his words, that indeed He meant nothing so dreadful as they supposed! but so far from this, He only reasserts what has already offended them so deeply, and this in words than which none in Holy Scripture have contributed more to the fast fixing of the doctrine concerning the relations of the Father and the Son.

CHAPTER XVI.

The Miraculous Feeding of Five Thousand

MATT. xiv. 15-21; MARK vi. 34-44; LUKE ix. 12-17; JOHN vi. 5-14.

THIS miracle, with that of the walking on the sea, which may be regarded as an appendix to it, is the only one which St. John has in common with the other Evangelists; but this he shares with them all. It is thus the only one of which a fourfold record exists. In what I write on the matter it will be my endeavour to keep all the narratives in view, as they mutually complete one another. St. Matthew connects the Lord's retirement to the desert place on the other side of the lake,[1] with the murder of John the Baptist; St. Mark and St. Luke place the two events in juxtaposition, but without making one the motive of the other. St. Mark, indeed, gives another as the immediate motive, namely, that the Apostles, who were just returned from their mission, might have time at once for bodily and spiritual refreshment, might not be always in a crowd, always ministering to others, never to themselves. But thither, *into a desert place belonging to the city called Bethsaida*, the multitude followed Him; not necessarily *afoot*, but *by land*, as distinguished from Him and his company, who made the passage *by sea*. They lost so little time on their journey, that although their way was much longer about than his, who had only to

---

[1] Dean Stanley, *Sinai and Palestine*, p. 371: "The eastern shores of the lake have been so slightly visited and described, that any comparison of their features with the history must necessarily be precarious. Yet one general characteristic of that shore, as compared with the western side, has been indicated, which was probably the case in ancient times, though in a less degree than at present, namely, its desert character. Partly this arises from its nearer exposure to the Bedouin tribes; partly from its less abundance of springs and streams. There is no recess in the eastern hills, no towns along its banks corresponding to those in the Plain of Gennesareth. Thus the wilder region became a natural refuge from the active life of the western shores. It was 'when he saw great multitudes about him' that 'he gave commandment to depart unto the *other side*;' and again He said, 'Come ye yourselves apart into a desert place, and rest a while; for there were many coming and going, and they had no leisure so much as to eat.' "

cross the lake, they *outwent* Him, anticipated his coming, so that when He *went forth*, not, that is, from the ship, but from his solitude, and for the purpose of graciously receiving those who followed Him with such devotion, He *saw much people* waiting for Him. This presence of theirs entirely defeated the intention with which He had sought that solitude; yet not the less He *received them, and spake unto them of the kingdom of God, and healed them that had need of healing.* St. John's apparently casual notice of the fact that *the passover, a feast of the Jews, was nigh,* is introduced, some say, to explain from whence this great multitude came; that they were on their road to Jerusalem, there to keep the feast. But what should they have done in that remote region, so far withdrawn from all the usual lines of communication? St. John accounts in another way for their presence. They were there, "because they saw his miracles which He did on them that were diseased." The mention of the passover here, if it is to find an explanation, and is anything more than the fixing of a point in the chronology of our Lord's ministry, must be otherwise explained.

The way is prepared for the miracle somewhat differently by the three earlier Evangelists, and by St. John. According to them, *when it was evening, his disciples came to him, saying, This is a desert place, and the time is now past; send the multitude away, that they may go into the villages, and buy themselves victuals.* The first suggestion comes here from the disciples; while in St. John it is the Lord Himself who, in his question to Philip, *Whence shall we buy bread, that these may eat?* (vi. 5) first contemplates the difficulty. This difference, however, is capable of an easy explanation. Our Lord may have put this question to Philip at a somewhat earlier period of the afternoon; then left the difficulty which He had suggested to work in the minds of the Apostles; bringing them, as was so often his manner, to see that there was no help in the common course of things; and when they had acknowledged this, then, and not before, stepping in with his higher aid.[2]

St. John, ever careful to avert a misconception of his Lord's words (ii. 21; xxi. 22), above all, one which might seem to derogate from his perfect wisdom or love, does not fail to inform us that He asked this question, not as needing any counsel, not as being Himself in any real embarrassment, *for he himself knew what he would do,* but *tempting him,* as Wiclif's translation has it, or to *prove him,* as has our own; which here rightly gives to the word of the original its mildest sense (cf. Gen. xxii. 1). It was *to prove him,* and what measure of faith he had in that Master whom he had himself already acknowledged as "him, of whom Moses in the law, and the prophets, did write" (John i. 45). It should now be seen whether Philip, calling to mind the great things which Moses had done, giving to the people bread from heaven in the wilderness, and the notable miracle which Elisha, though on a smaller scale, had performed (2 Kin. iv. 43, 44), could so lift up his thoughts as to believe that He whom he had recognized as the Christ, greater therefore than Moses or the prophets, would meet the present need. Why Philip was singled out for proof it is impossible to say; but whatever the motive may have been, he does not abide it. Long as he has been with Jesus, he has not yet seen, he had not seen at a later day, the Father in the Son (John xiv. 9); he does not understand that the Lord whom he serves upon earth is even the same on whom all creatures wait, who "openeth his hand, and filleth all things living with plenteousness," who has sustained them from the creation of the world, and who therefore can feed these few thousands that are this day more particularly dependent on his bounty. He can conceive of no other supplies save such as natural means could procure, and at once comes to the point: *Two hundred pennyworth of bread is not sufficient for them,*

---

[2] For the reconciliation of any apparent contradiction, see Augustine, *De Cons. Evang.* ii. 46.

that every one of them may take a little. The sum he names, about some seven pounds sterling, was much larger — for so much he would imply — than any which the common purse could yield.

Having drawn from the mouth of Philip this confession of inability to meet the present need, He left it to work; — till, somewhat later in the day, the disciples came with their proposal that He should dismiss the assemblage. But bringing now the matter to a head, He replies, *They need not depart; give ye them to eat.* They repeat with one mouth what Philip had before affirmed, how far, namely, the outlay exceeded their means, *Shall we go and buy two hundred pennyworth of bread, and give them to eat?* We may compare the remonstrance which on a somewhat similar occasion Moses had made: "Shall the flocks and the herds be slain for them to suffice them?" (Num. xi. 22; cf. Ps. lxxviii. 19, 20); there is the same mitigated infidelity in both; the same doubt whether the power of the Lord is equal to that which his word, expressly or implicitly, has undertaken. But not heeding this He proceeds, *How many loaves have ye? go and see.* They return and tell Him that the utmost which they have at command is five loaves and two fishes, the little stock which a single lad among the multitude has to sell; and which they have purchased, or may purchase if they will.

With this slender stock of homeliest fare, for St. John informs us that the loaves were of barley (cf. 2 Kin. vii. 1; Jud. vii. 13; Ezek. iv. 12), the Lord undertakes to satisfy all that multitude (Chrysostom quotes aptly here Ps. lxxviii. 19: "Shall God prepare a table in the wilderness?"); for *He commanded them to make all sit down by companies upon the green grass,* at that early spring season a delightful resting-place. *So the men³ sat down, in number about five thousand.* The mention

---

³ Godet: "In keeping with Eastern customs, according to which the women and children were kept apart, the men alone appear to have sat down in the order indicated. This explains why, as say the synoptic Gospels, they alone were counted, as Luke (vers. 14), Mark (vers. 44), and still more distinctly Matthew (vers. 21), besides women and children."

of this *green grass,* or *much grass,* is another point of contact between St. Mark and St. John. The former adds a further graphic touch, how they sat in companies, *by hundreds and by fifties,* and how these separate groups showed in their symmetrical arrangement like so many garden-plots. It was a prudent precaution. The vast assemblage was thus subdivided and broken up into manageable portions; there was less danger of tumult and confusion, or that the weaker, the women and the children, should be passed over, while the stronger and ruder unduly put themselves forward; the Apostles were able to pass easily up and down among the groups, and to minister in orderly succession to them all.

The taking of the bread in hand was a formal act which went before the blessing or giving of thanks for it (Luke xxiv. 30; 1 Cor. xi. 23). This eucharistic act Jesus accomplished as the head of the household, and according to that beautiful saying of the Talmud, "He that enjoys aught without thanksgiving, is as though he robbed God." Having blessed, He *brake, and gave the loaves to his disciples, and the disciples to the multitude;* — the marvellous multiplication taking place, as some affirm, first in the Saviour's own hands, next in the hands of the Apostles, and lastly in those of the eaters. This may have been so; but whether thus or in some other way, *they did all eat, and were filled* (Ps. cxlv. 16). Christ was herein fulfilling for this multitude his own promise, "Seek ye first the kingdom of God, and his righteousness; and all these things shall be added unto you" (Matt. vi. 33). They had come taking no thought, for the time at least, of what they should eat or what they should drink, only desirous to hear the word of life, only seeking the kingdom of heaven; and now the lower things, according to the word of the promise, were added unto them.

This miracle, even more than that of the water changed into wine, when we endeavour to realize to ourselves *the manner* of it, evermore eludes our grasp, and baffles imagination. Nor is this strange; for indeed, how can it be possible to bring within forms of our conception, or in thought to bridge over the gulf between not-being and being, which yet is bridged over in every creative act? And this being so, there is no force in the objection which one has made against the historical truth of this narrative, namely, that "there is no attempt by closer description to make clear in its details the manner and process by which this wonderful bread was formed." It is true wisdom, to leave the indescribable undescribed, and without so much as an attempt at the description. They who bear record of these things appeal to the same faith, on the part of their readers or hearers, as that which believes "that the worlds were framed *by the word of God,* so that things which are seen were not made of things which do appear" (Heb. xi. 3).

An analogy, and, so to speak, a help to the understanding of this miracle has been found, in that which year by year is accomplished in the field, where a single grain of corn multiplies itself, and in the end unfolds in numerous ears; — and, with this analogy in view, many beautiful remarks have been made; as this, that while God's every-day miracles had grown cheap in men's sight by continual repetition, He had therefore reserved something, not more wonderful, but less frequent, to arouse men's minds to a new admiration. Others have urged that here, as in the case of the water made wine, Christ did but compress into a single moment all those processes which in ordinary circumstances He, the same Lord of nature, causes more slowly to succeed one another. But, true as in its measure is this, the analogy is good only to a certain point. For that which finds place in the field is the unfolding of the seed according to the law of its own being. Thus, if the Lord had taken a few grains of corn and cast them into the ground, and if, a moment after, a large harvest had sprung up, to this the name of such a "divinely-hastened nature-process" might have been fitly applied. But with bread it is otherwise; since, before that is made, there must be new interpositions of man's art, and those of such a character that by them the very life, which up to this point has unfolded itself, must be crushed and destroyed. A grain of wheat left to itself could never, according to the laws of natural evolution, issue in a loaf of bread. And, moreover, the Lord does not start here from the simple germ, from the lifeful rudiments, wherein all the seeds of a future life might be assumed to be wrapt up, and by Him rapidly developed, but with the latest artificial product. The oak is folded up in the acorn, but not in a piece of timber hewn and shaped from itself. This analogy then, even as such, presently fails; and renouncing all helps to faith to be gotten from this quarter, we must be content to behold in this multiplying of the bread an act of divine omnipotence,[4] — not indeed now, as at the first, of absolute creation out of nothing, since there was a substratum to work on in the original loaves and fishes, but an act of creative accretion; a *quantitative,* as in the water turned into wine there was a *qualitative,* miracle, the bread *growing* in the Lord's hands, so that from that little stock the whole multitude were abundantly supplied. Thus He, all whose works were "signs," embodied and visible words, did in this miracle proclaim Himself the true bread of the world, the unexhausted and inexhaustible upholder of all life, in whom there should be enough and to spare for the spiritual needs of all hungering souls in all ages. For, in Augustine's language, once already quoted, "He was the Word of God; and all the acts of the Word are themselves words for us; they are not as pictures, merely to look at and admire, but as letters, which we must seek to read and understand."

When all had eaten and were satisfied, the disciples *took up*

---

[4] Augustine (*In Ev. Joh. tract.* ix.): "The omnipotence of the Lord was the source, as it were, of the bread;" and again (*Enarr.* ii. *in Ps.* cx. 10): "The sources of the bread were in the hands of the Lord."

of the fragments that remained twelve baskets full, — for every Apostle a basket; St. Mark alone records that it was so done with the fishes also; the existence of these fragments witnessing that there had been enough for all, and to spare (2 Kin. iv. 43, 44; Ruth ii. 14). Only St. John mentions that they do this at their Lord's bidding, and only he the motive, *that nothing be lost.* For thus with the Lord of nature, as with nature herself, the most prodigal bounty goes hand in hand with the nicest and exactest economy; and He who had but now shown Himself God, again submits Himself to the laws and conditions of his life upon earth, so that, as in the miracle itself his power, in this command his humility, shines eminently forth. *The fragments,* or perhaps "broken pieces" would be better, which remained over must have immensely exceeded in bulk the original stock; and we have thus a visible symbol of that love which exhausts not itself by loving, but after the most prodigal outgoings upon others, abides itself far richer than it would else have done; of the multiplying which there ever is in a true dispensing; of the increasing which may go along with a scattering (Prov. xi. 24; cf. 2 Kin. iv. 1-7).

St. John, — always careful to note whatever actively stirred up the malignity of Christ's enemies, and thus hastened the final catastrophe, — which nothing did more to bring about than the utterances of the people's favour, — alone tells us of the impression which this miracle left upon the multitude; how *those men when they had seen the miracle that Jesus did, said, This is of a truth that prophet that should come into the world* (cf. vii. 40), the prophet of whom Moses spake, like to himself, whom God would raise up (Deut. xviii. 15), the Shiloh of Jacob's blessing (Gen. xlix. 10), the Star and the Sceptre of Balaam's vision (Num. xxiv. 17; cf. John i. 21; Mal. iii. 1). He tells us too how they would fain, with or without his consent, have made Him their king; for they recognized the kingly, as well as the prophetic, character of their future Messiah (John i. 50): and, as St. John's word implies, would fain have hurried Him, willing or unwilling, to Jerusalem, and installed Him there in the royal seat of David. It was not merely the power which He here displayed that moved them so mightily, but the fact that a miracle exactly of this character was looked for from the Messiah. He was to repeat, so to say, the miracles of Moses. As Moses, the first redeemer, had given bread of wonder to the people in the wilderness, even so should the later Redeemer do the same. Thus too, when the first enthusiasm which this work had stirred was spent, the Jews compare it with what Moses had done, not any longer to find evidence here that as great or a greater prophet was among them, but invidiously to depress the present miracle by comparison with the past; and in the inferiority of the later to find proof that He who wrought it was no Messiah after all, with the right to rebuke and to command. "What sign shewest Thou then, that we may see, and believe Thee? What dost *Thou* work? Our fathers did eat manna in the desert, as it is written, He gave them bread *from heaven* to eat" (John vi. 30, 31; cf. Exod. xvi. 4; Ps. lxxviii. 24); "while the bread which Thou hast given," for so much they would imply, "is but this common bread of earth, wherewith Thou hast once nourished a few thousands."[5]

But whatever resemblance may exist between that miracle and this, there is another in the Old Testament, one indeed already referred to, which this resembles more nearly, that namely which Elisha wrought, when with the twenty loaves of barley he satisfied a hundred men (2 Kin. iv. 42-44). All the *rudiments* of this miracle there appear; the two substances, one artificial, one natural, from which the many persons are fed; as here bread and fish, so there bread and fresh ears of corn. As the

---

[5] Tertullian (*Adv. Marc.* iv. 21): "Not for one day, but for forty years, not on the inferior food of bread and fish, but on the manna of heaven, He preserved the lives, not of about five thousand, but of six hundred thousand men."

disciples are incredulous here, so there the servitor asks, "Should I set this before a hundred men?" As here twelve baskets of fragments remain, so there "they did eat, and left thereof." Yet were they only the weaker rudiments of this miracle; a circumstance which the difference between the servants and the Lord sufficiently explains. The prophets having grace only in measure, so in measure wrought their works; but the Son, working with infinite power, and with power not lent Him, but his own did all with much superabundance.

CHAPTER XVII.

The Walking on the Sea

MATT. xiv. 22-33; MARK vi. 45-52; JOHN vi. 14-21.

THE three Evangelists who record this miracle agree to place it in immediate sequence to the feeding of the five thousand, and on the evening of the same day. The two earlier relate, that when all were fed, and the Lord was now about to dismiss the multitude, *straightway he constrained his disciples to get into the ship.* Why He should have found it necessary to *constrain* these, they do not tell us.[1] The key to the phrase is obtained when we compare the parallel record of St. John. There we learn that the multitude desired to take Jesus by force and make Him a king; and were so much in earnest about this, that, as the only means of defeating this purpose, *He departed again into a mountain himself alone.* The disciples could not avoid being aware of the shape which the popular enthusiasm, roused to the highest pitch by the recent miracle, was taking. This was precisely this which they had long hoped would arrive; so that they must have been most reluctant to quit their Master at the moment of his approaching exaltation. Thus, however, it must be, and while He dismisses the people, they must *go before him unto the other side,* or *unto Bethsaida,* as St. Mark has it. There is no contradiction between this account and St. John's, that they *went over the sea towards Capernaum;* since this Bethsaida, not identical with that just before mentioned by St. Luke, lay on the western side of the lake, in the same direction as Capernaum. St. Matthew, and St. Mark with him, make two evenings to this day, — one which had already commenced before the prepara-

---

[1] Jerome: "He constrains them to get into the ship, since from love of their teacher they are loth to be parted from him even for a moment."

tions for the feeding of the multitude had begun (ver. 15),
the other now when the disciples had entered into the ship, and
set forth on their voyage (ver. 23). And this was an ordinary
way of counting among the Jews, the first evening being very
much our afternoon (see Luke ix. 12, where the *evening* of
Matthew and Mark is described as the season *when the day began to wear away*) ; the second evening being the twilight, or
from six o'clock to twilight; on which absolute darkness followed. It was the first evening, or afternoon, when the preparations for feeding the five thousand commenced; the second,
when the disciples took ship.

*And when he had sent the multitudes away, he went up into
a mountain apart to pray; and when even was come, he was
there alone.* From thence, with the watchful eye of love, *He saw
them toiling in rowing* (cf. Exod. iii. 7; Ps. lvi. 8) ; for in their
Lord's absence they were able to make no effectual progress:
the wind was contrary, and the sea rough: their sails, of course,
could profit them nothing. It was now *the fourth watch of the
night,* near morning therefore, and notwithstanding all their exertions they had not accomplished more than *five and twenty or
thirty furlongs,* scarcely, that is, more than half of their way,
the lake being forty or forty-five furlongs in breadth.[2] Suddenly
they see their Lord *walking on the sea,* and already close to their
bark.

It was his purpose in all the events of this night, as Chrysostom well brings out, to train his disciples to higher things
than hitherto they had learned. That first storm, of which we
have heard already (Matt. viii. 24), was by day, this by night.

---

[2] Thomson (*The Land and the Book,* pt. ii. c. 25): "My experience in this
region enables me to sympathize with the disciples in their long night's contest with
the wind. I spent a night in that Wady Shukalyif, some three miles up it, to the
left of us. The sun had scarcely set when the wind began to rush down toward
the lake, and it continued all night long with constantly increasing violence, so that
when we reached the shore next morning the face of the lake was like a huge boiling
caldron. The wind howled down every wady from the north-east and east with such
fury that no efforts of rowers could have brought a boat to shore at any point
along that coast. In a wind like that, the disciples must have been driven quite
across to Gennesaret, as we know they were."

Then He was present in the ship with them. But they must learn to walk by faith and not by sight. This time He puts them forth into the danger alone, even as some loving mother-bird thrusts her fledglings from the nest, that they may find their own wings and learn to use them. Nor shall the happy issue of all fail to waken in them an abiding confidence in his everready help. He, when He has tried them to the uttermost, *in the fourth watch of the night,* the same morning watch in which He had wrought of old another deliverance, not really more significant, though on a mightier scale (Exod. xiv. 24), appears beside them; thus teaching them for all their after life, in all coming storms of temptation, that He is near them; unseen it may be by their bodily eyes, yet indeed a very present help in the needful time of trouble.

Nor should we miss the symbolic character which this whole transaction wears. As it fared with that bark upon those stormy billows, so fares it oftentimes with the Church, tossed to and fro on the waves of a troublesome world. It seems as though its Lord had forgotten it. But his eye is on it still. And when at length the extremity of the need has arrived, He is suddenly with it in marvellous ways; then all that before was so laborious is easy, and the toiling rowers are anon at the haven where they would be.

And when the disciples saw him walking on the sea they were troubled, saying, It is a spirit; and they cried out for fear. It is often so. Let that Lord only come to his people, as they have not hitherto known Him, in the shape of some affliction, in the way of some cross, and they recognize Him not. Their Lord, and charged with blessings for them, He yet seems to them as some terrible phantom of the night; and they too cry out for fear.[3] The disciples on this occasion might perhaps have pleaded that there was that in his approach to their bark, which would

---

[3] Bengel: "They were troubled. We often take Christ for another rather than for Christ."

not allow them to recognize Him for what He was. He *would have passed them by*. How could they suppose that this was their Lord, hastening to the help of his own? The circumstance perplexed *them* for a moment; it has perplexed others lastingly. Such as are on the watch to detect inner inconsistencies in the Gospels have asked, "Why appear to pass them by and to escape them, when the only aim of his coming was to re-assure and to aid them? Doubtless this is hard to be understood of those to whom the life of faith is altogether strange. He will seem to pass them by, appear to forsake them, and so evoke their prayer and their cry. We have here no exceptional dealing, but one finding its analogies everywhere in the Scripture and in the Christian life. What part does Christ sustain here different from that which in the parable of the Unjust Judge (Luke xviii. 2) He ascribes to God? or different from that which He himself sustained when He came not to the help of the sisters of Bethany in what seemed the utmost extremity of their needs (John xi. 6)? And are not all the complaints of the faithful in the Psalms, as that God hides his face, confessions that He does so deal with his own, that by delaying and seeming to pass them by, He quickens their faith, and calls out their prayers that He would come to them soon, and abide with them always?

And now, as one by that cry of distress arrested and detained, He at once scatters and rebukes their fears: *Straightway Jesus spake unto them, saying, Be of good cheer; it is I; be not afraid.* How often has He to speak this word of encouragement even to his own; almost always when they are brought suddenly or in any unusual way face to face with Him (Gen. xvi. 1; Jud. vi. 23; Dan. x. 12, 19; Matt. xvii. 7; Luke i. 20; Rev. i. 17). And now follows that characteristic rejoinder of Peter, which, with all that follows from it, St. Matthew alone records: *Lord, if it be thou, bid me come unto thee on the water.* That *if* must not be interpreted as implying a doubt whether it was the

Lord or not. Peter's fault would be of another kind. His words mean rather: "*Since* it is Thou, command me to come unto Thee"; for he feels rightly that Christ's command must go before his own coming. And, doubtless, it was the promptness and forwardness of love which made him ask for this command, which made him desire to be where his Lord was (John xxi. 7). In that *Bid me,* the fault may be found. He will outdo and outdare the other disciples; will signalize himself by a mightier testimony of faith than any one of them will venture to render. It is but in another shape, "Although all shall be offended, yet will not I."

Let us observe, and with reverence admire, the wisdom and love of the Lord's answer. With more gracious and discriminating wisdom the great Master of souls; who yet, knowing what the event must prove, pledges not Himself for the issue of his coming. Peter had said, *come unto Thee;* the *unto Me* disappears from our Lord's answer; which is only *Come;* that is, "if thou wilt; make the experiment, if thou desirest." It is a merely permissive *Come.* Doubtless it contained an implicit pledge that Peter should not be wholly swallowed up by the waves, but none for the successful issue of the feat. What the issue should be, depended upon Peter himself, — whether he should keep the beginning of his confidence firm unto the end. And He who knew what was in man, knew that he would not; that this was not the pure courage of faith; that what of carnal over-boldness there was in it would infallibly be exchanged, when the stress of the trial came, for fear and unbelief.

It was even so. *And when Peter was come down out of the ship, he walked on the water, to go to Jesus.* So long as he looked to his Lord and to Him only, he also was able to walk upon the unsteady surface of the sea, to tread upon the *waters,* which for him also were not *waves.* But when he took counsel of flesh and blood, when he saw something else besides Jesus,

then, because *he saw the wind boisterous, he was afraid; and
beginning to sink, he cried, saying, Lord, save me.* He who
had thought to make a show before all the other disciples of
a courage which transcended theirs, must now in the presence
of them all confess his terror, and reveal the weakness, as he
had thought to display the strength, of his faith.

But Peter has to do with One who will not allow him greatly
to fall. His *Lord, save me,* is answered at once. *Immediately
Jesus stretched forth his hand, and caught him.* And then how
gracious the rebuke! *O thou of little faith!* He does not say
"of none!" and *Wherefore didst thou doubt?* not "Wherefore
didst thou come?" thus, instead of checking, as He then would
have done, the future impulses of his servant's boldness, encour-
aging them rather: showing him how he could do all things
through Christ strengthening him, and that his error lay, not
in undertaking too much, but in relying too little upon that
strength which would have triumphantly borne him through all.[4]
And not until by that sustaining hand He has restored confidence
to the fearful one, and made him feel that he can indeed tread
under foot those waves of the unquiet sea, does He speak even
this word of a gentle rebuke. The courage of the disciple has
already returned, so that the Master speaks of his doubt as of
something which is already past; *Wherefore didst thou doubt?*
Before the doubt arose in thy heart, thou didst walk on these
waves, and now that thy faith has returned, thou dost walk on
them again; thou seest that it is not impossible, that it lies but
in thy faithful will; that all things are possible to him that
believeth.

We must look at this episode of the miracle as itself also
symbolic. Peter represents to us here the faithful of all times
in the seasons of their unfaithfulness and fear. So long as they
are strong in faith, they are able to tread under foot the most

---

[4] Bengel: "He was not blamed because he came out of the ship, but because he
did not remain in the firmness of faith."

turbulent agitations of an unquiet world; but when they are afraid, when, instead of "looking unto Jesus," they look at the stormy winds and waters, anon these prevail against them, and they begin to sink; and were it not for their Lord's sustaining hand, stretched out in answer to their cry, they would be wholly overwhelmed and swallowed up.

And when they were come into the ship, the wind ceased. They willingly received him into the ship. Those who a little before cried out with fear at his approach, as though it had been a spirit, were now glad[5] to receive Him in their midst, and did so receive Him; *and immediately the ship was at the land whither they went.*

St. Mark, as his wont is (cf. ii. 12; v. 42; vii. 37; ix. 15), records the infinite astonishment of the disciples at all which they witnessed; *they were sore amazed in themselves beyond measure and wondered;* while from St. Matthew we learn that the impression was not limited to them alone; for *they that were in the ship,* others who were sailing with them, sailors and passengers, caught a momentary glimpse of the greatness of Him in whose presence they stood; and *came and worshipped him, saying Of a truth thou art the Son of God* (cf. John i. 49; Matt. xxvii. 54).

It was *the will* of Christ, which bore Him triumphantly above those waters; even as it was the will of Peter, that will, indeed, made in the highest degree active and potential by faith in the Son of God, which should in like manner have enabled him to walk on the great deep, and, though with partial and transient failure, did so enable him. There was here a sign of the lordship of man's will, when that will is in absolute harmony with God's will, over external nature.

---

[5] Grotius: "Not that they did not receive him, but. as Syrus shows, that they received him with exceeding eagerness."

CHAPTER XVIII.

The Opening of the Eyes of One Born Blind

JOHN ix.

IT IS on the whole most probable that this work of grace and power crowned the day of that long debate with Jewish adversaries, which, beginning at John vii. 34, reaches to the end of chapter x.; — the history of the woman taken in adultery being only an interruption, and an intercalation easily betraying itself as such. Our Lord then, as He passed from the temple, to escape those stones which were the last arguments of his foes (viii. 59), will have paused — probably in the immediate neighbourhood of the temple, where beggars, cripples, and other afflicted persons took their station (Acts iii. 2, 10), to accomplish this miracle. Nothing in the narrative indicates a break. That long "contradiction of sinners" which the Lord endured found place, we know, on a Sabbath, the last day of the feast of tabernacles (vii. 37) being always such; and on a Sabbath, to all appearance the same Sabbath. He opened this blind man's eyes (ix. 14). Moved by these reasons, the ancient interpreters see here a narrative continuous and unbroken, and with them most of the modern consent.

But how, it has been sometimes urged, could the disciples know of this man that he *was blind from his birth?* One way or other the fact had come to the knowledge of the disciples, and out of it their question grew. Perplexed at this more than ordinary calamity, they ask their Master to explain to them its cause: *Who did sin, this man or his parents, that he was born blind?* But what they had in their minds when they suggested the former alternative, namely that a man for his *own* sins should have been *born* blind, has naturally enough been often demanded.

I believe they failed to perceive at the moment when they asked their question, the self-contradiction involved in the first alternative which they put before their Lord. While they rightly, and by a most true moral instinct, discerned the intimate connexion in which the world's sin and the world's suffering stand to one another, yet in this case they did not realise how it must have been the sin and suffering, not of this individual man, but of him as making part of a great whole, which were thus connected together. They did not at the moment perceive that the mere fact of this calamity reaching back to his birth at once excluded and condemned the uncharitable suspicion, that wherever there was a more than ordinary sufferer, there was also a more than ordinary sinner, — leaving only the most true thought, that a great sin must be cleaving to a race, of which any member could so greatly suffer.

This, as it is continually affirmed in Scripture, so we cannot suppose that our Lord intended to deny it. His words, *Neither hath this man sinned, nor his parents,* — or better, *Neither did this man, nor his parents, sin,* — words which need for their completion — "that he should have been born blind," neither deny the man's own sin, nor that of his parents; they as little deny that sicknesses are oftentimes the punishment of sins (Deut. xxviii. 22; Lev. xxvi. 16; 1 Cor. xi. 30; Jam. v. 15), or that the sins of parents are often visited on their children (Exod. xx. 5). All that the Lord does is to check in his disciples that most harmful practice of diving down into the secrets of other men's lives, and, like the friends of Job, ascribing to them great transgressions in explanation of their unusual sufferings (Job. iv. 7; viii. 6). "This blindness," He would say, "is the chastening of no *peculiar* sin on his own part, nor on his parents." Seek, therefore, its cause elsewhere. The purpose of the lifelong blindness of this man is *that the works of God should be made manifest in him*. Not, indeed, as though this man had been used merely *as a means,* visited with this blindness to the end that the power of God in Christ might be manifested to others in its removal.[1] The manifestation of the works of God has here a wider reach: it includes, indeed, the manifestation of those works to the world and *on* the man; but it does not exclude, rather of necessity includes, their manifestation also *to* him and *in* him. It entered into the plan of God for the bringing of this man to the light of everlasting life, that he should thus for a while be dark outwardly; that so upon this darkness, and upon the darkness of his heart, a higher light might break, and the Sun of righteousness arise on him, with healing in his wings for all his bodily and all his spiritual infirmities; which, except for that long night of darkness and sorrow, might have never been: while again this was part of a larger whole, and fitted in, according to his eternal counsels, to the great scheme for the revelation of the glory and power of the Only-begotten to the world (cf. John xi. 4; Rom. v. 20; ix. 17; xi. 25, 32, 33).

At the same time we must not accept this as the entire and exhaustive solution of this man's blindness. God, though not the author, is yet the disposer of evil, — who distributes that which He did not Himself bring in, and distributes it according to the counsels of his wisdom and righteousness and grace, had willed that on this man should be concentrated more than the ordinary penalties of the world's universal sin, that a more than ordinary grace and glory might be revealed in their removing.

With this the Lord girds up Himself to the work which is before Him, and justifies Himself in undertaking it: *I must work the works of Him that sent Me,*[2] *while it is day,* or, adopting the preferable reading, *We must work the works of Him*

---

[1] Leo the Great (*Serm.* 45): "That which He had not given to the principles of nature, He had reserved for the manifestation of his own glory."

[2] This was a favourite passage with the Arians; see Augustine, *Serm.* cxxxv. 1-4, and his answer there to their abusive interpretation.

that sent Me, while it is day, the Lord associating the disciples in this blessed work with Himself; so the R. V.; *The night cometh, when no man can work* (cf. xi. 9, 10; Rom. xiii. 12). Whatever perils attended that work, yet it must be accomplished; for his time, *the day* of his open activity, was drawing to an end. *The night,* when He should no longer have the opportunity of working, with his own hands at least, works like these, was approaching. And then, with prophetic allusion to the work before Him, *As long as I am in the world, I am the light of the world* (cf. i. 4) ; "what work then will become Me better than this of opening the blind eyes? where should I find so fit a symbol of my greater spiritual work, the restoring of the darkened spiritual vision of mankind?"

And now He who at the old creation had said, "Let there be light, and there was light" (Gen. i. 3), will in this, a little fragmentary specimen of the new creation which hereafter shall be, display the same almighty power. *When he had thus spoken, he spat on the ground, and made clay of the spittle, and he anointed the eyes of the blind man with the clay.* A medicinal value was attributed in old time to saliva, neither are we altogether without examples of a medicinal use of clay." Still we must not suppose that, *besides* his divine power, the Lord *also* used natural remedies, or that these were more than conductors, not in themselves needful, but such as of his own free will He assumed, as channels to convey his grace (cf. 2 Kin. iv. 41; Isai. xxxviii. 21) ; for other blind eyes He opened without employing any such means (Matt. ix. 27-30; xx. 30-34). Probably the reasons which induced their use were ethical. It may have been a help to the weak faith of this man to find that something external was done. Nor may we leave out of sight a symbolic reference to Gen. ii. 7. The same creative hand which wrought at the beginning is again at work.

This done, Christ *said unto him, Go, wash in the pool of Siloam.* The command was certainly something more than a mere test of obedience. Did St. John see anything significant and mystical in the name of the pool, that he should add for his Greek readers an interpretation of it, *which is by interpretation, Sent?* How can we suppose that St. John did *not* see a prophetic significance in the name *Siloam,* or that, except for this, he would have paused to insert in his narrative the meaning of the word (cf. i. 38, 42)? Christ, the Sender indeed in this particular instance, was the Sent of God, when we contemplate his work as a whole;[3] so He ever contemplated it Himself (John iii. 17, 34; v. 36, 38; vii. 29; viii. 42). These waters of Siloam, in which the blind man washed and was illuminated, may well have been to St. John a type of the waters of baptism (cf. 1 Pet. iii. 21), or indeed of all the operations of grace by which the eyes spiritually blind are opened; the very name of the pool having therefore for him a presaging fitness, which by this notice he would stamp as more than accidental.

The man is no Naaman, resenting the simplicity of the means by which his cure should be effected, and with difficulty persuaded to be healed (2 Kin. v. 11, 13). He at once fulfilled the conditions imposed: *he went his way therefore, and washed, and came seeing* (cf. xi. 37); returned, probably to the place where the Lord had met him; but not finding Him there, went to his own house. His neighbours and those familiar with his former life are the first to take note of the cure; — persons, as would appear, not ill disposed, but altogether under the influence of the Pharisees. They wonder, debate whether it be indeed he whom they had known so long; for the opening of the eyes, those windows of the soul, had no doubt altered the whole character of the countenance. *Some said, This is he; others said, He is like him;* these last denying the identity, and allowing only a fortuitous resemblance; and so the debate proceeded, until the man himself cut it short, and *said, I am he.* The admission

---

[3] Augustine (*Serm.* cxxxv. I): "Who is he that is sent save He who said, in this very context, 'I am come to do the works of him that sent me?'"

on his part is at once taken up. *Therefore said they unto him, How were thine eyes opened?* and having heard from his lips of the wonder-worker who had wrought the cure, and of the means by which He had wrought it, they desire to see Him, and demand where He might be found. The man cannot tell them. In the end, as the safest course, and they possibly having some misgivings about a work thus wrought upon the Sabbath, *they brought to the Pharisees him that aforetime was blind,* — not, that is, to the great Sanhedrim, for that was not always sitting, but the lesser. The Sanhedrim, it is true, did not exclusively consist of members of this party (for Caiaphas was a Sadducee, and see Acts xxiii. 6), but these were the most numerous and influential party there, and the bitterest enemies of the Lord.

More formally examined by them, the man can only repeat his simple tale: *He put clay upon mine eyes, and I washed, and do see.* He speaks of the clay only, for that only came within the scope of his knowledge, who judged by the feeling alone; *how* the clay had been tempered he was ignorant. Already there is a certain curtness in his reply, reduced as it is to the fewest possible words, as contrasted with the greater particularity of his first explanation (see ver. 11). And now the Pharisees discuss the matter among themselves. Some seek to rob the deed of its significance by a charge against the doer: *This man is not of God, because he keepeth not the Sabbath day.* Admitting the reality of the miracle, it proved nothing in favour of Him that wrought it; rather was it to be inferred, since he was thus an evident transgressor of God's commandment, that He was in connexion with the powers of evil.

But there was throughout all these events, which were so disastrously fixing the fortunes of the Jewish people, a truer and better party in the Sanhedrim, of which Nicodemus and Joseph of Arimathea were the worthiest representatives. These from time to time made their voices to be heard in the cause of right-

eousness and truth. Thus, on the present occasion, they claim
that He should not at once be prejudged a sinner and a breaker
of God's law, who had done such miracles as these (cf. x. 19-21).
Even their own doctors were not altogether at one concerning
what was permitted on the Sabbath, and what not. They could
therefore plead that the Spirit of God might well have directed
him in this that He did, and they ask, *How can a man that is
a sinner do such miracles?* Yet the shape which their interference takes, the form of a question, betrays the timidity of
men, who do not dare more than to hint their convictions; who
"lack the courage of their opinions." No wonder that they
should be in the end overborne and silenced by their more
unscrupulous adversaries, even as now they prove unequal to
the obtaining of a fair and impartial hearing of the matter. All
which the Evangelist notes for the present is that *there was a
division among them.*

To the interrogation in the verse following, *What sayest thou
of him, that he hath opened thine eyes?* (What conclusion draw-
est thou from thence?) the answer is to the point, *he said, He is
a prophet;* — not yet the Messiah, not yet the Son of God; of
these higher dignities of his healer the man as yet has no guess;
but what he believes Him he boldly declares Him, *a prophet,* —
one furnished with a message from above, and attesting that
message by deeds which no man could do, except God were
with him (John iii. 2; iv. 19; vi. 14). They who asked this,
cared not in the least for the judgment of the man; but they
hoped to mould him into an instrument for their own wicked
purposes. The intention of the question is that he, perceiving
what would be welcome to them, and following the suggestions
which they had thrown out, should turn against his benefactor,
and ascribe the opening of his eyes to the power of an evil
magic. But a rare courage from above is given to him, and he
dares, in the face of these formidable men whom he is making

his foes, to avouch his belief that the work and the doer of the work were of God.

But the Jews did not believe concerning him that he had been blind, and received his sight, until they had called the parents of him that had received his sight. To these they address themselves now. There is something selfish, and almost cowardly, in their manner of extricating themselves from a danger in which they are content to leave their son. The questions put to them are three: *Is this your son?* — *Who ye say was born blind?* — *How then doth he now see?* The first two they answer in the affirmative: *We know that this is our son* — *And that he was born blind:* on the third they altogether decline to give any opinion — *By what means he now seeth, we know not; or who hath opened his eyes, we know not: he is of age; ask him: he shall speak for himself.* The parents could not tell the truth without saying something to the honour of Jesus; and they will not do this, fearing to come under the penalties which the Sanhedrim had lately pronounced against any that should *confess that He was Christ.* We are not to understand by this that the Sanhedrim had formally declared Jesus to be an impostor, a false Christ, — but only that, so long as the question of the truth or falsehood of his claims to be the Messiah was not yet clear, — and they, the great religious tribunal of the nation, had not given their decision, — none were to anticipate that decision; and any who should thus run before, or, as it might prove, run counter to, their decision, *should be put out of the synagogue,* — that is, should be excommunicated (cf. xii. 42). There were two, or as some say three, kinds of excommunication among the Jews, greatly differing in degrees and intensity; and Christ often speaks of them, as among the sharpest trials which his followers would have to endure for his name's sake (John xvi. 2). The mildest form was exclusion for thirty days from the synagogue. To this period, in case the excommunicated showed no sign of repentance, a similar or a longer period, according to the will of those that imposed the sentence, was added: in other ways too it was made sharper; it was accompanied with a curse; none might hold communion with him now, not even his family, except in cases of absolute necessity. Did the offender show himself obstinate still, he was in the end absolutely separated from the fellowship of the people of God, cut off from the congregation, — a sentence answering, as many suppose, to the delivering to Satan in the apostolic Church (1 Cor. v. 5; 1 Tim. i. 20).

The man had been removed, while his parents were examined. The Pharisees now summon him again. Our *Give God the praise* sets the English reader on a wrong track. The Pharisees do not mean, "Give the glory of thy cure to God, and not to this sinful man, who in truth could have contributed nothing to it." They who did not allow that any cure had taken place at all could not mean this; professing, as they did, to believe that the alleged healing was a fraud and conspiracy throughout, contrived between Christ and the man who was before them. The words are rather an adjuration to him that he should speak the truth[4] (cf. Josh. vii. 19; 1 Sam. vi. 5; 1 Esdr. ix. 8). *"We know that this man is a sinner,* a more than ordinary transgressor, one, therefore, to whom last and least of all would God have given this higher power; your story then cannot be true; we who have the best opportunities of knowing, know this." They will overbear him with the authority of their place and station, and with their confident assertion.

The man, whom we must recognize throughout as ready-witted, genial, and brave, declines altogether to enter on a question which lay plainly beyond his knowledge: *Whether he be a sinner or no, I know not;* yet, as Chrysostom observes, not in the least allowing the alternative that such He was. He will

---

[4] Seneca (Ep. 95) speaks very nobly of this giving glory to God, as the great work of every man: "The first worship of the Gods is to believe in the Gods, and then to attribute unto them their majesty, to attribute unto them their goodness, without which there is no majesty."

speak, however, of that which lies within it; and they may draw their own conclusions: *One thing I know, that, whereas I was blind, now I see.* They perceive that they can gain nothing in this way, and they bid him to tell over again the manner and method of his cure: *Then said they to him again, What did he to thee? how opened he thine eyes?* hoping either to detect on a second repetition some contradictions in his story, or to find something which they can better lay hold on, and wrest into a charge against the Lord; or perhaps utterly perplexed how to escape from their present embarrassment, they ask for this repetition to gain time, and in the hope that some light may break upon them presently.

But the man has grown weary of the examinations to which they are submitting him anew, and there is something of defiance in his answer: *I have told you already, and ye did not hear: wherefore would ye hear it again?* — and then, with an evident irony, *Will ye also be his disciples?* Nothing could have stung the Pharisees more than the bare suggestion of such a discipleship on their parts: *Then they reviled him and said, Thou art his disciple, but we are Moses' disciples* — setting, as was their wont, Moses against the Lord, and contrasting their claims: *we know that God spake unto Moses;* he had a commission and an authority; but *as for this fellow, we know not from whence He is;* there is no proof that God has given Him a commission, no one can certainly affirm whether He be from above or from beneath. On a former occasion their charge against Him had been that they knew whence He was (John vii. 27), so impossible is it to convince those who are resolved to remain unconvinced.

This confession that they are unable to explain so new and wonderful an appearance, still further emboldens the man. There is an irony keener still in his present retort than in his last: *Why herein is a marvellous thing, that ye know not from whence He is, and yet He hath opened mine eyes.* This is wonderful; here is one evidently clothed with powers mightier than man's, able to accomplish a work like this; and you, the spiritual rulers of our nation, you that should try the spirits, should be able to pronounce of each new appearance whether it be of God or not, here acknowledge your ignorance, and cannot decide whence He is, whether of earth or of heaven. *Now we know,* for you have yourselves declared the same (see ver. 24), *that God heareth not sinners;* but this man He *hath* heard, and enabled Him to do a work without parallel; therefore I know whence He is; for *if this man were not of God, he could do nothing* — being the same conclusion at which one of themselves had arrived (John iii. 2).

It is interesting to observe how rapidly this poor man's faith and insight and courage have grown during this very examination. He who had said a little while before, *Whether he be a sinner or no, I know not,* evading the answer, now declares boldly, *We know that God heareth not sinners.* Nor need we take exception, as many have taken, at his statement. They may well be allowed to stand, and that in the intention of the speaker. For the term *sinner* has more than one application in Scripture. Sometimes it is applied to all men, as they are the fallen guilty children of Adam. Were it true that in this sense *God heareth not sinners,* such were a terrible announcement indeed: nothing short of this, God heareth not any man; or if by *sinners* were understood more than ordinary transgressors, and the words implied that such would not be heard, though they truly turned, this too would be an impeaching of God's grace. But the Scripture knows another and emphatic use of the term *sinners,* — men *in their sins,* and not desiring to be delivered out of them (Isai. xxxiii. 14; Gal. ii. 15); and in this, which is the sense of the speaker here, as of the better among the Pharisees, who a little earlier in the day had asked, *How can a man that is a sinner do such miracles?* (ver. 16; cf. x. 21), it is most true *that God heareth not sinners;* their prayer is an abomination;

and even if they ask, they obtain not their petitions (Isai. i. 11-15; Prov. i. 28; Ps. 1. 16; Job xi. 15; Jer. vi. 20; Amos v. 21-23; Mic. iii. 4; Jam. iv. 3) ; or only obtain them for their own worse confusion in the end (Num. xxii. 10; Ps. lxxviii. 29-31). *But if any man be a worshipper of God, and doeth his will, him He heareth* (Job xi. 13-15; xlii. 8; 1 Tim. ii. 8; 1 John iii. 22; v. 14).

This was what least of all the Pharisees could endure, that the whole relations between themselves and this man should be reversed, — that he should thus be *their* teacher; and while it was now plain that he could neither be cajoled nor terrified from his simple yet bold avowal of the truth, their hatred and scorn break forth without any restraint: "*Thou wast altogether born in sins,* — not imperfect in body only, but, as we now perceive, maimed and deformed in soul also, that birth-sin, which is common to all (Ps. li. 5), assuming far more than a common malignity in thee" — for so much their words imply, — "*and dost thou teach us?*⁵ Thou that camest forth from thy mother's womb with the note of thy wickedness upon thee, dost thou school us, presuming to meddle and make in such high matters as these?" They take the same view of his calamity, namely, that it was the note of a more than ordinary guilt, which the disciples had suggested; but make hateful application of it. *And they cast him out,* — which does not merely mean, as some explain it, rudely flung him forth from the hall of judgment, wherever that may have been; but, according to the decree which had gone before, they declared him to have come under those sharp spiritual censures denounced against any that should recognize the prophetic office of the Lord (John vii. 13). Only so would the act have the importance which (ver. 35) is attached to it (cf. John xvi. 2; 3 John 10). No doubt the sign and initial act of this excommunication was the thrusting him

---

⁵ Calvin: "They revile him as if he had issued from his mother's womb with the mark of his sins."

forth and separating him from their own company (Acts vii. 58) ; and so that other explanation has its partial truth. Yet this was not all, or nearly all, involved in the words. This violent putting of him forth from the hall of audience was only the beginning of the things which he should suffer for Christ's sake. Still there was, to use the words of Fuller on this very occasion, this comfort for him, that "the power of the keys, when abused, doth not shut the door of heaven, but in such cases only shoot the bolt beside the lock, not debarring the innocent person entrance thereat."

And in him were eminently fulfilled those words, "Blessed are ye when men shall hate you, and when they shall separate you from their company, and shall reproach you, and cast out your name as evil, for the Son of man's sake" (Luke vi. 22; cf. Isai. lxvi. 5; John xvi. 2). He is cast out from the meaner fellowship, to be received into the higher, — from that which was about to vanish away, to be admitted into a kingdom not to be moved. *Jesus heard that they had cast him out,* and, Himself the Good Shepherd, went in search of this sheep for making it his own for ever. *And when he had found him,* it may be in the temple (cf. John v. 14), *He said unto him, Dost thou believe on the Son of God?* with an emphasis in the original on *thou.* The man knows what this title *Son of God* means, that it is equivalent to Messiah, but he knows of none with right to claim it for his own: such trust, however, has he in his Healer, that whomsoever he will point out to him as such, he will recognize. *He answered and said, Who is he, Lord, that I might believe on him? And Jesus said unto him, Thou hast both seen him, and it is he that talketh with thee* (cf. John iv. 26). This *Thou hast seen Him,* is a reply to the question, *Who is He, Lord, that I might believe on Him?* "He is one whom thou hast seen already; ever since thou hast been speaking with Me thine eyes have beheld Him, for He is no other than this Son of man that talketh with thee."

And now the end to which all that went before was but as the prelude, has arrived: *He said, Lord, I believe; and he worshipped him:* not that even now we need suppose him to have known all which that title, *Son of God,* contained, nor that, by *worshipping* the Lord, he intended to render to Him that supreme adoration, which is indeed due to Christ, but only due to Him because He is one with the Father. For God manifest in the flesh is a mystery far too transcendent for any man to embrace in an instant. There were, however, in him the preparations for that crowning faith. The seed which should unfold into this perfect flower was securely laid in his heart; and he fell down at the feet of Jesus as of one more than man, with a deep religious reverence and fear and awe. And thus the faith of this poor man was accomplished. Step by step he had advanced, following faithfully the light which was given him. In him was grandly fulfilled the prophecy of Isaiah, and this at once literally and spiritually: "In that day the eyes of the blind shall see out of obscurity and out of darkness" (xxix. 18).

So wonderful was the whole event, so had it brought out the spiritual blindness of those who should have been the seers of the nation, so had it ended in the illumination, spiritual as well as bodily, of one who was counted among the blind, that it called forth from the Saviour's lips those remarkable words in which He moralized the whole: *For judgment I am come into this world, that they which see not might see, and that they which see might be made blind.* He would say, "I am the touchstone; much that seemed true shall at my touch be proved false, to be merely dross; much that for its little sightliness was nothing accounted of, shall prove true metal. Many, whom men esteemed to be seeing, such as the spiritual chiefs of this nation, shall be shown to be blind; many, whom men counted altogether unenlightened, shall, when my light touches them, be shown to have powers of spiritual vision undreamt of before" (Matt. xi. 25; Luke v. 25; xv. 7).

CHAPTER XIX.

The Restoring of the Man with a Withered Hand

MATT. xii. 9-13; MARK iii. 1-5; LUKE vi. 6-11.

THIS is not the first among our Lord's cures on the Sabbath day[1] which stirs the ill-will of his adversaries, or which is used by them as a pretext for accusing Him. Twice already we have seen the same results follow, the same offence taken; but I have reserved till now the consideration, once for all, of the position which our Lord Himself assumed in respect of the Sabbath. For in the discourse which immediately precedes this miracle, our Lord Himself deals with the question, and delivers the weightiest words which at any time on this matter fell from his lips.

The Pharisees were offended with the disciples for plucking ears of corn and eating them upon the Sabbath. It was not the act itself which offended, for the very law which they stood forward to vindicate had expressly permitted as much: "When thou comest into the standing corn of thy neighbor, then thou mayest pluck the ears with thine hand" (Deut. xxiii. 25). Not in what they did, but in the day on which they did it, the fault of the disciples, if any lay. The Pharisees accuse them to their Lord: *Why do they on the Sabbath day that which is not lawful?* Either He shall be obliged to confess his followers transgressors of the law; or, defending them, shall become a defender of the transgression; — in either case a triumph for his foes. So they calculate, but the issue disappoints their calculation (cf. Matt.

---

[1] The sabbatical cures recorded in the Gospels are seven in number, namely, that of the demoniac in the Synagogue of Capernaum (Mark i. 21); of Simon's wife's mother (Mark i. 29); of the impotent man at Bethesda (John v. 9); of this man with a withered hand; of the man born blind (John ix. 14); of the woman with a spirit of infirmity (Luke xiii. 14); of the man who had a dropsy (Luke xiv. 1). We have a general intimation of many more, as at Mark i. 34.

195

xxii. 15-22). The Lord seeks in his reply to raise the objectors
to a truer point of view from which to contemplate the act of
his disciples; and by two examples, and these drawn from that
very law which they believed they were asserting, show them how
the law must be spiritually handled and understood.

The first, David's claiming and obtaining the shew-bread from
the High priest (1 Sam. xxi. 1-6), might be expected to carry
weight with them, David being for them the great pattern and
example of Old Testament holiness: "Will ye affirm that they
did wrong, — David who in that necessity claimed, or the High
priest who gave to him, the holy bread?" The second example
came yet nearer home, being one grounded in the very constitution of the Levitical service: "Ye do yourselves practically
acknowledge it right that the rest of the Sabbath should give
place to a higher interest. The sacrifices, with all the laborious
preparations which they require, do not cease upon the Sabbath
(Num. xxviii. 9, 10); yet no one accounts the priests to be
therefore in any true sense violators of the law; such they would
rather be if they left these things undone. And then, lest the
Pharisees should retort, or in their hearts make exception, that
the work referred to was wrought in the service of the temple,
and was therefore permitted, while there was no such serving
of higher interests here, He adds, *But I say unto you, That in
this place is One greater than the temple.* He contemplates his
disciples as already the priests of the New Covenant, of which
He is Himself the living Temple. It was in their needful service
and ministration to Him, which left them no leisure regularly
to prepare food or to eat, that they were an hungered, and pro-
faned, as their adversaries esteemed it, the Sabbath. But if those
who ministered in that temple which was but the shadow of the
true, might without fault accomplish on the Sabbath whatsoever
was demanded by that ministry of theirs, by how much better
right were they free from all blame, who ministered about the

Temple not made with hands, the true Tabernacle, which the
Lord had pitched and not man!

But it is not enough to absolve his disciples; the malignant
accusation must not pass without rebuke. *But if ye had known
what that meaneth, I will have mercy, and not sacrifice, ye would
not have condemned the guiltless.* If with all their searching into
the Scripture, they had entered into the spirit of that law, they
would not have blamed them who indeed were blameless. The
citation, not now made for the first time (cf. Matt. ix. 13), is
from Hosea (vi. 6). He is declaring that what God longs for
is not the outward observance, the sacrifice in the letter, but the
inward outpouring of love, that which the *sacrifice* symbolizes,
the giving up of self in the self-devotion of love (cf. Heb.
x. 5-10; Ps. xl. 6-8; l. 8-14; li. 16, 17; Jer. vii. 22, 23). This
must underlie every outward sacrifice and service which shall
have any value in his sight; and when a question arises between
the form and the spirit, so that the one can only be preserved
at the expense of the other, then the form must yield to the life,
as the meaner to the more precious.

But the application of the words in the present instance still
remains unsettled. They might be taken thus: "If you had at all
known what God desires of men, you would then have understood that my disciples, who in love and pity for perishing souls
had so laboured and toiled as to go without their necessary food,
were offering that very thing; you would have seen that their
loving violation was better than other men's cold and heartless
fulfilment of the letter of the commandment." Or else the words
may refer more directly to the Pharisees: "If you had understood
the service wherein God delights, you would have sought to
please Him by mercy, — by a charitable judgment of your
brethren, — by that love out of a pure heart, which to Him is
more than all whole burnt-offerings and sacrifices (Mark xii. 33),
rather than in the way of harsh and unrighteous censure of your

brethren" (Prov. xvii. 15; Isa. v. 23).[2] "No pure zeal for the
cause of God urged them on. Rather sought they out of envy
and an inner bitterness to bring something against the disciples.
They *condemned the guiltless;*" for the disciples had not for
mere pastime's sake, plucked those ears, but out of hunger (ver.
1). They stood in the same position as David the servant of
God, who, in like manner, with them that were with him,
hungered in the service of the Lord; as the priests, who in the
temple must labour on the Sabbath, and so for the Lord's sake
seem to break the law of the Lord. While this was so, *they* also
might without scruple eat of the shew-bread of the Lord: what
was God's, was also theirs.

St. Mark has alone preserved for us the important words:
The Sabbath was made for man, and not man for the Sabbath.
The end for which the Sabbath was ordained was that it might
bless man; the end for which man was created was not that he
might observe the Sabbath. A principle is here laid down, which
must extend to the whole circle of outward ordinances. Man
was not created to the end that he might observe these; but
these were given, that they might profit man, discipline and
train him, till he should be ready to serve God from the free
impulses of his spirit. And all this being so, *therefore the Son of
man is Lord also of the Sabbath.* To conclude that the Sabbath
being *made for man,* man therefore can deal with the Sabbath
as he will, is a serious error. Among all the bold words with
which St. Paul declares man's relations to the law, he never
speaks of him, even after he is risen with Christ, as being its
lord. The redeemed man is not, indeed, *under* the law; he is
released from his bondage to it, so that it is henceforth *with
him,* as a friendly companion, not *over him,* as an imperious
master. But for all this it is God's law, the expression of his

---

[2] Wolf (*Curae,* in loc.): "I cannot doubt that these words were spoken to
confront the harsh and rigid judgment of the Pharisees, which they had passed on
the disciples as Sabbath-breakers."

holy will concerning man; and he, so long as he bears about a body of sin and death, and therefore may at any moment need its restraints, never stands *above* it; rather, at the first moment of his falling away from the liberty of a service in Christ, will come *under* it anew. But the *Son of man,* who is also Son of God, has power over all these outward ordinances. It was He who first gave them as a preparatory discipline for the training of man; and when they have done their work, when this preparatory discipline is accomplished, it is for Him to remove them (Heb. ix. 11-15). "Made *under* the law" in his human nature (Gal. iv. 4), He is *above* the law, and lord of the law, by right of that higher nature which is joined with his human. *He, therefore,* may pronounce *when* the shadow shall give place to the substance, *when* his people have so made one their own that they may forego the other. Christ is "the end of the law," and that in more ways than one. To Him it pointed; in Him it is swallowed up; being Himself living law; yet not therefore in any true sense the destroyer of the law, as the adversaries charged Him with being, but its transformer and glorifier, changing it from a bondage to a liberty, from a shadow to a substance, from a letter to a spirit (Matt. v. 17, 18).

To this our Lord's clearing of his disciples, or rather of Himself in his disciples, the healing of the man with a withered hand is by St. Matthew immediately attached, although from St. Luke we learn that it was on *another Sabbath* that it actually found place. There, in *their synagogue,* the synagogue of those with whom He had thus disputed, He encountered *a man who had his hand withered;* his *right hand,* St. Luke tells us (cf. xxii. 50). His disease showed itself in a gradual wasting of the bulk of the limb, with a loss of its powers of motion, and ending with the total cessation in it of all vital action.

The apparent variation in the different records of this miracle, that in St. Matthew the question proceeds from the Pharisees, in the other Gospels from the Lord, is no real one. The Pharisees first ask Him, *Is it lawful to heal on the Sabbath days?* He answers question with question, as was so often his custom (see Matt. xxi. 24): *I will ask you one thing. Is it lawful on the Sabbath days to do good, or to do evil? to save life or to destroy it?* With infinite wisdom He shifts the whole argument, lifts it up altogether into a higher region; and then at once it is evident on which side the right lies. They had put the alternative of doing or not doing; there might be a question here. But He shows that the alternative is, the doing good or the failing to do good, — which last He puts as identical with doing evil (Prov. xxiv. 11, 12). Here there could be no question; this under no circumstances could be right. Therefore it is not merely allowable, but a duty, to do some things on the Sabbath. "Yea," He goes on, "and works much less important and urgent than that which I am about to do, you would not yourselves leave undone. *What man shall there be among you, that shall have one sheep, and if it fall into a pit on the Sabbath day, will he not lay hold on it, and lift it out? How much then is a man better than a sheep?* You have asked Me, Is it lawful to *heal* on the Sabbath? I reply, It is lawful *to do well* on that day, and therefore to heal." *They held their peace,* having nothing to answer more.

Then, — that is, *when He had looked round about on them with anger, being grieved for the hardness of their hearts* (Mark iii. 5), — *saith He to the man, Stretch forth thy hand.* The presence of grief and anger in the same heart at the same time is no contradiction. Indeed, with Him who was at once perfect love and perfect holiness, grief for the sinner must ever go hand in hand with anger against the sin; and this anger with Him was perfectly pure; for it is not the agitation of the waters, but the sediment at the bottom, which troubles and defiles them; and where no sediment is, no impurity will follow on their agitation. The man obeyed the word, which was a word of power; *he stretched it forth, and it was restored whole, like as the other.*

Hereupon the exasperation of Christ's enemies rises to the highest pitch. He has broken their traditions; He has put them to silence and to shame before all the people. *They were filled with madness,* as St. Luke tells us; or, in the words of St. Matthew, *went out, and held a council against him, how they might destroy him* (cf. John xi. 53). In their blind hate they do not even shrink from joining league with the Herodians, the Romanizing party in the land, — if between them they may bring to nothing this new power which equally menaces both. Thus it is ever with the sinful world. Its factions, divided against one another, can yet lay aside for the moment their mutual jealousies and enmities, to join in a common conspiracy against the truth. The kingdom of lies is no longer a kingdom divided against itself, when the kingdom of the truth is to be opposed. Between lie and lie, however seemingly antagonistic, there are always points of contact; it is only between a lie and the truth that there is absolute opposition, and no compromise possible. The Lord, aware of the machinations of his enemies, withdraws from their malice to his safer retirements in the immediate neighbourhood of the sea of Galilee (Mark iii. 7; John xi. 53, 54).

CHAPTER XX.

The Restoring of the Woman with a Spirit of Infirmity

LUKE xiii. 10-17.

WE have here another of those cures, which, having been accomplished on the Sabbath, awoke the indignation of the rulers of the Jewish Church. We are not told where this healing took place; but only that *He was teaching in one of the synagogues on the Sabbath.* There were synagogues in every place; and in these, on every Sabbath, prayer was wont to be made, and the Scriptures of the Old Testament read and expounded (Luke iv. 16, 17; Acts xiii. 14, 15; xv. 21). *And, behold, there was a woman which had a spirit of infirmity eighteen years, and was bowed together, and could in no wise lift up herself.* Had we only this account of what ailed her, namely that she *had a spirit of infirmity,* we might doubt whether St. Luke meant to trace up her complaint to any other than the natural causes. But the Lord's later commentary on these words — *whom Satan hath bound,* — shows that her calamity had a deeper spiritual root. Her sickness having its first seat in her spirit, had brought her into a moody melancholic state, of which the outward contraction of the muscles of her body was but the sign and the consequence.

And when Jesus saw her, he called her to him, and said unto her, Woman, thou art loosed from thine infirmity, — not waiting till his aid was sought (cf. John v. 6), though possibly her presence may have been, on her part, a tacit seeking of that aid. As much seems implied in the words of the ruler of the synagogue, bidding the multitude upon other days than the Sabbath to *come and be healed. And he laid his hands on her,*[1] — this

---

[1] Chrysostom (in Cramer, *Catena*): "He lays also his hands on her, that we may learn that the holy body possessed the power and energy of the Word of God."

act of power, no doubt, accompanying those words of power; and from Him there streamed into her the currents of a new life, so that the bands, spiritual and bodily, by which she was holden, were loosened; *and immediately she was made straight, and glorified God* (Luke xvii. 15; xviii. 43); others, no doubt, of those present glorifying God with her (Matt. ix. 8; xv. 31). Some part of this glory could not but redound to Him who was the immediate author of her cure. But there was one who could ill endure to be a witness of this (cf. Matt. xxi. 15, 16). He, *the ruler of the synagogue,* interrupting, and so far as in him lay, marring that festival of joy, *answered with indignation, because that Jesus had healed on the Sabbath day, and said unto the people, There are six days in which men ought to work: in them therefore come and be healed, and not on the Sabbath day!* Not venturing to come into direct collision with the Lord, he seeks circuitously and covertly to reach Him through the people. Rebuking them for coming to be healed, he indeed has another in his eye, and means that rebuke to glance off on Him, who upon this day had been willing to be a Healer.

The Lord takes him up with unusual severity. *Thou hypocrite!* He calls him — zeal for God being only the cloak which he wore, to hide from others, or perhaps from himself as well, his hatred to all which was holy and divine. And this his hypocrisy Christ proceeds to lay bare to him, making him to feel that, however he might plead the violation of the Sabbath as the cause of his indignation, its real ground lay in the fact that Christ was glorified by the cure upon that day wrought. The Lord proceeds: *Doth not each one of you on the Sabbath loose his ox or his ass from the stall, and lead him away to watering? And ought not this woman, being a daughter of Abraham, whom Satan hath bound, lo, these eighteen years, be loosed from this bond on the Sabbath day?* Every word of this answer *tells.* He does not so much defend his breach of the Sabbath, as deny that He has broken it at all: "You have your relaxations of the Sabbath's strictness, required by the very nature and necessities of your earthly condition. Your ox and your ass are precious in your sight, and, whatever you may hold or teach concerning the strictness with which the Sabbath should be kept, you loose them on that day; yet are angry now that I should loose a human spirit, which is of more value than many beasts. And these animals, when you loose them, have not been tied up for more than a few hours; while I, in your thoughts, may not loose from the thraldom of Satan this captive of eighteen years. Yours too is a laborious process of unfastening and leading away to water, — which yet (and rightly) you do not omit; being for all this offended with Me, who have but spoken a word, and with that word have released a soul."[2] There lies at the root of this argument, as of so much else in Scripture, an implied assertion of the specific difference between man, the lord of creation, for whom everything else was made, on the one side, and all the inferior creatures which inhabit the same earth with him on the other. But besides the common claims of humanity, this woman had other and still stronger claims to this help from Him. She was a *daughter of Abraham;* compare Luke xix. 9 — an inheritress, as perhaps the Lord would imply, of the faith of Abraham, — however, for the saving of her soul in the day of the Lord, she had come under the scourge of Satan. The narrow-hearted Scribe might grudge to behold her a partaker of this grace; but in his eyes it was only meet that she should receive it.

---

[2] Chemnitz (*Harm. Evang.* 112): "He brings the question of time also into the comparison. The cattle are probably tied to their stall for a single night or for a few days. But this woman is especially worthy of every one's compassion, if only for the length of time she had suffered."

CHAPTER XXI.

The Healing of the Man with a Dropsy

LUKE xiv. 1-6.

ALL which is most remarkable in the circumstances of this miracle has been already anticipated in others, chiefly in the two just considered, to which the reader is referred. Our Lord in his great long-suffering did not even at this late period of his ministry treat the Pharisees as wholly and finally hardened against the truth. So far from this, and still seeking to win them for his kingdom, He had accepted the invitation of a chief among them *to eat bread* in his house. This was upon the Sabbath, with the Jews a favourite day for their festal entertainments: for it is an entire mistake to regard the day with them as one of rigorous austerity; on the contrary, the practical abuse of the day was rather a turning of it into a day of riot and excess.[1] The invitation, though accepted in love, yet had not been given in good faith; in the hope rather that close and more accurate watching might furnish matter of accusation against Him. They *watched him.*

And behold, there was a certain man before him which had the dropsy. Some have suggested that this sufferer was of design placed before Him. But, although it is quite conceivable of these malignant adversaries, that they should have laid such a snare as this, still there is no ground for ascribing to them such treachery here. At any rate, if such plot there was, the man himself was no party to it; for the Lord *took him, and healed him, and let him go.*

But before He did this, He justified the work which He would accomplish, demanding of these lawyers and Pharisees, inter-

---

[1] Compare Plutarch (*Symp.* iv. 6): "The Hebrews honour the Sabbath chiefly by inviting each other to drinking and intoxication."

preters of the law, *Is it lawful to heal on the Sabbath day?*
Here, as in so many matters of debate, it only needs for the
question to be rightly stated, and all is so clear, that the question
itself has for ever disappeared. But as this answer they would
not give, they did what alone was possible, *they held their
peace.* He proceeds: *Which of you shall have an ass or an ox
fallen into a pit, and will not straightway pull him out on the
Sabbath day?* Olshausen says, "As on other occasions (Matt. xii.
11; Luke xiii. 15), the Lord brings back those present to their
own experience, and lets them feel the keen contradiction in
which their blame of Christ's free work of love sets them with
themselves, in that, where their worldly interests were at hazard,
they did that very thing whereof they made now an occasion
against Him." As in that other case, where the woman was
bound, He adduces the example of *unbinding* a beast (Luke
xiii. 15), so in this, where the man was dropsical, a sufferer
from water, the example He adduces has an equal fitness.[2] Why
do you not love your neighbour as yourselves? why do you
grudge that *he* should receive the help which you would freely
render to your own? *And they could not answer him again to
these things.* The truth, which did not win them, did the only
other thing which it could do, exasperated them the more; they
replied nothing, biding their time (cf. Matt. xii. 14).

---

[2] Grotius: "The man with a dropsy He compared to a beast drowning, the crooked woman to a beast bound."

CHAPTER XXII.

The Cleansing of Ten Lepers

LUKE xvii. 11-19.

THE Jews in Galilee, in their journeys to keep the passover at Jerusalem, commonly took the longer route, leading them across the Jordan, and through the region of Peraea, so to avoid the inhospitable land of the Samaritans. For these were naturally most unfriendly of all to the pilgrims who, travelling up to the great feasts at Jerusalem, thus witnessed in act against the will-worship of Mount Gerizim, and against the temple of Samaria in which was no presence of the living God (John iv. 22). It is generally understood that, notwithstanding the discomforts and dangers of that inhospitable route (see Luke ix. 51-56; John iv. 9), our Lord, with his disciples, on this his last journey to the holy city, took the more direct way which led Him straight from Galilee, *through the midst of Samaria* to Jerusalem. Certainly the words which we have translated, *And it came to pass, as he went to Jerusalem, that he passed through the midst of Samaria and Galilee, may* bear this meaning; in our Version they must bear it.

And as he entered into a certain village, there met him ten men that were lepers, which stood afar off. Their common misery had drawn these poor outcasts together (cf. 2 Kin. vii. 3), and had caused them to forget the fierce national antipathy which kept Jew and Samaritan apart; for a Samaritan, as presently appears, had found admission into this forlorn company. There has been already occasion to speak of leprosy. It was the outward symbol of sin in its worst malignity, as involving therefore entire separation from God; not of spiritual sickness only, but of spiritual death. These poor outcasts, in obedience to the

209

commandment (Lev. xiii. 46; Num. v. 2; cf. 2 Kin. xv. 5), *stood afar off;* and out of a deep sense of their misery, yet not without hope that a Healer was at hand, and all of them in earnest now to extort the benefit, *lifted up their voices, and said, Jesus, Master, have mercy on us!* All who have studied this terrible disease tell us that an almost total failure of voice is one of the symptoms which accompany it. It is not then for nothing that we are presently told of one who had been restored to health that he returned *with a loud voice* glorifying God; while here the earnestness with which the boon was sought, is sufficiently indicated by the fact that they *lifted up their voices,* found such an utterance as it might have seemed beforehand the disease would have denied them.

And when he saw them, he said unto them, Go, show yourselves unto the priests. Most instructive is it to observe the *manifold* wisdom of the great Physician, varying his treatment according to the varying needs of his patients. There are no doubt reasons why these ten are dismissed as yet uncleansed, and bidden to show themselves to the priests; whilst that other, whose healing was before recorded (Matt. viii. 2-4), is first cleansed, and not till afterwards bidden to present himself in the temple. There was here, in the first place, a keener trial of faith. With no signs of restoration as yet upon them, they were bidden to do that which implied that they were perfectly restored. In their prompt obedience they declared plainly that some weak beginnings of faith were working in them: which yet in the end was only perfectly unfolded in one. So much they declared, for they must have known very well that they were not sent to the priests for these to heal them. That was no part of the priest's office; who did not cure, but only pronounce cured (Lev. xiv. 3, 4).

As there was a keener trial of faith than that to which the leper of Matt. viii. 2 was exposed, so also there was here a stronger temptation to ingratitude. *It came to pass, that as they*

went, they were cleansed. When these poor men first felt and
found the benefit whereof they were partakers, it is likely that
they were some way upon their journey.[1] At all events to return
and render thanks to Him was an effort greater than the most
of them cared to make: *one of them, when he saw that he was
healed, turned back, and with a loud voice glorified God, and
fell down at his feet, giving him thanks: and he was a Samaritan.*
Some, indeed, suppose that the return of this one did not take
place till after he had fulfilled all which was commanded him.
The record of the miracle which we have here seems to me to
leave no room for such an interpretation. It was *when he saw
that he was healed* — that he turned back. He, as I take it, and
his whole company, having advanced some way on their commanded journey, felt and knew themselves cleansed. Hereupon
this Samaritan, from whom it could least have been expected,
turned back to give glory to God and thanks to his great Healer
and Saviour; the others meanwhile enduring to carry away the
benefit without one grateful acknowledgment rendered unto Him
from whom it came.[2]

Even He, who "knew what was in man," marvelled at the
greatness of the ingratitude: for He asked, *Were there not ten
cleansed?* or rather, *Were not the ten cleansed? but where are
the nine? There are not found that returned to give glory to God,
save this stranger.* Him now He dismisses with a second blessing,
and one better than the first. Gratitude for a lower mercy obtains
for him a higher. That which the others missed, to which their
bodily healing should have introduced them, and would so have
done, if they had received it aright, he has obtained; for to him,
and to him only, it is said, *Arise* — for he was kneeling still —
go thy way; thy faith hath made thee whole (Luke vii. 50; Matt.
ix. 22; Mark x. 52).

---

[1] Calvin suggests another reason, which may have kept them away: "They slipped
away to banish the memory of their disease."
[2] So too Bernard: "Importunate to receive, restless till they receive, ungrateful
when they have received." Calvin: "So want and hunger give birth to faith, which
fulness kills."

It gives a special significance to this miracle that this thankful one should have been a Samaritan. It was involved in this that the Gentiles were not excluded from the kingdom of God; nay rather, might obtain a place in it before others who by nature and birth were children of the kingdom; that the ingratitude of these might exclude them, while the faith of those might give to them an abundant entrance into all its blessings.

How aptly does the image which this history supplies set forth the condition of the faithful in this world! They too are to take Christ's word that they will be cleansed, that in some sort they are so already (John xv. 3) ; for in baptism they have the pledge and promise and the initial act of it all. And this they must believe, even while they still feel in themselves the leprous taint of sin, — must go forward in faith, being confident that in the use of his Word and his sacraments, and all his appointed means of grace, they will find that health which according to the sure word of promise is in some sort already theirs; and as they go, believing this word, using these means, they *are* healed. And for them, too, a warning is here — that they forget not the purging of their old sins (2 Pet. i. 9) after the manner of those nine. Let those who now are clean through the word spoken to them, keep ever in memory the times of their past anguish, — when they saw themselves as "unclean, unclean," shut out from all holy fellowship of God and men, and cried out in their anguish, *Jesus, Master, have mercy upon us.* Let each remembrance of the absolving word which was spoken to them, bring them anew to the Saviour's feet, giving glory to God by Him; lest, failing in this, their guilt prove greater than even that of these unthankful nine. For these carried away temporal mercies unacknowledged; but we should in such an event be seeking to carry away spiritual; not, indeed, that we should succeed in so doing; since the spiritual mercy which is not evermore referred to its Author, sooner or later inevitably ceases from him who thinks on any other conditions to retain it.

CHAPTER XXIII.

The Healing of the Daughter of the Syrophoenician Woman

MATT. xv. 21-28; MARK vii. 24-30.

WE have no reason to think that at any time during his earthly ministry our Lord passed beyond the borders of the Holy Land; not even when He *departed into the coasts of Tyre and Sidon*. It was only *into the borders of Tyre and Sidon* as St. Mark expressly tells us (vii. 24), that He went. The general fitness of things, and more than this, his own express words on this very occasion, *I am not sent but unto the lost sheep of the house of Israel*, combine to make it most unlikely that He had now brought his healing presence to any other but the people of the Covenant; moreover, when St. Matthew speaks of the *woman of Canaan* as *coming out* of that district or *of the same coasts*, he clearly shows that he did not intend to describe the Lord as having more than drawn close to the skirts of that profane land.

Being there, He *entered into an house, and would have no man know it: but*, as "the ointment bewrayeth itself," so He, whose "Name is like ointment poured out," *could not be hid;* and among those attracted by its sweetness was a woman of that country, — *a woman of Canaan*, as St. Matthew terms her; *a Greek, a Syrophoenician*, as St. Mark has it, but the first term indicating her religion, that it was not Jewish, but heathen; by the second, the stock of which she came, being no other than that accursed race once doomed of God to excision root and branch (Deut. vii. 2), but of which some branches had been spared that should have destroyed all (Judg. ii. 2, 3). Everything seemed banded against her; yet this did not prevent her

213

from drawing nigh, from seeking, and obtaining, the boon that
her soul longed after. She had heard of the mighty works which
the Saviour of Israel had done. And she has a boon to ask for
her daughter; — or say rather for herself, so entirely has she
made her daughter's misery her own: *Have mercy on me, O
Lord, thou Son of David; my daughter is grievously vexed with
a devil.*

But she finds Him at a first encounter very different from
that gracious helper and healer which report had described. He,
who of Himself had anticipated the needs of others (John v. 6),
withdrew Himself from hers; *He answered her not a word.* The
Word has no word. At last the disciples, wearied out with her
persistent entreaties, *came and besought him, saying, Send her
away.* They reveal at the same time the root of selfishness out of
which this compassion of theirs grew; for why is He to satisfy
her and dismiss her? *for she crieth after us;* she is drawing on
them unwelcome observation. Here, as so often, behind a seeming severity lurks the real love, while under the show and
semblance of a greater easiness selfishness lies hid.

Christ stops their mouth with words which seem to set the
seal of hopelessness on her suit: *He answered and said, I am
not sent but unto the lost sheep of the house of Israel* (cf. Matt.
x. 5, 6). In what sense was this true? All prophecy which went
before declared that in Him, the promised seed, not one nation
only, but all nations of the earth, should be blest (Ps. lxxii. 11;
Luke ii. 32; Rom. xv. 9-12). He Himself declared, "Other
sheep I have, which are not of this fold; them also I must bring,
and they shall hear my voice" (John x. 16). Clearly it must
have been in his own personal ministry.[1] That ministry, for wise
purposes in the counsels of God, should be restricted to his

---

[1] Augustine (*Serm.* lxxvii. 2): "He said that *He was not sent but unto the lost
sheep of the house of Israel?* We understand then by this that it behoved him to
manifest his bodily presence, his truth, the exhibition of his miracles, and the power
of his resurrection among that people." Jerome (*Comm. in Matt.* in loc.): "He was
reserving the perfect salvation of the Gentiles for the time of his passion and
resurrection."

own nation; and every departure from this was, and was clearly marked as, an exception. Here and there, indeed, there were first drops of that gracious shower which should one day water the whole earth (John xii. 20-22). It was only as by a rebound from them that the grace was to light upon the heathen world; while yet that issue, which seemed thus accidental, was laid deep in the counsels of God (Acts xiii. 44-49; xix. 9, 10; xxviii. 25-28; Rom. xi.). In Christ's reply, as St. Mark gives it, *Let the children first be filled,* the refusal does not appear so absolute and final, and a glimpse is vouchsafed of the manner in which the blessing might yet pass on to others, when as many of these, *the children,* as were willing, should have accepted it. But there, too, the *present* repulse is absolute. The time is not yet; others intermeddle not with the meal, till the children have had enough.

The woman hears the repulse which the disciples receive; but is not daunted or disheartened thereby. Hitherto she had been crying after the Lord, and at a distance; but now *came she and worshipped him, saying, Lord, help me.* On this He breaks the silence which hitherto He has maintained towards her; but it is with an answer more discomfortable than that silence itself had been: *He answered and said, It is not meet to take the children's bread, and to cast it to dogs. The children* are, of course, the Jews, "the children of the kingdom" (cf. Matt. viii. 12). He who spoke so sharply *to* them, speaks thus honourably *of* them; for here He is speaking of the position which God has given them in his kingdom; there, of the manner in which they have realized that position. On the other hand, extreme contempt was involved in the title of *dog* given to any one, the nobler characteristics of this animal being never brought out in Scripture.

There are very few for whom this would not have been enough. Not so, however, this heathen woman; she is mighty in faith; and from the very word which seems to make most against her, draws with the ready wit of faith an argument in her own behalf. She entangles the Lord, Himself most willing to be so entangled, in his own speech:[2] *Truth, Lord: yet the dogs eat of the crumbs which fall from their masters' table.*

She accepts the Lord's declaration to show how *in that very declaration* is involved the granting of her petition. "Saidest Thou *dogs?* it is well; I accept the title and the place; for the dogs *have* a portion too; — not indeed the first, not the children's portion, but a portion still, — the crumbs which fall from the masters' table. In this very putting of the case, Thou bringest us heathen, Thou bringest *me,* within the circle of the blessings which God, the great Householder, is ever dispensing to his family. We also belong to his household, though we occupy but the lowest place therein. According to thine own showing, I am not wholly an alien, and therefore I will abide by this name, and will claim all which in it is included." By the *masters* she intends the great Heavenly householder Himself. She uses the plural, *masters,* to correspond with the plural, *dogs,* which Christ had used just before; while yet it is the one Son only, the Only-begotten of the Father, who is intended there.[3] He who fills all things living with plenteousness spreads a table for all flesh; and all that depend on Him are satisfied from it, each in his own order and place.

She has conquered at last. She, who before heard only those words of a seeming contempt, now hears words of a most gracious commendation: *O woman, great is thy faith!* He who showed at first as though He would have denied her the smallest boon, now opens to her the full treasure-house of his grace, and bids her to help herself, to carry away what she will: *Be it unto thee even as thou wilt.* He had shown to her for a while, the aspect of severity; but He would not maintain it an instant longer than was needful, and after that mighty word of an

---

[2] Corn. a Lapide: "She entangles Christ in his own words, seizes and takes him. The argument He had used against her she gently retorts upon himself."
[3] Maldonatus: "She speaks in the plural because of the dogs, each of which has his own master."

undaunted faith, it was needful no more: *For this saying go thy way; the devil is gone out of thy daughter.*

Like the centurion at Capernaum (Matt. viii. 13) she made proof that his word was as effectual spoken far off as near. She offered in her faith a channel of communication between her distant child and Christ. With one hand of that faith she laid hold on Him in whom all healing grace was stored, with the other on her suffering daughter, — herself a living conductor by which the power of Christ might run, like an electric flash, from Him to the object of her love. *And when she was come to her house, she found the devil gone out, and her daughter laid upon the bed,* weak and exhausted, as these words imply, from the paroxysms of the spirit's going out; — unless, indeed, they indicate that she was now taking that quiet rest, which hitherto her condition had excluded.

The question remains, *Why* this anguish was not spared her, *why* the Lord should have presented Himself under so different an aspect to her, and to most other suppliants? Doubtless because He saw in it a faith which would stand the proof, knew that she would emerge victorious from this sore trial; and not only so, but with a mightier and purer faith than if she had borne away her blessing at once and merely for the asking. She has learned "that men ought always to pray, and not to faint;" she has won the strength which Jacob won from his wrestling with the Angel. God Himself yields to the might of faith and prayer.

Yet, when we thus speak of man overcoming God, we must never for an instant lose sight of this, that the power whereby he overcomes the resistance of God, is itself a power supplied *by* God. Thus when St. Paul speaks of himself as *striving* for the Colossians (Col. i. 29), striving, that is, with God in prayer (see iv. 12), he immediately adds, "according to *his* working, which worketh in me mightily."

CHAPTER XXIV.

The Healing of One Deaf and Dumb

MARK vii. 31-37.

S T. MATTHEW tells us that when the Lord had returned from those coasts of Tyre and Sidon unto the sea of Galilee, "great multitudes came unto Him, having with them those that were lame, blind, dumb, maimed, and many others, and cast them down at Jesus' feet, and He healed them" (xv. 30). Out of this number of cures St. Mark selects one to relate more in detail, and this, no doubt, because it was signalized by some incidents which had not occurred on any other like occasion. *They bring unto him one that was deaf, and had an impediment in his speech,* one who, if not wholly dumb, was yet incapable of uttering articulate sounds. His case differs, apparently, from that of the dumb man mentioned Matt. ix. 32; for while that man's evil is traced up distinctly and directly to a spiritual source, nothing of the kind is intimated here. Him his friends now brought to the great Healer, *and they beseech him to put his hand upon him.* It is not, however, exactly in the way they designate that He will heal him who is brought to Him now.

It has been already observed, that there must lie a deep meaning in all the variations which mark the different healings of different sick and afflicted, a wisdom of God ordering all the circumstances of each particular cure. Were we acquainted as accurately as He who "knew what was in man," with the spiritual condition of each who was brought within the inner circle of his grace, we should then perfectly understand why one was healed in the crowd, another led out of the city before the work of restoration was commenced; why for one a word effected a cure, for another a touch, while a third was sent to wash in

219

the pool of Siloam ere "he came seeing;" why for this one the process of restoration was instantaneous, while another saw at first "men as trees, walking." We are not for an instant to suppose in cures gradually accomplished any restraint on the power of the Lord save such as He willingly imposed on Himself, — and this, doubtless, in each case having reference to, and being explicable by, the moral and spiritual state of the person at that time passing under his hand. Our ignorance may prevent us from at once and in every case discerning "the manifold wisdom" which ordered each work of his, but we are not less sure that this wisdom ordered them all.[1]

This man He first *took aside from the multitude.* But with what intent did He isolate him thus? His purpose was that the man, apart from the tumult and interruptions of the crowd, in solitude and silence, might be more receptive of deep and lasting impressions; even as the same Lord does now so often lead a soul apart, sets it in the solitude of a sick chamber, or in loneliness of spirit, or takes away from it earthly companions and friends, when He would speak to it words of help and of healing — so that in the hush of the world's din it may listen to Him.

Having this done, Christ *put his fingers into his ears, and he spit, and touched his tongue.* These are symbolic actions, which it is easy to see why He should have employed in the case of one afflicted as this man was. Christ by these signs would awaken his faith, and stir up in him the lively expectation of a blessing. The fingers are put into the ears as to pierce through the obstacles which hindered sounds from reaching the seat of hearing. This was the fountain-evil; this man did not *speak* plainly, because he did not *hear;* this defect, therefore, is first removed.

---

[1] Maldonatus: "Christ even seems to have willed not to manifest his divinity and power always in the same degree, judging, although the cause be hidden from us, that this was not always fitting. At times by his mere word He casts out devils and raises the dead, showing himself to be wholly God: at times He heals the sick by a touch, by spittle or by clay, accommodating in a manner his power to the method of working of natural causes, and to the sense and usage of men."

Then, with the moisture of his own mouth upon his finger He touched the tongue which He would release from the bands that held it fast (cf. John ix. 6). It is not for any medicinal virtue that use is made of this moisture, but as the apt symbol of a power residing in, and going forth from, Himself.

St. Mark, abounding as he does in graphic touches, tells us how, this doing *and looking up to heaven, He sighed.* He has further preserved for us the very word which He spake, in the very language in which He spake it; He *saith unto Him, Ephphatha, that is, Be opened.* The *looking up to heaven* was a claiming of the divine help (Acts vii. 55); or rather an acknowledgment of his oneness with the Father, and that He did only those things which He saw the Father do (cf. Matt. xiv. 19; John v. 19, 20; xi. 41, 42). *He sighed,* or *He groaned,* which is the rendering of the Rhemish Version; we may suppose that this poor helpless creature now brought before Him, this living proof of the malice of the devil in deforming the fair features of God's original creation, wrung that groan from his heart. Thus on another still more memorable occasion, "He groaned in the spirit and was troubled" (John xi. 33), with a trouble which had in like manner its source in the thought of all the desolation which sin and death had effected. In the preservation of the actual Aramaic *Ephphatha,* which Christ spoke, as in the "Talitha, cumi" of Mark v. 41, we recognize the narrative of an eye- and ear-witness. Christ's word of power now as at all other times showed itself, for *straightway his ears were opened, and the string of his tongue was loosed, and he spake plain.*

The injunction, *He charged them that they should tell no man,* implies that the friends of this afflicted man had accompanied or followed Jesus out of the crowd, were now included in the same command not to divulge what they had seen. On the reasons which induced the Lord so often to give this charge of silence something has been said already. On this, as on other occasions (see Matt. ix. 31; Mark i. 44, 45), the charge is nothing regarded by those on whom it is laid; *the more he charged them, so much the more a great deal they published it.* The exclamation in which men's surprise and admiration find utterance, *He hath done all things well,* reminds us of the words of the first creation (Gen. i. 31), upon which we are thus not unfitly thrown back, for Christ's work is in the highest sense "a new creation." The notice of St. Matthew, *and they glorified the God of Israel* (xv. 31) implies that many of those present were heathens, as we might expect in that half-hellenized region of Decapolis; who, beholding the mighty works which were done, confessed that He who had chosen Israel for his own possession was God above all gods.

CHAPTER XXV.

The Miraculous Feeding of Four Thousand

MATT. xv. 32-39; MARK viii. 1-9.

ALMOST all which might be said upon this miracle, the preceding miracle, moving in precisely the same sphere of things, has anticipated already. Most probably the scene of it was almost the same; for thither the narrative of St. Mark has brought the Lord. The fact that immediately after the miracle He took ship and came to the region of Magdala (Matt. xv. 39), points the same way; since Magdala was certainly on the western side.

With many points of likeness, there are also some points of unlikeness in the two miracles. Here the people had continued with the Lord three days, while on the former occasion nothing of the kind is noted; the provision too is somewhat larger, *seven loaves and a few little fishes* instead of five loaves and two fishes; while the number fed is somewhat smaller, *four thousand* now instead of the five thousand then; and the remaining fragments in this case are only *seven baskets full,* while in the former they were twelve. These trivial differences do not in the slightest measure affect the miraculous element in this work of power. At the same time they are well worthy of note, seeing that nothing is more certain than that these miraculous features of the second miracle would have surpassed those of the first, had we here to do with mythical and unhistorical traditions.

At first it excites some surprise that the disciples, with that other miracle fresh in their memories, should on this later occasion have been as seriously perplexed. It is evermore thus in times of difficulty and distress. All former deliverances are in danger of being forgotten;[1] the mighty interpositions of God's hand in former passages of men's lives fall out of their remembrance. He may have divided the Red Sea for his people, yet no sooner are they on the other side than they murmur against Moses, and count that they must perish for thirst, crying, "Is the Lord among us, or not?" (Exod. xvii. 1-7). It is only the man of a full-formed faith, of a faith which Apostles themselves at this time did not possess, who argues from the past to the future, and truly derives confidence from God's former dealings of faithfulness and love (cf. 1 Sam. xvii. 34-37; 2 Chron. xvi. 7, 8). Only a strange unacquaintance with the heart of man could have led any to argue that the disciples, with their previous experience of one miracle of this kind, *could not* on a second similar occasion have been perplexed how the wants of the multitude should be supplied; that we have therefore here an illustration of the general inaccuracy which prevails in the records of our Lord's life, of a loose tradition, which has told the same event twice over.

Moreover their perplexity is capable of another explanation. The disciples might have doubted whether He would choose a second time to put forth his creative might; — whether there was in these present multitudes that spiritual hunger, which was worthy of being met and rewarded by such an interposition of divine power. But such earnest seekers, for the time at least, they were; and as others had faith to be healed, so these had faith to be fed; and the same bounteous hand which fed the five thousand before, fed the four thousand now.

---

[1] Calvin: "But because a like languor is daily creeping over us, therefore we should be the more watchful never to let our minds be distracted from the consideration of God's benefits, that the experience of the past may teach us to expect for the future the same favour which God has already once, or repeatedly, bestowed upon us."

CHAPTER XXVI.

The Opening the Eyes of One Blind at Bethsaida

MARK viii. 22-26.

THIS miracle, peculiar to St. Mark, in many of its circumstances resembles another, which he has recorded a little while before (vii. 31-37). Its treatment therefore in some most important features has been anticipated. As the Lord took that other sufferer, of whom the same Evangelist alone keeps a record, "aside from the multitude" (vii. 33), even so *He took the blind man by the hand, and led him out of the town;*[1] and with the same moisture from his own mouth wrought his cure. The Lord, as was so often his custom, links his power to means already in use among men, clothing the supernatural in the forms of the natural. Thus did He, for example, when He bade his disciples to anoint the sick with oil, — one of the most esteemed helps for healing in the East (Mark vi. 13; cf. Jam. v. 14). Not the oil, but his word, should heal; yet without the oil the disciples might have found it too hard to believe in the power which they were exerting, — those who could only be healed through their faith, to believe in the power which should heal them.

The feature which most distinguishes this miracle is the progressive character of the cure. This is not itself without analogies in other cases; yet the steps of the progress are marked with greater emphasis here than in any other instance. For, first, after the Lord *Had spit on his eyes, and put his hands upon him, He asked him if he saw aught. And he looked up, and said, I see men, as trees, walking.* Certain moving forms he saw about him, but without the power of discerning their shape or magnitude. But the good Physician leaves not his work un-

---

[1] Bengel: "To the blind man on recovering sight, the aspect of heaven, and of the divine works in nature, was more joyous than that of man's works in the village."

finished: *After that he put his hands again upon his eyes,*[2] *and made him look up; and he was restored, and saw every man clearly.*

Chrysostom and others find the explanation of this gradual cure in the imperfection of this blind man's faith. Proof of this imperfection they see in the fact that this man was brought to Him by others, as one who himself scarcely expected a benefit. The gracious Lord, who would not reject, but who could as little cure so long as there was on his part this desperation of healing, vouchsafed to him a glimpse of the blessing, so to awaken in him a longing for its fulness, and, this longing once awakened, presently satisfied him with that fulness. This healing step by step is a testimony of the freeness of God's grace, which is linked to no single way of manifestation, but works in divers manners, sometimes accomplishing only little by little what at other times it brings about in a moment. And certainly no symbol more suitable could be found of the progressive steps by which He who is the Light of the world "makes sometimes the souls that come to Him partakers of the illumination of his grace. Not all at once do men see clearly: for a while there is much of their old blindness remaining, much for a season impairing the clearness of their vision. Yet in good time Christ completes the work which He has begun. "The author," He is also "the finisher of their faith."

And he sent him away to his house, saying, Neither go into the town, nor tell it to any in the town (cf. Matt. ix. 30; Mark i. 44; vii. 36). The first of these commands contains the second; for if he did not *go into the town,* it is certain he could not *tell it to any in the town.* Whether on this occasion the Lord was better obeyed than on very many similar (Matt. ix. 31; Mark i. 45; vii. 36) we are not told.

---

[2] Chemnitz (*Harm. Evang.* 84): "He lays on his hands to show that his flesh is the instrument through which and with which the Eternal Word himself accomplishes all his life-giving works."

CHAPTER XXVII.

The Healing of the Lunatic Child

MATT. xvii. 14-21; MARK ix. 14-29; LUKE ix. 37-42.

THE Scribes had taken advantage of the absence of our Lord on the Mount of Transfiguration, to win a temporary triumph over such of his disciples as He had left behind Him. These had undertaken to cast out an evil spirit of a peculiar malignity, and had proved unequal to the task; *they could not* — weakened as they were by the absence of their Lord; and with Him, the three in whom, as habitually the nearest to Him, we may suppose his power most mightily resided. The Scribes were pressing to the uttermost the temporary advantage which they had gained.[1] A great multitude were gathered round, spectators of the defeat of Christ's servants; and the strife was at the highest, when suddenly He about whom the strife was, appeared, returning from the holy Mount, his face and person yet glistening, as there is reason to believe, with traces of the glory which had clothed Him there. But very different was the impression which that glory made from the impression made by the countenance of Moses. When the multitude saw the lawgiver of the elder Covenant, as he came down from *his* mountain, the skin of his face shining, "they were afraid to come nigh him" (Exod. xxxiv. 30); for that glory upon his face was a *threatening* glory, the awful and intolerable brightness of the law. But the glory of God shining in the face of Christ Jesus, though awful too, is an *attractive* glory, full of grace and beauty; it draws men to Him, does not drive them from Him; and thus, indeed, *all the people, when they beheld Him, were greatly amazed,* such

---

[1] Calvin: "The Scribes triumph in victory, and not only mock at the disciples, but wax bold against Christ, as if in the person of the disciples his power had been made nought."

gleams of brightness arrayed Him still; yet did they not therefore flee from Him; but rather, as being the more allured by that brightness, *running to Him, saluted Him* (cf. 2 Cor. iii. 18).

Yet the sights and sounds which greeted Him on his return to our sinful world, how different were they from those which He had just quitted upon the holy Mount! There the highest harmonies of heaven; here some of the wildest and harshest discords of earth. There He had been receiving from the Father honour and glory (2 Pet. i. 17); here those to whom his work had been intrusted in his absence, had been procuring for Him shame, defeat, and dishonour. But as when some great captain, suddenly arriving upon a battle-field, causes the tide of victory to turn, and everything to right itself again, so was it now. The Lord arrests the advancing and victorious foe with the words, *What question ye with them?* taking the baffled and hard-pressed disciples under his own protection. The Scribes, so forward to dispute with the servants, do not so readily accept the challenge of the Master. The disciples are as little forward to proclaim their own defeat; and thus *one of the multitude,* the father of the afflicted child on whom the ineffectual attempt at healing had been made, is the first to speak; *kneeling down to him, and saying, Lord, have mercy on my son;* and with this declaring the miserable case of his child, his only one, as St. Luke informs us (cf. vii. 12), and the little help he had obtained from the disciples.

All the symptoms exactly agree with those of epilepsy; — not that we have here *only* an epileptic; but this was the ground on which the deeper spiritual evils of this child were super-induced. The fits were sudden and lasted remarkably long; the evil spirit *hardly departeth from him;* — a *dumb spirit,* St. Mark calls it, a statement which does not contradict that of St. Luke, *he suddenly crieth out;* this dumbness was only in respect of articulate sounds. Nor was it a natural defect, as where the string of the tongue has remained unloosed (Mark vii. 32), or the needful organs for speech are wanting, but the consequence of this possession. When the spirit took him in its might, it tare him, till he foamed and gnashed with his teeth: and altogether he pined away like one the very springs of whose life were dried up. And while these accesses of his disorder might come upon him at any moment and in any place, they exposed him to the worst accidents: *ofttimes he falleth into the fire, and oft into the water.* In St. Mark the father attributes these fits to the direct agency of the evil spirit: *ofttimes it hath cast him into the fire, and into the waters, to destroy him;* yet such calamities might equally be looked at as the natural consequences of his unhappy condition.

The father concludes his sad tale with a somewhat reproachful reference to the futile efforts of the disciples to aid him: *I spake to thy disciples that they should cast him out, and they could not.* We have two explanations of our Lords words of sorrowful indignation which follow, *O faithless and perverse generation, how long shall I be with you? how long shall I suffer you?* For some, as for Origen, this *faithless generation* is the disciples, and they only; and this an utterance of holy impatience at the weakness of their faith; and the after discourse (Matt. xvii. 20) favours such an application. But Chrysostom, and generally the early interpreters, pointedly apply it to the surrounding multitude alone. It will be best, I think, to understand the words as not exclusively aimed at the disciples, nor chiefly; but addressed primarily to the multitude and the father. They, however, with all others that are present, are included in the rebuke; their unfaithfulness and unbelief had for the time brought them back to a level with their nation, and they must share with it all in a common condemnation. *How long shall I be with you?* are words not so much of one longing to put off the coil of flesh,[2] as of a master, complaining of the slowness and dulness of his scholars; "Have I abode with you all this time, and have you profited so little by my teaching?" Till their task is learned, He must tarry with them still.[3]

And now He exclaims, *Bring him hither to Me.* As the staff in Gehazi's hand could not arouse the dead child, but the prophet himself must arrive and undertake the work, so is it now (2 Kin. iv. 31). Yet the first bringing of the child to Jesus causes another of the fearful paroxysms of his disorder, so that *when he saw Him, straightway the spirit tare him, and he fell on the ground, and wallowed foaming.* The kingdom of Satan is ever stirred into a fiercer activity by the coming near of the kingdom of Christ. But as the Lord on another occasion (Mark v. 9) began a conversation with the sufferer, seeking thus to bring back something of calmness to his soul, so does He now with the representative of the sufferer, being precluded by the child's actual condition from doing this with himself: *How long is it ago since this came unto him?* The father answers, *Of a child,* and, for the stirring of more pity, describes again the miserable perils in which these fits involved his child; at the same time ill content that anything should come before the healing, if a healing were possible, having, also, present to his mind the recent discomfiture of the disciples, he adds, *If Thou canst do anything, have compassion on us, and help us* — "Thou," that is, "more than these, whose failure is so conspicuous." In that *"us"* we see how entirely his own life is knit up with his child's. At the same time he reveals by that *if,* that he has come with no unquestioning faith in the power of

---

[2] Jerome (*Comm. in Matt.* in loc.): "Not that He, the mild and gentle, was overcome with impatience . . . . but after the manner of a physician who should see his patient ordering his life contrary to his rules, saying: 'How long shall I visit you, how long shall I waste my diligent skill, I ordering one thing and you doing another?' "

[3] Bengel: "He was hastening to the Father, and yet knew that He could not make his departure until He had led his disciples unto faith. Their slowness was irksome."

Christ to aid, but is rendering the difficult cure more difficult still by his own doubts and unbelief.

Our Lord's answer is not without its difficulty; but its sense is plainly the following: "That *if* of thine is to be resolved by thee, and not by Me. The absence of faith on thy part, and not any overmastering power in this malignant spirit, is that which straitens Me; the question is, *if thou canst believe;*" this is the hinge upon which all must turn — and then with a pause, and not merely completing the sentence, as in our Version, *all things are possible to him that believeth.* Thus faith is here, as in every other case, set as the condition of healing; on other occasions it is the faith of the person; but here, that being impossible, the father's is accepted instead; even as the Syrophoenician mother's in the room of her daughter's (Matt. xv. 22). And thus too the Lord appears as helping the birth of faith in that travailing soul; even as at length, though with pain and sore travail, it comes to the birth, so that the father *cried out and said with tears, Lord, I believe;* and then, the little spark of faith which has been kindled in his soul revealing to him the abysmal depths of unbelief which are there, he adds this further: *help Thou mine unbelief.*

When now this prime condition of healing is no longer wanting, the Lord, meeting and rewarding even the weak beginnings of faith, accomplishes the cure; and the more promptly when *He saw that the people came running,* that an agitation and excitement was beginning which he desired at once to check. How majestic, in his address to the foul spirit, is that *I charge thee.* No longer those whom thou mayest hope to disobey, but I, having all power in heaven and on earth, *charge thee, come out of him* (cf. Luke iv. 35). Nor is this all: he shall *enter no more into him;* his return is barred; the cure shall be at once perfect and lasting. The wicked spirit must obey; but he does so most unwillingly; what he can no longer retain he would, if he might, destroy; as Fuller expresses it, "like an outgoing tenant, that cares not what michief he does." So fearful was this last paroxysm, that *he was as one dead; insomuch that many said, He is dead; but Jesus took him by the hand and lifted him up;* and life from that touch of the Lord of life flowing into him anew, *he arose.* Of the son of the widow of Nain we are expressly told that the Lord *delivered him to his mother* (Luke vii. 15). The same Evangelist records of this child whom Christ had thus healed, that He *delivered him again to his father,* crowning so the work of grace.

Then, — when He was come into the house, as we learn from St. Mark — *came the disciples to Jesus apart, and said, Why could not we cast him out?* Where, they would fain know, was the secret of their defeat, seeing that they were not exceeding their commission (Matt. x. 8), and had on former occasions found the devils subject to them (Luke x. 17)? *And Jesus said unto them, Because of your unbelief,* because of their lack of that to which, and to which only, all things are possible. They had made but a languid use of the means for stirring up and increasing faith; being certain to be foiled whenever they encountered an enemy of peculiar malignity. And such they encountered here; for the phrase *this kind* marks that there are orders of evil spirits, that as there is a hierarchy of heaven, so is there an inverted hierarchy of hell. The same is intimated in the mention of the unclean spirit going and taking "seven other spirits more wicked than himself" (Matt. xii. 45). *This kind,* He declares, *goeth not out but by prayer and fasting.* The faith which shall be effectual against this must be a faith exercised in prayer, that has not relaxed itself by an habitual compliance with the demands of the lower nature, but has often girt itself up to an austerer rule, to rigour and self-denial.

But as the secret of all weakness is in unbelief, so of all strength in faith: *For verily I say unto you, if ye have faith as*

*a grain of mustard-seed, ye shall say unto this mountain, Remove
hence to yonder place, and it shall remove; and nothing shall be
impossible unto you.* We have here a tacit contrast between a
grain of mustard-seed,[4] a very small thing (Matt. xiii. 31, 32),
and a mountain, a very great. That smallest shall be effectual to
work on this largest. The least spiritual power, which is really
such, shall be strong to overthrow in the end the mightiest powers which are merely of this world.

---

[4] Augustine (*Serm.* ccxlvi.) "A grain of mustard seems a little thing: nothing
is more contemptible to look at, nothing is stronger to taste. What then is this but
the highest ardour and inward strength of faith in the Church?"

CHAPTER XXVIII.

The Finding of the Stater in the Fish's Mouth

MATT. xvii. 24-27.

ST. MATTHEW alone among the Evangelists relates this gracious little incident. Before we close our study of it, it will be abundantly clear why, if one gospel only were to record it, then it fell most fitly to that of St. Matthew, which is eminently the Gospel of the kingdom, of the King and the King's Son. Slight as the incident may seem, it is one full of the profoundest teaching. We read then here: *And when they were come to Capernaum, they that received tribute money came to Peter, and said, Doth not your Master pay tribute?* I should much prefer to read the last words here, *Doth not your Master pay the half-shekel?* as indeed in the R. V. has been done. The reader may not at once understand what is meant, but he is put on the right track for understanding; *tribute* on the other hand, almost inevitably leads him astray, so that he identifies the question here with that which the Pharisee propounded to the Lord, whether it was lawful to pay tribute to Caesar or not (Matt. xxii. 17). But the evidence is overwhelming that we have nothing here to do with tribute to Caesar nor with any civil impost whatever; but rather and only with a theocratic payment, due to the temple and the temple's God. Questions altogether different in fact are here at issue and there.

The evidence that the payment demanded here is not tribute to Caesar, but dues to the temple, is such as may well convince every one before whom it is fairly brought. In the first place, this *half-shekel* which the collectors here demand was exactly the ransom of souls, the half-shekel (Exod. xxx. 11-16; xxxviii. 25-26) to be paid by every Israelite above twenty years old to the service and current expenses of the tabernacle, or, as it afterwards would be, of the temple. It does not, indeed, appear at first as an annual payment, but only as payable on the occasions, not frequently recurring, of the numbering of the people. But it became annual, whether this had been intended from the first, or out of a later custom. Thus there are distinct notices of this payment in the times of the Kings. Joash devotes to the reparation of the temple funds to be derived from three sources; the first of these being this half-shekel, "the money that every man is set at" (2 Kin. xii. 4); "the collection that Moses, the servant of God, laid upon Israel in the wilderness," as it is called in the parallel record in Chronicles (2 Chron. xxiv. 9). It was an annual payment in the time of Josephus.[1] Philo attests the conscientious and ungrudging accuracy with which it was paid by the Jews of the Dispersion. Vespasian diverted this temple rate into the imperial fisc, but only after city and temple had been destroyed. Of Vespasian Josephus writes: "He imposed a tribute on the Jews wheresoever they lived, requiring each to pay yearly two drachms to the Capitol, as before they were wont to pay them to the temple at Jerusalem." But of Pompeius he merely affirms, that "he made Jerusalem tributary to the Romans," with no mention of this tax at all. We have already had abundant evidence that long after his time it continued to be rendered to the temple. Titus refers to this fact, when, upbraiding the Jews with the unprovoked character of their revolt, he reminds the revolters that the Romans had permitted them to collect their own sacred imposts.

We note further that it is not publicans who demand this money, as the collectors would certainly have been called, had this been an ordinary tax. As little is the tone of the demand,

---

[1] *Antt.* xviii. 9. 1. It should be paid between the 15th and 25th of the month Adar (March), that is, about the feast of the passover. Yet no secure chronological conclusions in regard to our Lord's ministry can be won from this; as, through his absence from Capernaum, the money might have been for some time due. Indeed, the feast of tabernacles was probably now at hand.

Doth not your Master pay the half-shekel? that of a rude Roman tax-gatherer, who had detected a Jew in the act of evading the tax; but is exactly what we might expect, where the duty was one of imperfect obligation, which, if any declined, the payment could scarcely have been enforced.[2] Theophylact suggests that having seen or heard of the wonderful works which Christ did, they may have been uncertain in what light to regard Him. In this uncertainty they may have suffered Him to pass by them unchallenged; and it is only to his disciple, that they put their question directly.

Peter, zealous for his Master's honour, pledges Him without hesitation to the payment: *he saith, Yes.* Certainly Peter was over-hasty here. Not in this spirit had he exclaimed a little while before, "Thou art the Christ, the Son of the living God" (Matt. xvi. 16). For the time at least he had lost sight of his Lord's true position and prerogative, that it was *to Him in* his Father that offerings were to be made, not *from Him* to be received. He who should give Himself a ransom for all other souls could not properly pay a ransom for his own; and it seriously obscured the true relation between Him and all other men that He should even seem to admit the payment of it as an obligation lying upon Him. Willing therefore to bring back Peter, and in him the other disciples, to the true recognition of Himself, from which they had in part fallen, the Lord puts to him the question which follows. With the same intention, being thus engaged through Peter's hasty imprudence to the rendering of the half-shekel, He yet does it by a miracle which should testify that all things served Him, from the greatest to the least, — that he was Lord over nature, and, having nothing, yet, in his Father's care for him, was possessed of all things. Here, as so often in the life of our Lord, the depths of his humiliation are lighted up by a

---

[2] Kuinoel (in loc.), one of the right interpreters of this incident, observes this: "The Roman taxgatherers would undoubtedly have exacted the tribute payable to Caesar with greater harshness."

gleam of his glory; He pays, but in the manner of his payment reasserts the true dignity of his person, which might else have been compromised in the eyes of some. The miracle, then, meets a real need — outwardly a slight one, for the money could assuredly have been in some other and more ordinary way procured; but as an inner need, most real: in this, then, essentially differing from the apocryphal miracles, which are so often mere sports and freaks of power, with no ethical motive or purpose whatever.

We may trace the same purpose throughout. The Lord does not wait for Peter to inform Him what he had answered, and to what engaged Him; but *when he was come into the house, Jesus prevented him,* or *spake first to him* (so the R. V.), anticipating his communication, showing Himself a discerner of the thoughts of the heart, and, though not having been present, perfectly aware of all which had passed.[3] *What thinkest thou, Simon? Of whom do the kings of the earth* (with an emphasis on the last words, for there is a silent contrasting of these with the King of heaven, as at Ps. ii. 2), *take custom or tribute? of their own children or of strangers?* On what principle had he made that engagement? was not all the analogy of things earthly against it? These earthly things, it is true, cannot *prove* the heavenly, yet are they shadows of the true, and divinely appointed helps for the better understanding of them. When Peter confesses that such kings of the earth take tribute not of their own children, but *of strangers,* then at once He brings him to the conclusion whither He was leading him, namely that *the children,* or, as it would have been better rendered, *the sons,* were *free.*

We have here proof absolute that what was here demanded of the Lord was God's money, to be rendered to God, and not

---

[3] Jerome: "Without any prompting from Peter the Lord puts his question, that the disciples might not be scandalized at the demand for tribute, perceiving his knowledge of what was done in his absence."

Caesar's, to be rendered to Caesar; seeing that only on this assumption could He have claimed immunity for Himself, as He does in those words, *Then are the children free;* or *Surely, then, the sons are free.* With a payment owing to Caesar it would have been quite a different thing. Christ was no son of Caesar. The fact that the sons are free would have involved no exemption for Him. He might, indeed, have asserted his freedom on other grounds; though this He would not, since He had come submitting Himself during his earthly life to every ordinance of man.

The plural here, *the sons,* rather than a singular *the son,* has perplexed some. The explanation is easy. In making a general statement of the worldly relations from which He borrows his analogy, as there are many *kings of the earth,* or as one king might have many sons, He naturally throws his speech into a plural form; and it is just as natural, when we come to the heavenly order of things which is there shadowed forth, to re-strain it to the singular, to the only Son; seeing that to the King of heaven there is but One, the only-begotten of the Father. As little can there be drawn from it the conclusion, that the Lord intended to include in this liberty not Himself only, but all his people, all that in this secondary sense are "sons of God." This plainly is not true concerning dues owing to God; none are so bound to render them as his *sons.* Were the payment in question a civil one, it would be equally untrue. Not as the eldest among many brethren, but as the true and only Son of God, He challenges this liberty for Himself; and "we may observe, by the way, that the reasoning itself is a strong and convincing testimony to the proper Sonship, and in the capacity of Son to the proper relationship of Jesus Christ to the Father, which those who deny that relationship will not easily evade or impugn." It is true that for those determined not to be con-vinced, there is always a loophole of escape; in the present instance, the plural *sons* affords, for those who seek it, the desired opportunity of evasion.

Under this protest Christ will pay the money. *Notwithstanding, lest we should offend them, go thou to the sea, and cast an hook, and take up the fish that first cometh up;* the fish, that is, which shall first ascend from the deeper waters to his hook; *and when thou hast opened his mouth, thou shalt find a piece of money.* Christ will put no stumblingblock in the way of any. Were He now to refuse this payment, it might seem to those who knew not the transcendent secret of his birth that He was affecting a false liberty,[4] was come not to fulfill the law, but to destroy it. There was indeed no need, only a decorum, in the payment; as there was no necessity for his Baptism; nor yet for the Circumcision which He received in his flesh (Luke ii. 21); but He took on Himself the humiliations of the law, that He might in due time deliver from under the law.

And here is the explanation of the very significant fact that the Lord should make this payment not for Himself only, but also for Peter, the representative of all the faithful. He came under the same yoke with men, that they might enter into the same freedom with Him. *That take, and give unto them for me and thee.* Capernaum was the place of Peter's domicile (Matt. viii. 5, 14) as well as the Lord's; the place therefore where his half-shekel, no less than the Lord's, would be due. Christ says not "for *us*," but *for me and thee;* as elsewhere, "I ascend unto *my* Father and *your* Father, and to *my* God, and *your* God" (John xx. 17); for, even while He makes common part with his brethren, He yet does this by the condescension of grace, not by a necessity of nature; here was a delivered and a Deliverer, a ransomed and a Ransomer. Also is there here a protest of

---

[4] Chrysostom (*Hom.* lxiv. *in Joh.*) gives to these words, *Lest we should offend them,* another turn—lest, when this secret of our heavenly birth, and our consequent exemption from tribute, is told them, they should be unable to receive it; and we should thus have put a stumbling-block in their path, revealing to them mysteries which at this present they are unable to receive.

Christ's immunity from the present payment, first in own declaration, *Then are the children free;* and next in the notable device by which He meets the necessity which Peter has so heedlessly created for Him.

It is remarkable, and is a solitary instance of the kind, that the issue of this bidding is not told us. We are meant beyond doubt to understand that Peter went to the neighbouring lake, cast in his hook, and in the throat of the first fish that rose to it, found, according to his Lord's word, the coin that was needed. As little here as at Luke v. 4, 6 did the miraculous in the miracle consist in a mere foreknowledge on the Lord's part that this first fish should yield the stater which was needed: He did not merely foreknow; but by the mysterious potency of his will which ran through all nature, drew such a fish to that spot at that moment, and ordained that it should swallow the hook. We see here as at Jonah i. 17 that in the lower spheres of creaturely life there is unconscious obedience to Him; that these are without knowing it, for grace or for judgment, the active ministers of his will (1 Kin. xiii. 24; 2 Kin. xvii. 25; Job v. 22, 23; Jer. v. 6; Ezek. xiv. 15; Amos ix. 3).

All attempts to exhaust this miracle of its miraculous element, as that of the rationalist Paulus, who will have it that the Lord bade Peter go and catch as many fish as would sell for the required sum, and maintains that this actually lies in the words, — are hopelessly absurd. In an opposite extreme, they multiply miracles without a warrant who assume that the stater was *created* for the occasion; nay more, they step altogether out of the proper sphere of miracle. That divine power which dwelt in Christ never passed over on any one occasion into the region of absolute creation.

The allegorical interpretations, or rather uses, of this miracle, have not much to attract. It is superfluous to press further a miracle already so rich in teaching as this has approved itself to be.

CHAPTER XXIX.

The Raising of Lazarus

JOHN xi. 1-54.

IT is a remarkable statement which St. John makes at the close of the twentieth chapter of his Gospel: "And many other signs truly did Jesus in the presence of his disciples, which are not written in this book; but these are written that ye might believe that Jesus is the Christ, the Son of God" (ver. 30, 31; cf. xxi. 35). He has indeed shown a noteworthy restraint, even a parsimony, in the number of miracles which he has actually recorded. He has in no instance more than one miracle of the same kind; thus one healing of the lame (v. 9), one opening of blind eyes (ix. 7), one raising from the dead, namely this of Lazarus; and, as wrought by the Lord in the days of his flesh, only seven miracles in all — these seven again dividing themselves into two groups, of four and of three; four wrought in Galilee, and three in Judaea. When we call to mind the frequent grouping by seven both in his Gospel and in the Apocalypse, we can hardly account this number accidental. We have now reached the last of this seven; it is not for nothing that it is thus the last, occupying the place which it does just at the close of Christ's ministry on earth. He who was Himself so soon to taste of death will show Himself by this infallible proof the Lord of life and conqueror of death; who, redeeming the soul of another from the grave, would assuredly not lack the power to redeem his own from the same.

Now a certain man was sick, named Lazarus, of Bethany, the town of Mary and her sister Martha. This *Now,* — or *But,* which would be preferable, — connects what follows with what just has gone before, indicates how it came to pass that the

safer and more retired life of the Lord (see x. 39-42) was
brought to a close, and He once more drawn into the perilous
neighbourhood of that city, the head-quarters of his bitterest foes.
Lazarus appears now for the first time in the Evangelical history;
he is described, if we give full force to the two prepositions, as
from Bethany, of the town of Mary and Martha. The latter
clause is added to make plain, *which* Bethany was intended.
There were two villages of this name. In addition to the Bethany
which we know so well, there was another "beyond Jordan;" for
"Bethany" or "Bethania," not "Bethabara," is the proper reading of John i. 28.[1] Lazarus might be unknown even by name to
St. John's readers, but with Mary and Martha they were familiar.
It is true that St. John has not himself named them yet; but
here as everywhere (thus see iii. 24; vi. 70; xi. 2), he assumes
an acquaintance on the part of his readers with the preceding
Gospels, and in St. Luke's the two sisters, though not the
brother, appear (x. 38-42). When therefore he designates
Bethany as *the town of Mary and her sister Martha,* he at once
makes evident which Bethany he intends.

What the exact constitution of the household of Bethany
may have been, it is impossible to say, the Gospels being
singularly sparing in circumstantial notices concerning the persons
they introduce, only relating so much as is absolutely necessary
to make their part in the divine story intelligible. I pass on to
the miracle before us. *It was that Mary,* the Evangelist proceeds
to say, *which anointed the Lord with ointment, and wiped his
feet with her hair, whose brother Lazarus was sick.* He will
distinguish her by that notable deed of hers from all the other
Maries of the Evangelical history; even as with his commemora-
tion of the deed the fulfilment of Matt. xxvi. 13 begins. As he
has not thus far himself recorded that anointing, however he

---

[1] It was so read, Origen assures us, in nearly all copies of his day; and having
the authority of all the best MSS. and of most of the older Versions, has now obtained a place in our best critical editions.

may do so when the fit time shall arrive (xii. 2-8), here too
he assumes a familiarity on the part of his readers with those
two earlier Gospels in which that story is related at length
(Matt. xxvi. 6; Mark xiv. 3).

*Therefore his sisters sent unto him, saying, Lord, behold he
whom thou lovest is sick.* We know not how often the Lord had
honoured that house at Bethany with his presence. One memorable occasion, with its word of warning love, had occurred already (Luke x. 41, 42); and when later than this, during the
great Week, He lodged, as we are told, in Bethany (Matt. xxi.
17; Mark xi. 11, 19), returning thither for the night after the
day's task in the hostile city was over, and again repairing with
the early morning to Jerusalem, He can scarcely have graced
with his presence any other roof but this. Now therefore, when
there is sorrow there, the sisters turn in their need to Him, whom
they may have themselves already proved an effectual helper in
the day of trouble, who at any rate has shown Himself such in
the worst necessities of others. He is at a distance, beyond Jordan;
having withdrawn there thither from the malice of his adversaries (John x. 39, 40; cf. i. 28); but the place of his retirement
is known to the friendly household, and their messenger finds
his way to Him with the tidings of danger and distress. Very
beautiful is their confidence in Him; they speak no word urging
Him to come, and to come quickly; they only state their need.
This, they take for granted, will be sufficient; for He does not
love and forsake them whom He loves.[2] It is but a day's journey
from the one Bethany to the other; they may securely count that
help will not tarry long.

*When Jesus heard that, he said, This sickness is not unto
death, but for the glory of God, that the Son of God might be
glorified thereby.* This saying, addressed to the messenger for

---

[2] Augustine (*In Ev. Joh. tract.* xl.): "They did not say, Come. For to him
that loved him only the news need be given. . . . It is enough that Thou knowest:
for Thou dost not love and forsake."

him to carry back to them who sent him, is indeed spoken to them (see ver. 40, where Christ with his, *Said I not unto thee,* refers Martha to these very words). They are purposely enigmatical, and must have sorely tried the faith of the sisters. By the time that the messenger brought them back, Lazarus was already dead. Greatly therefore must this confident assurance of a happier issue have perplexed them. Had their heavenly Friend deceived them? or had He been Himself deceived? Why had He not excluded all room for mischance by Himself coming; or, if aught had hindered this, by speaking that word which, far off as near, was effectual to heal (Matt. viii. 13; John iv. 50). But, as with so many other of the divine promises, which seem to us for the moment to have utterly failed, and this because we so little dream of the resources of the divine love and the divine power, and are ever putting human limitations on these, so was it with this word, — a perplexing riddle, till the event made it plain. Even now, in the eyes of Him who saw the end from the beginning, that sickness was *not unto death;* and this they too should acknowledge, when, through the grave and gate of death their brother should enter on a higher life than any which hitherto he had known. For this we may confidently assume, that it *was* a higher life than any which he had before lived to which Lazarus was recalled. That sickness of his was *for the glory of God;* in which *glory* was included the perfecting of his own spiritual being, as no doubt it *was* perfected through this wondrous crisis of his life. But all this, which was so much for him, was also a signal moment in the gradual revelation of the glory of Christ to the Church and to the world. The Son of God was first glorified *in* Lazarus, and then *on* and *through* him to the world; compare the exact parallel, John ix. 2, 3.

What follows, *Now Jesus loved Martha, and her sister, and Lazarus,* is best connected not with *one,* but with *two* verses which follow. St. John would say: Jesus loved Martha and the others; *when he had heard therefore that he was sick, he abode two days still in the same place where he was; then after that, saith he to his disciples, Let us go into Judea again,* as one who could not endure to remain longer away from those so loved, and so urgently needing his presence. To conceive any other reason for his tarrying where He was during those two days, than that He might have scope for that great miracle, as, for example, that He had in hand some important work for the kingdom of God where He was, is extremely unnatural (see x. 41, 42). This tarrying was rather a part of the severe yet gracious discipline of divine love. The need must attain to the highest, before He interferes. It is often thus. He intervenes with mighty help, but not till every other help, not until, to the weak faith of man, even his own promise seems utterly to have failed.

This mention of Judaea brings out the danger more vividly than Bethany of itself would have done. The wondering and trembling disciples remonstrate: *Master, the Jews of late sought to stone thee* (see x. 31, 39), *and goest thou thither again?* The necessity of hiding from their malice had brought Him to those safer haunts beyond Jordan, and will He now affront that danger anew? In these remonstrances of theirs there spake out a true love to their Master; but mingled with this love apprehensions for their own safety, as is presently made plain by the words of Thomas (ver. 16), who takes it for granted that to return with Him is to die with Him. To keep this in mind, will help us to understand the answer of the Lord: *Are there not twelve hours in the day?* or, rather, *Are not the hours of the day twelve?* And then He proceeds: *If any man walk in the day, he stumbleth not, because he seeth the light of this world.* This saying of his we may paraphrase thus: "Is there not a time which but consists of twelve full hours, during any part of which a man may

walk and work without stumbling, being enlightened by the
natural sun in the heavens? Such a day there is now for Me, a
day during which I can safely accomplish the work given Me
by my Father, whose light I, in like manner, behold. So long
as the day appointed by my Father for my earthly walk, endures,
I am safe, and you are safe in my company." And then, leaving
all allusion to Himself, and contemplating his disciples alone,
He warns them that they never walk otherwise than as seeing
Him who is the Light of men, — that they undertake no task,
and affront no danger, unless looking to Him, who can alone
make their darkness to be light; *but if a man walk in the night,
he stumbleth, because there is no light in him.* In these last words
there is a forsaking of the figure, which would have required
something of this kind, "because there is no light *above* him;"
but in the spiritual world it is one and the same thing not to see
the light above us, and not to have it in us; they only having
it in them, who see it above them (cf. xii. 35; 1 John ii. 8-11).

*These things said he: and after that he saith unto them, Our
friend*[3] *Lazarus sleepeth; but I go, that I may awake him out
of sleep.* We must not suppose the Lord to have received newer
and later tidings from the house of sickness; but rather by the
inner power of his spirit He knows how it has fared with his
friend. In language how simple does He speak of the mighty
work which He is about to accomplish: Lazarus has fallen asleep,
and needs to be awakened. *Then said his disciples, Lord, if he
sleep, he shall do well;* for, as the Evangelist informs us, *they
thought that he had spoken of taking of rest in sleep.* This often
marks the favourable crisis in sickness; and they, eagerly seizing
upon any plea for not returning as into the jaws of destruction,
take for granted that it does so here. What need that their beloved Lord should expose Himself and them to uttermost peril,
when without his presence all was going well? The contempla-

---

[3] Bengel, on the words *Our friend:* "With what an entirely human feeling
Jesus communicates his friendship to his disciples."

tion of death as a sleep is so common, has been so taken up
into the symbolism, conscious or unconscious, of all nations,
that it was no difficulty in the image itself which occasioned the
misunderstanding upon their part; but, his words being capable
of a figurative or a literal sense, they erroneously accept them
in the latter. *Then said Jesus unto them plainly, Lazarus is dead;
and I am glad for your sakes that I was not there, to the intent
ye may believe.* He anticipates the thought which almost of
necessity must have risen up in their minds, namely, why He
had not been present to save. Through that absence of his there
should be a fuller revelation of the glory of God than could
have been from his earlier presence; a revelation that should
lead them, and in them all the Church, to loftier stages of faith,
to a deeper recognition of Himself, as the Lord of life and of
death. He is glad, for his disciples' sake, that it thus had befallen; for had He been upon the spot, He must have interfered
at an earlier moment.

Nevertheless let us go unto him. From the way in which
this summons is received, it is plain that for one disciple at
least the anticipation of death, as the certain consequence of
this perilous journey, is not removed. *Then said Thomas, which
is called Didymus, unto his fellow-disciples, Let us also go, that
we may die with him;* that is, with Christ; for to refer these
words, as some have done, to Lazarus, is idle. The words indicate not merely fellowship *in death,* but *in dying,* which was
manifestly impossible in the case of one already dead. On two
other occasions Thomas is introduced with the same interpretation of his name, the same reminder on the part of the
Evangelist to his Greek reader that Thomas in the Hebrew is
equivalent to Didymus, that is twin or double, in the Greek
(xx. 24; xxi. 2). Did St. John intend us to see any significance
in this name? Many, both in ancient times and in modern, have
thought he did. It is very possible that Thomas may have re-

ceived this as a new name from his Lord, even as Simon and
the sons of Zebedee received in like manner names from Him.
It was a name which told him all he had to fear, and all he had
to hope. In him the twins, unbelief and faith, were contending
with one another for mastery. It was for him to see that in and
through the regeneration he obtained strength to keep the
better, and to cast away the worse, half of his being. He here
utters words which belong to one of the great conflicts of his
life; and St. John very fitly bids us note that in this there was
the outcoming of all which his name embodied so well. For
indeed in this saying of his there is a very singular blending
of faith and unbelief — faith, since he counted it better to die
with his Lord than to live forsaking Him, — unbelief, since he
conceived it possible that so long as his Lord had a work to accomplish, He, or any under his shield, could be overtaken by a
peril which should require them to die together. Men of all
temperaments and all characters were to be found in that first
and nearest circle of disciples, that so there might be the representatives and helpers of all who hereafter, through struggles
of one kind or struggles of another, should attain at last to the
full assurance of faith. Very beautifully Chrysostom says of this
disciple, that he who now would hardly venture to go *with*
Jesus as far as to the neighbouring Bethany, afterwards *without*
Him, without, that is, his bodily presence, travelled to the ends
of the world, to the furthest India, affronting all the perils of
remote and hostile nations.

Lazarus probably died upon the same day that the messenger
announcing his illness had reached the Lord; otherwise it could
scarcely have been said that *when Jesus came, he found that he
had lain in the grave four days already.* The day of the messenger's arrival on this calculation would be one day; two other
our Lord abode in Peraea after He had received the message;
and one more, — for it was but the journey of a single day, —

He would employ in the journey to Bethany. Dying upon that day, Lazarus, according to the custom of the Jews that burial should immediately follow on death (Acts v. 6, 10), had been buried upon the same, as a comparison of this verse with ver. 39 clearly shows.

But before the arrival of Him, the true Comforter, other comforters, some formal, all weak, had arrived; drawn to this house of mourning by the providence of God, who would have many witnesses and heralds of this the most wondrous among the wondrous works of his Son. The nearness of Bethany to Jerusalem will have allowed these to be the more numerous; it is therefore noticed here: *Now Bethany was nigh unto Jerusalem, about fifteen furlongs off*, that is, about two miles; *and many of the Jews came to Martha and Mary, to comfort them concerning their brother*. It was part of the Jewish ceremonial of mourning, which was all most accurately defined,[4] that there should be a large gathering of friends and acquaintance, not less than ten, to condole with those that mourned for their dead (1 Sam. xxxi. 13; 1 Chron. vii. 22; Job ii. 11; Jer. xvi. 6, 7). Such condolence was sometimes, and on the part of some a reality; yet oftentimes a heartless form. But now *He* comes, who could indeed comfort the mourners and wipe away tears from their eyes. Yet He enters not the house; that was already occupied by *the Jews*, by those for the most part alien, even where they were not hostile, to Him. Not amid the disturbing influences of that uncongenial circle shall his first interview with the sorrowing sisters find place. Probably He tarried outside the town, and not very far from the spot where Lazarus was buried; for else, when Mary went to meet Him, the Jews could scarcely have exclaimed, *She goeth unto the grave to weep there* (ver. 31). From thence He may have suffered the tidings to go before Him that He was at hand.

---

[4] The days of mourning were thirty: of these the first three were days of *weeping* (fletus); then followed seven of *lamentation* (planctus); the remaining twenty of *mourning* (moeror).

Then Martha, as soon as she heard that Jesus was coming,
went and met him; but Mary sat still in the house. We are not,
in this hastening of the one and tarrying of the other, to trace,
as many have done, the different characteristics of the two sisters,
or to find an ethical parallel here to Luke x. 39. For on that
former occasion, when Mary chose to sit still, she did so because it was at *Jesus' feet* that she was sitting; this nearness to
Him, and not the sitting still, was then the attraction. The same
motives which kept her in stillness then, would now have
brought her on swiftest wings of love to the place where the
Master was. Moreover, so soon as ever she did hear that her
Lord was come and called for her, *she arose quickly, and came
unto him* (ver. 29). "It was not," to use Chrysostom's words,
"that Martha was now more zealous; but Mary had not heard."
This much charactersic of the two sisters may very probably lie
in the narrative, namely, that Martha, engaged in active employ-
ments even in the midst of her grief, may have been more in
the way of hearing what was happening abroad, while Mary, in
her deeper and stiller anguish, was sitting retired in the house,
and less within reach of such rumours from the outer world.
Martha too is ready to change words with "the Master;" while
the deeper anguish of Mary finds utterance in that one phrase:
Lord, if Thou hadst been here, my brother had not died; and
then she is silent. These words indeed are common to both;
for it is the bitterest drop in the cup of their common anguish,
that all might so easily have been otherwise. Had this sickness
befallen at another moment, when their Lord was within easier
reach, all might have been averted. At the same time to imagine that there is any the slightest reproach latent in the
words is quite to misconceive the spirit in which they are uttered.
In their way they are rather words of faith. But Martha has
much more to say. There are hopes, though she ventures only at a
distance to allude to them, which she is cherishing still: *But I
know that even now,* even now when all seems over, *whatsoever*

thou wilt ask of God, God will give it thee. High thoughts and poor thoughts of Christ cross one another here; — high thoughts, in that she sees in Him one whose effectual fervent prayers will greatly prevail; — poor thoughts, in that she regards Him as *obtaining* by prayer that which properly He *has* by the oneness of his nature with the Father.[5]

With words purposely ambiguous, being meant for the trying of her faith, Jesus assures her that the deep, though unuttered, longing of her heart shall indeed be granted; *Thy brother shall rise again.* But though her heart could take in the desire for so immense a boon, it cannot take in its actual granting (cf. Acts xii. 5, 15). She cannot believe that these words mean more than that he, with all other faithful Israelites, will stand in his lot at the last day; and with a slight movement of impatience at such cold comfort, she answers, *I know that he shall rise again in the resurrection at the last day.* Her love was as yet earthly, but needing to be infinitely exalted and purified. Unless the Lord had lifted her into a higher region of life, it would have profited her little that He had granted her heart's desire. This lower boon would only prove a boon at all, if both were alike made partakers of a higher life in Christ; then, indeed, death would have no more power over them, then they would truly possess one another, and for ever: and to this the wondrously deep and loving words of Christ would lead her. They are no unseasonable preaching of truths remote from her present needs, but the answer to the very deepest want of her soul; they would lead her from a lost brother to a present Saviour, a Saviour in whom alone that brother could be truly and for ever found. *Jesus said unto her, I am the Resurrection, and the Life;* the everlasting triumphs over death, they are *in Me* — no remote benefits, as thou speakest of now, to find place *at the last day;* no powers separate or separable from Me, as thou spakest of

---

[5] Grotius: "Here also her weakness is apparent. She deems that He has favour with God, but not that in him is the fulness of Divine power."

lately, when thou desiredst that I should ask of Another that which I possess evermore in Myself. In Me is victory over the grave, in Me is life eternal: by faith in Me that becomes yours which makes death not to be death, but only the transition to a better life.

Such is the general meaning and scope of these glorious words. When we ask ourselves what this title, *The Resurrection,* involves, we preceive that in one aspect it is something more, in another something less, than that other title of *The Life,* which Christ also challenges for his own. It is more, for it is life in conflict with and overcoming death; it is life being the death of death, meeting it in its highest manifestation, that of physical dissolution and decay, and vanquishing it there (Isai. xxv. 8; xxvi. 19; Dan. xii. 2). It is less, for so long as that title belongs to Him, it implies something still undone, a mortality not yet wholly swallowed up in life, a last enemy not yet wholly destroyed and put under his feet (1 Cor. xv. 25, 26). As He is *the Resurrection* of the dead, so is He *the Life* of the living — absolute life, having life in Himself, for so it has been given Him of the Father (John v. 26), the one fountain of life; so that all who receive not life from Him pass into the state of death, first the death of the spirit, and then, as the completion of their death, the death also of the body.

What follows, *He that believeth in me, though he were dead* — or better, *though he have died* — *yet shall he live; and whosoever liveth and believeth in me shall never die,* is not obscure in the sum total of its meaning; yet so to interpret it, as to prevent the two clauses of the sentence from containing a repetition, and to find progress in them, is not easy. If we compare this passage with John vi. 32-59, and observe the repeated stress which is there laid on the raising up at the last day, as the great quickening work of the Son of God (ver. 39, 40, 44, 54), we shall not hesitate to make the declaration, *yet shall he live,* in the first clause here, to be equivalent to the words, *I will raise him up at the last day,* there, and this whole first clause will then be the unfolding of the words, *I am the Resurrection;* as such He will rescue every one that believeth on Him from death and the grave. In like manner, the second clause answers to, and is the expansion of, the more general declaration, *I am the Life;* that is, "Whosoever liveth, every one that draweth the breath of life and believeth upon Me, shall know the power of an everlasting life, shall never truly die." Here, as so often in our Lord's words, the temporal death is taken no account of, but quite overlooked, and the believer in Him is contemplated as already lifted above death, and made partaker of everlasting life (John vi. 47; cf. Ephes. ii. 6; 1 John iii. 14).[6]

Having claimed all this for Himself, He demands of Martha whether she can receive it: *"Believest thou this,* — that I am this Lord of life and of death? Doth thy faith in the divine verities of the resurrection and eternal life after death centre in Me?" Her answer, *Yea, Lord, I believe that thou art the Christ, the Son of God, which should come into the world* (i. 9; vi. 14; ix. 35; Matt. xi. 3), is perhaps more direct than at first sight it appears. For one of the offices of Christ the Messiah was, according to the Jewish expectations, to raise the dead; and thus, confessing Him to be the Christ, she implicitly confessed Him also to be the quickener of the dead. Or she may mean, — "I believe all glorious things concerning Thee; there is nought which I do not believe concerning Thee, since I believe Thee to be Him in whom every glorious gift for the world is centered," — speaking like one whose faith, as that of most persons at all times must be, was implicit rather than explicit; she did not know all which that name, *the Christ, the Son of God,* involved, but all which it did involve she was ready to believe.

She says no more; for now she will make her sister partaker of the joyful tidings that He, the long waited for, long desired,

---

[6] Bengel. "The death of Christ deprived death of his power. After the death of Christ the death of believers is not death."

is arrived at last. Some good thing too, it may be, she expects from his high and mysterious words, though she knows not precisely what: a ray of comfort has found its way into her heart, and she would fain make her sister a sharer in this. Yet she told not her tidings openly, suspecting, and having sufficient cause to suspect (ver. 46), that some of their visitors from Jerusalem might be of unfriendly disposition towards the Lord. *She called Mary her sister secretly, saying, The Master is come, and calleth for thee.* The Master, as already suggested, was a name, probably *the* name, whereby the Lord was known in the innermost circle of his own (Matt. xxiii. 8; John xx. 16; xiii. 13). That He had asked for Mary, we had not hitherto learned. *As soon as she heard that, she arose quickly, and came unto him.* The Jews take it for granted that she is hastening in a paroxysm of her grief to the grave, to weep there; as it was the custom of Jewish women often to visit the graves of their kindred, and this especially during the first days of their mourning; — and they follow; for thus was it provided of God that this miracle should have many witnesses. *Then when Mary was come where Jesus was, and saw him, she fell down at his feet.* Nothing of the kind is recorded of Martha (ver. 20), whether this be the accident of a fuller narrative in one place than in the other; or, as is more probable, that we have here a characteristic touch differencing one sister from the other. But even if their demeanour is different, their first words are the same: *Lord, if thou hadst been here, my brother had not died.* The words with which her sister had greeted the Lord thus repeating themselves a second time from her lips, gives us a glimpse of all that had passed in that mournful house, since the beloved was laid in earth. Often during that four days' interval the sisters had said one to the other, how different the issues might have been, if the divine friend had been with them. Such had been the one thought in the hearts, the one word upon the lips, of both, and therefore was so naturally the first spoken by each, and that altogether independently of the other. She says no more. What the Lord can do, or will do, she remits altogether to Him, not so much as suggesting on her own part aught.

At the spectacle of all this grief, the sisters weeping, and even the more indifferent visitors from Jerusalem weeping likewise, the Lord also *groaned in the spirit, and was troubled.* The word which we translate *groaned* is far more expressive of indignation and displeasure than of grief; which last, save as a certain amount of it is contained in all displeasure, it means not at all. But at what and with whom was Jesus thus indignant?

It was the indignation which the Lord of life felt at all that sin had wrought. He beheld death in all its dread significance, as the wages of sin; the woes of a whole world, of which this was but a little sample, rose up before his eyes. For that He was about to wipe away the tears of those present, did not truly alter the case. Lazarus rose again, but only to taste a second time the bitterness of death; these tears He might stanch, only again hereafter to flow; and how many had flowed and must flow with no such Comforter to wipe them, even for a season, away. As He contemplated all this, a mighty indignation at the author of all this human anguish possessed his heart. And now He will no longer delay, but will at once do battle with death and with him that hath the power of death, the devil; and spoiling, though but in part, the goods of the strong man armed, will give proof that a Stronger is here. And that they may the sooner stand face to face, He demands, *Where have ye laid him? They said unto him, Lord, come and see. Jesus wept,* or, more accurately *shed tears,* Himself borne along with the high tide of sorrow, and not seeking to resist it. There are yet before Him two other occasions of tears (Luke xix. 41; Heb. v. 7). "The tears of the text," says Donne, "are as a spring, a well, belonging to one household, the sisters of Lazarus. The tears over Jerusalem are as a river, belonging to a whole country.

The tears upon the Cross are as the sea, belonging to the whole world."

Some of the Jews present, moved to good-will by this lively sympathy of the Lord with the sorrows of those around Him, exclaimed, *Behold how he loved him!* Not, however, all: *Some of them said, Could not this man, which opened the eyes of the blind, have caused that even this man should not have died?* It is an invidious suggestion. He weeps over this calamity now, but was it not in his power to avert it, if He had chosen? He who could open the eyes of the blind (they refer to the case which, through the judicial investigation that followed, had made so much noise at Jerusalem, John ix.), could He not (by his prayer to God) have hindered that this man should have died? There were indeed in this accusation, as so often in similar cases, assumptions mutually excluding one another; the assumption that He possessed such power and favour with God as would have enabled Him to stay the stroke of death, resting on the assumption of so eminent a goodness upon his part, as would have secured that his power should not be grudgingly restrained in any case suitable for its exercise. It is characteristic of the truth of this narrative, that they, dwellers in Jerusalem, should refer to this miracle which had so lately been performed there, rather than to the previous raisings from the dead, which in themselves were so much more to the point, as evidence of that dominion over death which He might have exerted had He willed. But those, accomplished at an earlier period of his ministry and in the remoter Galilee, they may have only heard of by obscure report, if indeed they had heard of them at all. This miracle on the contrary, so recently wrought, and at their very doors, which had roused so much contradiction, which it had been so vainly attempted to prove an imposture, was exactly the mighty work of the Lord that would be uppermost in their thoughts.

He meanwhile and they have reached the tomb, though not without another access of indignant horror — so dreadful did death seem to Him who, looking *through* all its natural causes, at which we often stop short, saw it altogether as the seal and token of sin: *Jesus therefore again groaning in himself cometh to the grave.* This, as the whole course of the narrative shows, was without the town (ver. 30), according to the universal custom of the East (Luke vii. 12), which did not suffer a depositing of the dead among the living. *It was a cave, and a stone lay upon it.* Such were commonly the family vaults of the Jews; sometimes natural (Gen. xxiii. 9; Judith xvi. 24), sometimes, as was this, artificial and hollowed out by man's labour from the rock (Isai. xxii. 16; Matt. xxvii. 60); in a garden (John xix. 41), or in some field the possession of the family (Gen. xxiii. 9, 17-20; xxxv. 18; 2 Kin. xxi. 26); with recesses in the sides wherein the bodies were laid (Isai. xiv. 15; Ezek. xxxii. 23); occasionally with chambers one beyond another. Sometimes the entrance to these tombs was on a level; sometimes, as most probably here, there was a descent to them by steps. The stone which blocked up the entrance, only with difficulty removed (Mark xvi. 3), kept aloof the beasts of prey, above all the numerous jackals, which else might have found their way into these receptacles of the dead, and torn the bodies. The tomb of our blessed Lord Himself, with its "door," appears rather to have had a horizontal entrance.[1]

Among many slighter indications that Mary and Martha were not among the poor of their people, this, that they should possess such a family vault, is one. The dead bodies of others would be brought "into the graves of the common people" (Jer. xxvi. 23). We have another indication of the same in the large concourse of mourners, and those certainly not of the meaner sort, who assemble from Jerusalem to console the sisters' in their bereavement. The pound of ointment of spikenard,

---

[1] See Winer, *Realwörterbuch*, s. v. Graber; and *Dict. of the Bible*, art. Burial.

"very costly," with which Mary anoints the Saviour's feet (John xii. 3), points the same way. She who was "troubled about many things" (Luke x. 41) was probably the mistress of a numerous household about which to be troubled.

Jesus said, Take ye away the stone. Martha, the sister of him that was dead, saith unto him, Lord, by this time he stinketh; for he hath been dead four days. Why does St. John designate Martha as *the sister of him that was dead,* when this was abundantly plain before? Probably to account for her remonstrance. The sister of the dead, she would be more shocked than another at the thought of the exposure of that countenance, upon which corruption had already set its seal. With the rapid decomposition that goes forward in a hot country, necessitating as it does an almost immediate burial, the *four days* might very well have brought this about; indeed, under actual conditions, could hardly have failed so to do. At the same time, it gives to this miracle almost a monstrous character, if we suppose it was actually the reanimating of a body which had already undergone the process of corruption. Rather He who sees the end from the beginning, and who had intended that Lazarus should live again, had watched over that body in his providence, that it should not hasten to corruption. No conclusion of an opposite kind can be drawn from Martha's words, spoken, as they plainly are, *before* the stone has been removed.

This much, however, her words do reveal — that her faith in Christ, as able even then to quicken her dead brother, had already failed. There is nothing strange in this. Faith, such as hers, would inevitably have these alternating ebbs and flows; from which, indeed, a much stronger faith would scarcely be exempt. All she concludes from this command to remove the stone is a desire on the Lord's part to look once more on the countenance of his friend; from this purpose she would fain recall Him, by urging how death and corruption must have been busy in that tomb. The Lord checks and rebukes her un-belief: *Said I not unto thee, that, if thou wouldest believe, thou shouldest see the glory of God?* Here, as ever, faith is set forth as the condition under which alone his miraculous power can be exerted. But when had He said this? These very words occur in the message which the Lord sends back to the sorrowing sisters when He first learns the sickness of his friend (ver. 4), the message itself furnishing the key to the whole subsequent nar-rative. To those words, so spoken, He refers.

And now Martha acquiesces: no longer opposes the hindrance of her unbelief to the work which the Lord would accomplish. *Then,* those nearest of kin thus consenting, *they took away the stone from the place where the dead was laid. And Jesus lifted up his eyes, and said, Father, I thank Thee that thou hast heard me.* The thanks *to* the Father are an acknowledgment that the power which He is about to display is *from* the Father (John v. 19, 20). But any such thanksgiving might easily have been misinterpreted by the disciples then, and by the Church after-wards; as though it would have been possible for the Father *not* to have heard Him; whereas the power was most truly his own, not indeed in disconnexion from the Father; but in his oneness with the Father, lay for Him the power of doing these mighty acts.[8] Therefore He explains, evidently not any more in a voice audible by all those present, but so that his disciples might hear Him, what this *Father, I thank thee,* meant, and why it was spoken: *And I knew that thou hearest me always: but because of the people which stand by I said it, that they may believe that thou hast sent me* (cf. 1 Kin. xviii. 36, 37). For them it was wholesome: they should thus understand that He claimed his power from above, and not from beneath; that there was no magic, no necromancy here.

---

[8] Chrysostom (*Hom.* lxiv. *in Joh.*) enters at large upon this point. Maldonatus observes: "Nothing else is signified by these words than unity of essence and of will." Cf. Ambrose, *De Fide,* iii. 4.

The Son renders by anticipation thanks to the Father, so confident is He that He too wields the keys of death and of the grave, that He too can quicken whom He will (John v. 21). *And when he had thus spoken, he cried with a loud voice, Lazarus, come forth* (cf. Mark v. 41; Luke vii. 14; viii. 54; Acts ix. 40). To this *cry with a loud voice*, calling the things which are not as though they were (Ezek. xxxvii. 4), and heard through all the chambers of death, the quickening power is everywhere in Scripture ascribed. Thus at John v. 28, 29: "The hour is coming, in the which all that are in the graves *shall hear his voice,* and shall come forth;" and again at 1 Thess. iv. 16, it is at the descent of the Lord "with a shout, with the voice of the Archangel," — which voice is his own, for Scripture knows of no other Archangel, — that the dead in Him will rise.

And he that was dead came forth,[9] *bound hand and foot with grave-clothes, and his face was bound about with a napkin.* Some, in their zeal for multiplying miracles, make it a new miracle, a wonder within a wonder, as St. Basil calls it, that Lazarus so bound was able to obey the summons. But in that case to what end the further word, *Loose him, and let him go?* Probably he was loosely involved in these grave-clothes, which hindering free action, yet did not hinder motion altogether; or possibly, in accordance with the Egyptian fashion, every limb was wrapped round with these stripes by itself, just as in the mummies each separate finger has sometimes its own wrapping.

St. John leaves us to imagine their joy, who thus beyond all expectation received back their dead from the grave.

Not attempting to picture this, he proceeds to trace the historic significance of the miracle, the permitted link which it formed in that chain of events, which should issue, according to the determinate decree and counsel of God, in the atoning death of the Son of God upon the cross. *Then many of the*

[9] Hilary (*De Trin.* vi. § 33): "Without any interval between the call and the life."

Jews which came to Mary, and had seen the things which Jesus did, believed on him; but some of them went their ways to the Pharisees, and told them what things Jesus had done. St. John does here what he does evermore, divides the light from the darkness, the belief from the unbelief, and marks the progressive growth of the one and of the other. Those who went and told the Pharisees were spectators of the miracle who on one plea or another refused to be convinced by it (Luke xvi. 31), and who, reporting to the professed enemies of the Lord this latest and most imposing work of his, would irritate them yet more against Him; St. John, it will be observed, links immediately with this report to the Pharisees a new and increased activity in their hostile machinations against the Lord.

They are indeed now seriously alarmed. They anticipate, and correctly (see xii. 10, 11, 17-19), the effect which this mighty work will have upon the people, and they gather in council together against the Lord and against his Anointed. They do not pause to inquire whether *this man,* as they contemptuously call Him, — who, even according to their own confession, *doeth many miracles* (cf. Acts iv. 16), may not be doing them in the power of God, may not be indeed the promised King of Israel. The question of the truth or falsehood of his claims seems never to enter into their minds, but only the bearing which the acknowledgment of these claims will have on the worldly fortunes of their order. This bearing they contemplate from a somewhat novel point of view: *If we let him thus alone, all men will believe on him; and the Romans shall come and take away both our place and nation.* The direct connexion which they traced between the recognition of Jesus as the Christ, and a collision with the Roman power, was probably this. The people will acknowledge Him for the Messiah; He will set Himself at their head, or they by compulsion will set Him there (John vi. 15); hereupon will follow an attempt to throw off the foreign yoke, an attempt to be crushed presently by the overwhelming power of Rome; which will then use the opportunity it has been waiting for long, and will make a general sweep, taking away from us wholly whatsoever survives of our power and independence, *our place and nation*. Or, without anticipating an actual insurrection, they may have assumed that the mere fact of the Jews acknowledging a Messiah or, in other words, a king of their own, would arouse the jealousy of Rome, would be accounted an act of rebellion, to be visited with these extreme penalties.[10] How sensitive that jealousy was, how easily alarmed, we have a thousand proofs. "Art Thou the King of the Jews?" (John xviii. 33; cf. Acts xvi. 21; xvii. 7, 8) is the point to which the Roman governor comes at once. The question will still remain, Did they who urged this danger, indeed feel the apprehension which they professed? or did they only pretend to fear these consequences from the ministry of Christ, if suffered to go on unhindered; urging this view on account of a party in the Sanhedrim (see John ix. 16), which could only be thus won over to the extreme measures now meditated against Him? The Greek expositors in general suppose that they did but feign this alarm; I must needs believe that herein they were sincere; however, besides this alarm, there may have been deeper and more malignant motives at work in their minds.

Probably many half-measures had been proposed by one member and another of the Sanhedrim for arresting the growing inclination of the people to recognize Jesus as the Christ, and had been debated backward and forward; such as forbidding them to hear Him; proclaiming anew, as had been done already, that any should be excommunicated who confessed Him to be Christ (John ix. 22). But these measures had been already tried, and had proved insufficient; and in that *Ye know nothing at all*

---

[10] Corn. a Lapide: "If all believe Jesus to be the Messias, the King of the Jews, the Romans, the masters of Judaea, will be irritated against us for setting up a new King and Messias, namely Jesus, and deserting Tiberius Caesar for him; therefore they will come in their arms, and will ravage and destroy Jerusalem and Judaea, with all the race and commonwealth of the Jews."

of Caiaphas, we have the voice of the bold bad man, silencing, with ill-suppressed contempt, his weak and vacillating colleagues, who could see the danger, while they yet shrank, though not for the truth's sake, from the one course which promised to remove it. He proceeds, *nor consider that it is expedient for us that one man should die for the people, and that the whole nation perish not.* Guilty or not guilty, this man, who threatens to imperil the whole nation, and, whether He means it or not, to entangle it in a hopeless conflict with the power of Rome, must be taken out of the way.

Caiaphas[11] was a Sadducee (Acts v. 17). Hengstenberg thinks we may trace in this utterance of his the rudeness and roughness which Josephus ascribes to these as compared with the Pharisees. St. John describes him as *being the High Priest that same year,* and repeats the same phrase ver. 51, and again xviii. 13; from which some have concluded, Strauss and Baur for example, that whoever wrote this Gospel accounted the High Priesthood a yearly office; and they have then deduced the further conclusion, that since it was impossible for St. John to have made this blunder, it was therefore impossible that he could be the author of this Gospel. They must be hardly set to find arguments against the authenticity of St. John's Gospel, who have recourse to this. If some historian were to write that Abraham Lincoln was President of the United States that same year in which the great civil war broke out, would any be justified in imputing to him the mistake that the Presidency was an annual office, or in concluding that the writer could not have been an American living at the time, and to whom the ordinary sources of information were open? And who has a right to ascribe to the words of St. John any further meaning than that Caiaphas was High Priest *then?* whether he had been so before, or should be after, was

---

[11] His proper name was Joseph. That other name by which he is better known he probably assumed with his assumption of the High Priesthood (Josephus, *Antt.* xviii. 2. 2; xviii. 4. 2). The High Priests were wont, on their election, to change their name, as the Popes do now.

nothing to his present purpose. It is significant to the Evangelist that he was this when he spake these words, obtaining as thus they did a weight and importance which else they would not have possessed. They were not the words of Caiaphas; they were the words of the High Priest: *This spake he not of himself; but being High Priest that year, he prophesied that Jesus should die for that nation.* This oracular, even prophetic, character which his utterance thus obtained requires some explanation. That a bad man should utter words which were so overruled by God as to become prophetic, would of itself be no difficulty. He who used a Balaam to declare that a Star should come out of Jacob and a Sceptre rise out of Israel (Num. xxiv. 17), might have used Caiaphas to fore-announce other truths of his kingdom. Nor is there any difficulty in such *unconscious* prophecies as this evidently is. How many prophecies of a like kind, — most of them, it is true, rather in act than in word, — meet us in the whole history of the crucifixion! What was the title over our blessed Lord, "Jesus of Nazareth, the King of the Jews," but another such scornful and contemptuous, yet most veritable, prophecy?

But the preplexing circumstance is the attribution to Caiaphas, because he was *High Priest*, of these prophetic words — for prophetic the Evangelist plainly pronounces them to be, and all attempts to rid his words of this intention, and to destroy the antithesis between *speaking of himself* and *prophesying,* are idle. There is no need, however, to suppose that he meant to affirm this to have been a power inherent in the High Priesthood; that the High Priest, as such, *must* prophesy; but only that God, the extorter of those unwilling, or even unconscious, prophecies from wicked men, ordained this further, that he in whom the whole theocracy culminated, who was "the Prince of the people" (Acts xxiii. 5), for such, till another High Priest had sanctified Himself, — and his moral character was nothing to the point,

— Caiaphas truly was, — should, because he bore this office, be the organ of this memorable prophecy concerning Christ and the meaning and end of his death.

What follows, *And not for that nation only, but that also he should gather together in one the children of God that were scattered abroad,*[12] is not a meaning involved in the words of Caiaphas, but is added by St. John, careful to disallow that limitation of the benefits of Christ's death, which otherwise they might seem to involve. Caiaphas indeed prophesied that Jesus should die for that nation, and (St. John himself adds) He indeed died not for that nation only, but also for the gathering in one of *all* the children of God scattered abroad through the whole world (cf. Isai. xlix. 6; lvi. 6-8). Elsewhere he has declared the same truth: "He is the propitiation for our sins; and not for ours only, but also for the sins of the whole world" (1 John ii. 2).

In pursuance of this advice of Caiaphas it came now to a solemn resolution on the part of the Sanhedrim, that Jesus should die. *Then from that day forth they took counsel together for to put him to death.* There had been purposes and schemes among "the Jews," that is, the Pharisees and their adherents, to put Him to death before (Matt. xii. 14; John v. 16, 18; vii. 1, 19, 25; viii. 37); but it was now the formal resolution of the chief Counsel of the nation (cf. Matt. xxi. 46). *Jesus, therefore, walked no more openly among the Jews* (cf. Deut. xxxii. 20), *but went thence unto a country near to the wilderness,* the wilderness, that is, which is mentioned Josh. viii. 15, 24; xvi. 1; xviii. 12; — *into a city called Ephraim, and there continued with his disciples,* — not indeed for long, for *the Jews' Passover was nigh at hand,* and He, the very Paschal Lamb of that Passover, must not be wanting at the feast.

---

[12] As Westcott says well: "The term *scattered abroad* marks a broken unity, and not only wide dispersion."

In the ancient Church there was ever found, besides the literal, an allegorical interpretation of this and the two other miracles of the like kind. As Christ raises those that are naturally dead, so also He quickens them that are spiritually dead. Here they found the whole process of the sinner's restoration from the death of sin to a perfect spiritual life shadowed forth. Nor was this all; for these three raisings from the dead were often contemplated in their connexion with one another, as setting forth one and the same truth under different and successive aspects. It was observed how we have the record of three persons that were restored to life, — one, the daughter of Jairus, being raised *from the bed;* another, the son of the widow, *from the bier;* and lastly, Lazarus *from the grave.* And in the same way Christ raises to newness of life sinners of all degrees; not only those who have just fallen away from truth and holiness, like the damsel who had just expired, and in whom, as with a taper newly extinguished, it was by comparison easy to kindle a vital flame anew; but He raises also them who, like the young man borne out to his burial, have been some little while dead in their trespasses. He quickens them also who, like Lazarus, have lain long festering in their sins, as in the corruption of the grave, who were not merely dead, but buried, — with the stone of evil customs and evil habits laid to the entrance of their tomb, and seeming to forbid all egress thence. Even this stone He rolls away, and bids them to come forth, loosing the bands of their sins so that presently they are sitting down with the Lord at that table, there where there is not the foul odour of the grave, but where the whole house is full of the sweet fragrance of the ointment of Christ (John xii. 1-3).

CHAPTER XXX.

The Opening of the Eyes of Two Blind Men near Jericho

MATT. xx. 29-34; MARK x. 46-52; LUKE xviii. 35-43.

THE adjusting of the several records of this miracle has put
the ingenuity of harmonists to the stretch. St. Matthew com-
mences his report of it as follows: *And as they departed from
Jericho, a great multitude followed him. And behold, two blind
men, sitting by the wayside, when they heard that Jesus passed
by, cried out, saying, Have mercy on us, O Lord, thou Son of
David.* Thus, according to him, there are two blind; and the
miracle is wrought as the Lord is departing from Jericho. St.
Luke mentions but *one;* and Christ effects his cure not as He
is quitting, but at his *coming* nigh to, the city. St. Mark with
St. Luke names one only who was healed; with St. Matthew he
places the miracle at the going out from, Jericho; so that the
three narratives in a way as curious as it is perplexing cross and
interlace one another. To escape all the difficulties thus presented to us, there is the convenient suggestion always at hand,
that the sacred historians are recording different events. But in
fact we do not thus escape embarrassments; we only exchange one
for another. Accepting this solution, we must believe that in the
immediate neighbourhood of Jericho, our Lord was thrice besought in almost the same words by blind beggars on the wayside
for mercy; — that on all three occasions there was a multitude
accompanying Him, who sought to silence the voices of the
claimants, but only caused them to cry the more earnestly, etc.

The three apparently discordant accounts can at once be reduced to two; the silence of one narrator is in itself no contradiction of the affirmation of another; thus the second and the
third Evangelist, making mention of *one* blind man, do not

contradict St. Matthew, who mentions *two*. There remains only
the circumstance that by one Evangelist the healing is placed at
the Lord's entering into the city, by the others at his going out.
Bengel's suggestion may perhaps be the right one, namely that
one cried to the Lord as He drew near to the city, whom yet
He cured not then, but on the morrow at his going out of the
city cured him together with the other, to whom in the mean
while he had joined himself. St. Matthew will then relate the
whole of the event there where he first introduces it, rather than,
by cutting it in two halves, and deferring his report of the conclusion, preserve a more painful accuracy, yet lose the effect
which the complete history related at a breath would possess.

I follow here the same course which I followed in treating
of the demoniacs in the country of the Gadarenes. I there dealt
with a single case, and will now do the same. The record of this
miracle which St. Mark has preserved for us will best serve our
turn. We read then in the second Gospel, *As he went out of
Jericho with his disciples and a great number of people, blind
Bartimaeus, the son of Timaeus, sat by the highway side, begging.*
We note here St. Mark's acquaintance with the name of the blind
man and the name of his father. In all likelihood Bartimaeus
having been drawn by this gracious dealing of the Lord into
the circle of his disciples, was sufficiently well known in the
Church to make it a matter of interest that he and no other was
the object of his healing power.

*And when he heard that it was Jesus of Nazareth, he began
to cry out, and say, Jesus, thou Son of David, have mercy on me.*
In the cry with which Bartimaeus sought to attract the Lord's
pity and help there lay a recognition of his dignity as the Messiah;
for this name, *Son of David,* was the popular designation of
the great expected Prophet (Matt. ix. 27; cf. Luke i. 32; Ezek.
xxxiv. 23, 24). There was wrapt up in it a double confession
of faith, to his power, and to his Person; that He could heal;

and this, as *the* Prophet at whose coming the eyes of the blind
should be opened, and the ears of the deaf unstopped (Isai.
xxix. 18; xxxv. 5). Here the explanation has been sometimes
found of what follows: *And many charged him that he should
hold his peace;* grudging, as has been suggested, to hear given
to Jesus titles of honour, which they were not themselves prepared to accord Him.[1] I cannot look at it in this way. It was
quite in the spirit of the envious malignant Pharisees to be vexed
with those Messianic salutations: but these well-meaning multitudes, rude and in the main spiritually undeveloped as no doubt
they were, were yet exempt from such spiritual malignities. They
for the most part sympathize with the Lord and his work (Matt.
ix. 8). While others said that his miracles were wrought in the
power of Beelzebub, they glorified God because of them. Nor
can I doubt that here too out of an intention of honouring Christ
they sought to silence this suppliant.

But the cry of need is not to be stifled so. On the contrary,
*he cried the more a great deal, thou Son of David, have mercy
on me.* Is there not here the story of innumerable souls? When
a man begins to be in earnest about his salvation, to cry that his
eyes may be opened, begins to despise the world and all those
objects which other men most desire, he will find a vast amount
of opposition, and that not from professed enemies of the Gospel
of Christ, but from such as seem, like this multitude, to be with
Jesus and on his side. Even they will endeavour to hinder any
earnest crying to the Lord. Augustine makes further application
of what follows. Arrested as ever by the cry of need, *Jesus stood
still, and commanded him to be called;* whereupon, as we read,
*they call the blind man, saying unto him, Be of good comfort,
rise; he calleth thee.* This too, he observes, repeats itself continually in the life of God's saints. If a man will only despise and

---

[1] Hilary: "Lastly the crowd rebukes them, because it was bitter to it to hear
from the blind men the assertion which it denied, that the Lord was the Son of
David."

overbear these obstacles from a world which calls itself Christian; if, despite all opposers, he will go on, until Christ is evidently and plainly with him, then those same who at the first checked and reprehended, will in the end applaud and admire; they who at first exclaimed, "He is mad," will end with exclaiming, "He is a saint."

And he, casting away his garment, ridding himself, that is, of every incumbrance *rose and came to Jesus.* In this his ridding himself of all that would have hindered, he has been often held forth as an example for every soul which Jesus has called, that it should in like manner lay aside every weight and every besetting sin (Matt. xiii. 44, 46; Phil. iii. 7). The Lord's question, *What wilt thou that I shall do unto thee?* is, in part, an expression of his readiness to aid, a comment in act upon his own words, spoken but a little while before, "The Son of man came not to be ministered unto, but to minister" (Matt. xx. 28); it is in part intended to evoke into livelier exercise the faith of the petitioner (Matt. ix. 28). The man, whose cry has been hitherto a vague indeterminate cry for mercy, now singles out the blessing which he craves,[2] *Lord, that I may receive my sight.* Only St. Matthew mentions that He *touched* the eyes which should be restored to vision (cf. ix. 29), and only St. Luke the word of power, *Receive thy sight,* by which the restoration was effected; while he and St. Mark record nearly similar words, passed over by St. Matthew: *Thy faith hath made thee whole — Thy faith hath saved thee* (cf. Matt. ix. 22; Mark ix. 23; Luke xvii. 19). The man who had hitherto been tied as to one place, now uses aright his new found faculty of free motion, for he uses it to follow Jesus in the way, at the same time with free outbreaks

---

[2] Gregory the Great (*Hom.* ii. *in Evang.*), commenting on this request of theirs, bids us, in like manner, to *concentrate* our petitions on the chief thing of all: "Not false riches, not earthly gifts, not fleeting honours, should we ask from the Lord, but *light*: and this not the light which is shut in by space, bounded by time, diversified by the interruption of night, and perceived by us in common with the brutes; but the light which we can see in common with only the angels, which no beginning inaugurates and no end limits."

of a thankful heart, himself *glorifying God* (cf. Luke xiii. 13, 17; xvii. 15), and being the occasion no less that *all the people, when they saw it, gave praise unto God* as well (Matt. ix. 8; Luke xiii. 17; Acts iii. 8-10).

CHAPTER XXXI.

The Cursing of the Barren Fig-Tree

MATT. xxi. 18-22; MARK xi. 12-14, 20-24.

THIS miracle was wrought upon the Monday in Passion week,
On the Sunday of Palms Christ had made his triumphal entry
into Jerusalem, and in the evening He retired to Bethany. On
the Monday morning, as He was returning to his ministry in the
city very early, the word against the fig-tree was spoken. That
same evening He with his disciples went back to Bethany to
lodge there, but probably at so late an hour that the darkness
prevented these from marking the effects which had followed
upon that word. It was not till the morning of Tuesday that
they saw the fig-tree dried up from the roots. Such is the exact
order of events, in the telling of which St. Mark shows himself
a more accurate observer of times and of the actual sequence
of events than the first Evangelist.

But while such differences as their several narratives offer are
easily set at one, and they who magnify them into serious difficulties are the true Pharisees of history, straining at gnats and
swallowing camels, there are perplexities in this narrative such
as we are bound not to evade. Let us address ourselves to these:
*Now in the morning, as he returned into the city, he hungered.
And when he saw a fig-tree in the way, he came to it, and found
nothing thereon but leaves only, and said unto it, Let no fruit
grow on thee henceforward for ever. And presently the fig-tree
withered away.* Thus how should our Lord, knowing, as by his
divine power He must, that there was no fruit upon that tree,
have gone to seek it there? Slight indeed as the insincerity would
have been, yet, if it was such, would it not trouble the clearness

of our image of Him, whom we conceive as the absolute Lord of truth? Further it is preplexing, that He should thus treat the tree as a moral agent. This becomes infinitely more so through a notice of St. Mark's: that *the time of figs was not yet.* He sought, and was displeased at failing to find, them. The symbol must needs be carried through; if by a figure we attribute guilt to the tree for not having fruit, we must be consistent, and show that it might have had such, that there was no justifying reason why it should have had none.

Upon the first point, namely that the Lord approached the tree, appearing to expect fruit upon it, and yet knowing that He should find none, deceiving thereby those who were with Him, it is sufficient to observe that a similar charge might be made against all figurative teaching, whether by word or by deed: for in all such there is a worshipping of truth in the spirit and not in the letter. A parable is told *as* true; and though the incidents are feigned, and the persons imagined, it *is* true, because of the moral or spiritual truth which sustains the outward framework of the story. Even so a symbolic action, although not meaning the thing which it professes to mean, is no deception, since it means something infinitely higher and deeper, of which the lower action is a type, and in which that lower is lost. What was it, for instance, here, if Christ did not intend really to look for fruit on that tree, being aware that it had none? yet He did intend to show how it would fare with a man or with a nation, when God came looking from it for the fruits of righteousness, and found nothing but the abundant leaves of a boastful yet empty profession.[1] As Fuller says, "He who *spake* many, here *wrought* a parable."

---

[1] Augustine (*Quaest. Evang.* ii. 51): "Not everything which we feign is a lie: but when we feign that which has no significance, then it is a lie. When our fiction refers to some significance, it is not a lie, but a figure of the truth. Otherwise everything which by wise and holy men, nay even by the Lord himself, has been said figuratively will be put down as a lie, because, taken in their ordinary meaning, such words have no foundation of truth. . . . But, as words, so also deeds are feigned without falsehood when their aim is to convey some significance; whence also is that act of the Lord in seeking fruit on a fig-tree at the time when the figs were not yet out."

But how, it is asked, shall we justify his putting forth of his anger on a tree? Say some, it was unjust to deal thus with a tree at all, which, being incapable of good or of evil, was as little a fit object of punishment as of reward. But this very objection does, in truth, involve that it was *not* unjust, that the tree was a *thing,* which might therefore lawfully be used merely as a means for ends lying beyond itself. Man is the prince of creation, and all things else are to serve him, and then rightly fulfil their subordinate uses when they do serve him. Christ did not attribute moral responsibilities to the tree, when He smote it because of its unfruitfulness; but He did attribute to it a fitness for representing moral qualities. All our language concerning trees, a *good* tree, a *bad* tree, a tree which *ought* to bear, is the same continual transfer to them of moral qualities, and a witness for the natural fitness of the Lord's language. He had already in some sort prepared his disciples for understanding and interpreting his act; and the not unfrequent use of this very symbol in the Old Testament, as at Hos. ix. 10; Joel i. 7, must have likewise assisted them here.

Yet, freely admitting all this, it may still be objected, Do not those words of St. Mark, *for the time of figs was not yet,* acquit the tree even of this figurative guilt, defeat the symbol, and put it, so to speak, in contradiction with itself? Does it not perplex us in Him, for whom we claim that highest reason should guide his every action, that He should look for figs, when they *could not* be found; — that He should bear Himself as one indignant, when He did not find them? The simplest, and as it appears to me, the entirely satisfying, explanation of this difficulty is the following. At that early period of the year, March or April, neither leaves nor fruit were naturally to be looked for on a fig-tree. But that tree, by putting forth leaves, made pretension to be something more than others, to have fruit upon it, seeing that in the fig-tree the fruit appears before the leaves. It was condemned, not so much for having no fruit, as that, not having fruit, it clothed itself abundantly with the foliage which, according to the natural order of the tree's development, gave pledge and promise that fruit should be found on it, if sought.

And this will then exactly answer to the sin of Israel, which under this tree was symbolized, — that sin being, not so much that it was without fruit, as that it boasted of having so much. The true fruit of that people, as of any people before the Incarnation, would have been to own that it had no fruit, that without Christ, without the incarnate Son of God, it could do nothing. But this was exactly what Israel refused to do. Other nations might have nothing to boast of, but they by their own showing had much.[2] And yet on closer inspection, the substance of righteousness was as much wanting on their part as anywhere among the nations round (Rom. ii. 1; Matt. xxi. 33-43).

And how should it have been otherwise? *for the time of figs was not yet;* — the time for the bare stock and stem of humanity to array itself in bud and blossom, with leaf and fruit, had not come, till its engrafting on the nobler stock of the true Man. All which anticipated this, which seemed to say that it could *be* anything, or *do* anything, otherwise than in Him and by Him, was deceptive and premature.

Here then, according to this explanation, there is no difficulty either in the Lord's going to the tree at that unseasonable time, — He would not have gone, but for those deceitful leaves which announced that fruit was there, — nor in the (symbolic) punishment of the unfruitful tree at a season of the year when according to the natural order, it could not have had any. It was punished not for being without fruit, but for proclaiming by the voice of those leaves that it had fruit; not for being barren, but for being false. And this was the guilt of Israel, a guilt

---

[2] It is not a little remarkable that it was with the fig-leaves that in Paradise Adam attempted to deny his nakedness, and to present himself as other than a sinner before God (Gen. iii. 7).

so much deeper than the guilt of the nations. The Epistle to the Romans supplies the key to the right understanding of this miracle; such passages as ii. 3, 17-27; x. 3, 4, 21; xi. 7, 10, above all. Nor should that remarkable parallel, "And all the trees of the field shall know that I the Lord have dried up the green tree, and made the dry tree to flourish" (Ezek. xvii. 24), be left out of account. And then the sentence, *No man eat fruit of thee hereafter for ever,* will be just the reversal of the promise that in them all nations of the earth should be blessed. Henceforth the Jewish synagogue is stricken with a perpetual barrenness. Once it was everything, but now it is nothing, to the world; the curse has come upon it, that no man henceforward shall eat fruit of it for ever.

And yet this *for ever* has its merciful limitation, when we come to transfer the curse from the tree to that of which the tree was as a living parable; a limitation which the word itself favours and allows; which is latent in it, to be revealed in due time. None shall eat fruit of that tree to the end of the present age, not until these "times of the Gentiles" are fulfilled. A day indeed will come when Israel, which now says, "I am a dry tree," shall consent to that word of its true Lord, which of old it denied: "from *Me* is thy fruit found" (Hos. xiv. 8), and shall be clothed with the richest foliage and fruit of all the trees of the field. The Lord, in his great discourse upon the last things (Matt. xxiv.), implies as much, when He gives this commencing conversion of the Jews, under the image of the re-clothing of the bare and withered fig-tree with leaf and bud, as the sign of the breaking in of the new aeon: "Now learn a parable of the fig-tree. When his branch is yet tender, and putteth forth leaves, ye know that summer is nigh: so likewise ye, when ye shall see all these things, know that it is near, even at the doors" (ver. 32, 33).

We conclude from St. Matthew that some beginnings of the threatened withering began to show themselves, almost as soon as the word of the Lord was spoken; a shuddering fear may have run through all the leaves of the tree thus stricken at its heart: for *presently the fig-tree withered away.* But it was not till the next morning, as the disciples returned, that they took note of its utter perishing, *dried up from the roots,* as now it was: whereupon *Peter calling to remembrance, saith unto him: Master, behold, the fig-tree which thou cursedst is withered away.* He will not let the occasion go by without its further lesson. What He had done, they might do the same and more. Faith in God would place them in relation with the same powers which He wielded, so that they might do mightier things even than this at which they marvelled so much.[3]

---

[3] It must have been in imitation of this act of his Lord that St. Bernard, quitting the scant hospitality of a castle which bore the name of Viride Folium, and where he had found nothing but resistance to the truth, exclaimed, "May God wither thee, thou green leaf," which word of his, as his biographer assures us, was not uttered in vain.

CHAPTER XXXII.

The Healing of Malchus' Ear

LUKE xxii. 49-51.

THE blow struck by a disciple, who would fain have fought for his Master, is recorded by all four Evangelists (Matt. xxvi. 51; Mark xiv. 47; Luke xxii. 50; John xviii. 10); but the miracle which followed belongs only to St. Luke. As a physician, this cure, sole of its kind which we know of our Lord's performing, the only miraculous healing of a wound inflicted by external violence, would attract his special attention. And then, further, nothing cohered more intimately with the purpose of his Gospel, than the portraying of the Lord on the side of his gentleness, his mercy, his benignity.

St. Luke, no doubt, knew very well, though he did not think good to set it down in his narrative, whose hand it was that struck this blow, — whether that the deed might still have brought him into trouble, though this appears an exceedingly improbable explanation, or from some other cause. The two earlier Evangelists preserve a like silence, and are content with generally designating him, — St. Matthew as *one of them who were with Jesus,* St. Mark as *one of them which stood by.* It is only from St. John we learn that it was Peter. He also tells us the name of the High Priest's servant who was wounded; *the servant's name was Malchus.* It is in entire consistency with all else which we read, that this fact should have come within the circle of St. John's knowledge; for he, in some way not explained to us, was acquainted with the High Priest (John xviii. 15), was so familiar with the constitution of his household that he is able to tell us concerning one, who later in the night provoked Peter to his denial of Christ, that he was "his kinsman whose ear Peter cut off" (ver. 26).

The whole incident is singularly characteristic; the *word*-bearer for the rest of the Apostles proves, when occasion requires, the *sword*-bearer also — showing himself prompter and more daring in action than them all. While they are inquiring, *Lord, shall we smite with the sword?* Peter waits not for the answer; but impelled by the natural courage of his heart,[1] and careless of the odds against him, aims a blow at one, probably the first that was daring to lay profane hands on the sacred person of his Lord. This was *a servant of the High Priest,* one therefore who, according to the proverb, "like master like man," may have been especially forward in this bad work. By God's good providence the stroke was turned aside, and grazing the head at which it was aimed, cut off the ear, — the *right ear,* as St. Luke and St. John tell us, — of the assailant, who thus hardly escaped with his life.

The words with which our Lord rebuked the untimely zeal of his disciple are differently given by different Evangelists, or rather each has given a different portion, each one enough to indicate the spirit in which all was spoken. St. Matthew records them most at length (xxvi. 52-54); while St. Luke passes them over altogether. That moment of uttermost confusion might seem unsuitable for so long a discourse. We may best suppose that while the healing of Malchus was proceeding, and all were watching and wondering, the Lord spoke these quieting words to his disciples. Possibly too his captors, who had feared resistance, now when they found that his words prohibited aught of the kind, may have been unwilling to interrupt Him. To Peter, and in him to all the other disciples, He says: *Put up again thy sword into his place; for all they that take the sword shall perish with the sword.* Christ refers, no doubt, to the primal

---

[1] Josephus characterizes the Galilaeans as pugnacious.

law, "Whoso sheddeth man's blood, by man shall his blood be shed" (Gen. ix. 6; cf. Rev. xiii. 10). The warning against taking the sword connects itself so closely with the command, *Put up again thy sword into his place,* that the meaning of the verse following (Matt. xxvi. 53) is plainly, "Thinkest thou that I need a feeble help like thine, when, instead of you, twelve weak trembling men, inexpert in war, I might even now at this latest moment *pray to my Father, and He shall presently give Me more than twelve legions[2] of Angels* to fight on my behalf? This mention of the *twelve legions of Angels,* whom it was free to Him to summon to his aid, brings the passage into striking relation with 2 Kin. vi. 17 (cf. 2 Chron. xxxii. 7; Job xxv. 3). *But how then shall the Scriptures be fulfilled, that thus it must be?* The temptation to claim the assistance of that heavenly host, — supposing Him to have felt the temptation, — is quelled in an instant; for how should that eternal purpose, that will of God, of which Scripture was the outward expression, *that thus it must be,* have then been fulfilled? (cf. Zech. xiii. 7). In St. John the same entire subordination of his own will to his Father's, which must hinder Him from claiming this unseasonable help, finds its utterance under another image: *The cup which my Father hath given Me, shall I not drink it?*

The words that follow, *Suffer ye thus far,* are still addressed to the disciples, and not to them who had just laid their hands on the Lord. We may paraphrase them thus, "Hold now; ye have gone thus far in resistance; but let this suffice." Having thus checked their too forward zeal, and now in act embodying his own precept, "Love your enemies, do good to them that hate you," He touched the ear of the wounded man, *and healed him.* Peter and the rest meanwhile, after this brief flash of a carnal courage, forsook their Master, and, leaving Him in the

---

[2] We are reminded here of the "multitude of the heavenly host" (Luke ii. 13), and other language of the same kind. Without falling in with the fancies of the Areopagite, we may see intimations here of a hierarchy in heaven. Bengel: "Angels are divided into their ranks and orders."

hands of his enemies, fled, — the wonder of the crowd at that gracious healing act, or the tumult with the darkness of the night, or these both together, favouring their evasion.

CHAPTER XXXIII.

The Second Miraculous Draught of Fishes

JOHN xxi. 1-23.

IF we regard John i. 1-14 as the prologue, this we might style the epilogue, of his Gospel. As that set forth what the Son of God was before He came from the Father, even so this, in mystical and prophetic guise, how He should rule in the world after He had returned to the Father.

After these things Jesus showed himself again to the disciples at the sea of Tiberias. St. John alone calls the lake by this name; his motive no doubt being that so it would be more easily recognized by those for whom he especially wrote — Tiberias, built by Herod Antipas in honour of Tiberius, being a city well known to the heathen world. On the first occasion of using this name, he has marked the identity of this lake with the lake of Galilee mentioned by the other Evangelists (vi. 1), but does not count it necessary to repeat this here. There is a significance in the words *showed himself,* or *manifested himself,* which many long ago observed, — no other than this, that his body after the resurrection was only visible by a distinct act of his will. It is not for nothing that in language of this kind all his appearances after the resurrection are related (Mark xvi. 12, 14; Luke xxiv. 34; Acts xiii. 31; 1 Cor. xv. 5-8). It is the same with angelic and all other manifestations of a higher heavenly world. Men do not *see* them; but they *appear* to men (Judg. vi. 12; xiii. 3, 10, 21; Matt. xvii. 3; Luke i. 11; xxii 43; Acts ii. 3; vii. 2; xvi. 9; xxvi. 16) ; being only visible to those for whose sakes they are vouchsafed, and to whom they are willing to show them-

285

selves.[1] Those to whom this manifestation was vouchsafed are enumerated. They are seven, which is scarcely an accident. *There were together Simon Peter, and Thomas called Didymus, and Nathanael of Cana in Galilee, and the sons of Zebedee, and two other of his disciples.* St. John has no list of Apostles. This is the nearest approach to one in his Gospel. It makes something for the opinion probable, and by some now accepted as certain, that the Nathanael of St. John is the Bartholomew of the other Evangelists, thus to find him named not after, but in the midst of, some of the chiefest Apostles. Who were the two unnamed disciples cannot certainly be known. They also could scarcely be other than Apostles, — a word, it should be remembered, which St. John nowhere uses to designate the Twelve, indeed uses only once (xiii. 16) in all his writings, — *disciples* in the most eminent sense of the word. Lightfoot supposes that they were Andrew and Philip; which is very likely; for where Peter was, there his brother Andrew would scarcely be wanting (Matt. iv. 18; Mark i. 29; Luke vi. 14; John vi. 8), and where Andrew there in all likelihood would be Philip as well (John i. 45; xii. 22; Mark iii. 18).

The announcement of Peter, *I go a-fishing,* is not, as it has been strangely interpreted, a declaration that he has lost all faith in Jesus as the Messiah, has renounced his apostleship, and will return to his old occupation. A teacher in that new kingdom which his Lord had set up, he is following the wise rule of the Jewish Rabbis, who were ever wont to have some manual trade or occupation on which to fall back in time of need. We all know of what good service to St. Paul was his skill in making

---

[1] Thus Ambrose on the appearing of the Angel to Zacharias (*Exp. in Luc.* i. 24): "He is appropriately said to have *appeared* to him who suddenly perceived him. And this phrase divine Scripture was wont to use specially in the case whether of the Angels or of God. . . . For things sensible are not seen in a like manner as is He in whose will it rests to be seen, and to whose nature it belongs that He is unseen, and to his will that He is seen. For if He wills not, He is not seen: if He wills, He is seen." And Chrysostom here: "By the phrase, *He manifested himself* it is made clear, that if He had not willed, and had not manifested himself in his condescension, He would not have been seen, his body being incorruptible."

tents (2 Thess. iii. 8). Peter's challenge to the old companions of his toil is at once accepted by them: *They say unto him, We also go with thee.* And hereupon *they went forth, and entered into a ship immediately; and that night they caught nothing.* It fared with them now, as it had fared with three, or perhaps four, among them on a prior occasion (Luke v. 5). Already a dim feeling may have risen up in their minds that this night should be the spiritual counterpart of that other. Had it been, however, more than the obscurest presentiment, they would have been quicker to recognize their Lord, who, *when the morning was now come,* or better, *when the day was now breaking, stood on the shore,* or rather, *stood on the beach.* It was an appropriate time; for "heaviness may endure for a night, but joy cometh in the morning (Ps. xxx. 5; cf. xix. 5; cxliii. 8). Nor was the place less appropriate; He now on the firm land, they still on the unquiet sea. As yet, however, their eyes were holden, *the disciples knew not that it was Jesus* (cf. xx. 14; Luke xxiv. 16); and in the language of a stranger He addressed them; *Children, have ye any meat?* putting this question, I should imagine, as with that friendly interest not unmixed with curiosity. *They answered Him, No.* The question was indeed asked to draw forth this acknowledgment from their lips: for it is well that the confessions of man's poverty should go before the incomings of the riches of God's bounty and grace (cf. John v. 6; vi. 7-9).

And he said unto them, Cast the net on the right side of the ship, and ye shall find. They take the counsel as of one possibly more skilful in their art than themselves: *They cast therefore, and now they were not able to draw it for the multitude of fishes* (Ezek. xlvi. 10). But this is enough; there is one disciple at least, *that disciple whom Jesus loved,* who can no longer doubt with whom they have to do. That other occasion, when at the bidding of their future Lord they enclosed so vast a multitude of fishes that their net brake, rises clear before his eyes (Luke

v. 1-11). And he says, not yet to all, but to Peter, to him with whom he stood in nearest fellowship (John xx. 3; Acts iii. 1), who had best right to be first made partaker of the discovery, *It is the Lord.* Each Apostle comes wonderfully out in his proper character:[2] he of the eagle eye first detects the presence of the Beloved; and then Peter, the foremost ever in act, as John is profoundest in speculation, unable to wait till the ship shall touch the land, *girt his fisher's coat unto him,* this for seemliness, *and cast himself into the sea,* that he might find himself the sooner at his Saviour's feet (Matt. xiv. 28; John xx. 6). He was before *naked,* stripped, that is, for toil, wearing only the tunic, or garment close to the skin, and having put off his upper and superfluous garments; for *naked* need mean no more. Some suppose that he walked on the sea; but we have no right to multiply miracles, and the words, *cast himself into the sea,* do not warrant, but rather forbid, this. Rather, he swam and waded to the shore, which was not distant more than about *two hundred cubits,* that is, about one hundred yards. The other disciples followed more slowly; for they were encumbered with the net and its weight of fishes. *As soon then as they were come to land, they saw a fire of coals there, and fish laid thereon, and bread —* by what ministry, natural or miraculous, has been often inquired; but we must leave this undetermined as we find it. The adjuncts of the scene and the whole tone of the narration certainly suggest the latter. *Jesus saith unto them, Bring of the fish which ye have now caught.* These shall be added to those already preparing.[3] Peter, again the foremost, *went up and drew the net to land full of great fishes, an hundred and fifty and three;* while

---

[2] Chrysostom: "On their recognizing him, the disciples Peter and John again display the peculiarities of their proper dispositions. Peter was more fervid, John the loftier; Peter the quicker, John the keener of vision." Tristram (*Natural History of the Bible,* p. 285): "The density of the shoals of fish in the sea of Galilee can scarcely be conceived by those who have not witnessed them."

[3] To the abundance and excellency of the fish in this lake many bear testimony. Thus Robinson (*Biblical Researches,* vol. ii. p. 261): "The lake is full of fishes of various kinds," and he instances sturgeon, chub, and bream; adding, "We had no difficulty in procuring an abundant supply for our evening and morning meal; and found them delicate and well-flavoured."

yet, setting a notable difference between this and a similar event of an earlier day (Luke v. 6), *for all there were so many, yet was not the net broken.*

It is hard to believe that all this should have happened, or should have been recorded with this emphasis and minuteness of detail, had it no other meaning than that which is ostensible and on the surface. There must be more here than meets the eye — an allegorical, or more truly a symbolic, meaning underlying the literal. Nor is this very hard to discover. Without pledging oneself for every detail of Augustine's interpretation, it yet commends itself as in the main worthy of acceptance. He puts this miraculous draught of fishes in relations of likeness and unlikeness with the other before the Resurrection (Luke v. 1-11), and sees in that earlier, the figure of the Church as it now is, and as it now gathers its members from the world; in this later the figure of the Church as it shall be in the end of the world, with the large incoming and sea-harvest of souls, "the fulness of the Gentiles" which then shall find place. On that prior occasion the "fishers of men" that should be, were not particularly bidden to cast the net on the right hand or on the left; for, had Christ said to the right, it would have implied that none should be taken but the good, — if to the left, that only the bad; while yet, so long as the present confusions endure, both bad and good are enclosed in the nets; but now He says, *Cast the net on the right side of the ship,* implying that all which are taken should be good; and this, because the *right* is ever the hand of good omen and of value. On that former occasion the nets were broken with the multitude of fishes, so that all were not secured which for a time were within them; and what are the schisms and divisions of the present condition of the Church, but rents and holes through which numbers, that impatiently bear the restraints of the net, break away from it? — but now, in the end of time, *for all there were so many, yet was not the net broken.* On that first occasion the fishes were brought into the ship, itself still tossed on the unquiet sea, even as men in the present time who are taken for Christ are brought into the Church, itself not in haven yet; but here the nets are drawn up to land, to the safe and quiet shore of eternity. Then the ships were wellnigh sunken with their burden, for so is it with the ship of the Church, — encumbered with evil-livers till it wellnight makes shipwreck altogether; but no danger of this kind threatens here. Then a great but indefinite multitude was enclosed; but here a definite number, even as the number of the elect is fixed and pre-ordained; and there small fishes and great, for nothing to the contrary is said; but here they are all *great,* for all shall be such who attain to that kingdom, being equal to the Angels.

Jesus saith unto them, Come and dine. And none of the disciples durst ask him, Who art thou? knowing that it was the Lord. But if they knew, why should they desire to ask? I take the Evangelist to imply that they knew *that it was the Lord;* yet would they willingly have had this assurance sealed and made still more certain to them by his own word, which for all this they shrank from seeking to obtain, so majestic and awe-inspiring was his presence now (cf. iv. 27; Judg. xiii. 6).

Jesus then cometh, and taketh bread, and giveth them, and fish likewise. What follows is obscure, and without the key which the symbolical explanation supplies, would be obscurer yet. What is the meaning of this meal which they found ready prepared for them on the shore, and which the Lord with his own hands distributed to them? For Himself, with his risen body, it was superfluous, nor does He seem to have shared, but only to have dealt to them, the food; as little was it needed by them, whose homes were near at hand; while indeed a single loaf or flat cake, and a single fish, for this is implied in the original, though not in our Version, would have proved a scanty meal for the seven. But we must continue to see an under-meaning, and a rich and deep one, in all this. As that large take of fish was to them the pledge and promise of a labour that should not be in vain, so the meal when the labour was done, a meal of the Lord's own preparing and dispensing, and *upon the shore,* was the symbol of the great festival in heaven with which, after their earthly toil was over, He would refresh His servants. The meal was sacramental in character, and had nothing to do with the stilling of their present hunger.

The most interesting conversation which follows hangs too closely upon this miracle to be passed over. Christ has given to his servants a prophetic glimpse of their work and their reward; and He now declares to them the sole conditions under which this work may be accomplished, and this reward obtained. Love to Him, the unreserved yielding up of self to God — these are the sole conditions, and all which follows is to teach this. *So when they had dined, Jesus saith to Simon Peter, Simon, son of Jonas, lovest thou Me more than these?* In that compellation, *Simon, son of Jonas,* there was already that which must have wrung the Apostle's heart. It was as though his Lord would say to him, "Where is that name Peter, which I gave thee (Matt. xvi. 18; John i. 42)? where is the Rock, and the rock-like strength, which I gave thee, which, when most needed, I looked for in vain (Matt. xxvi. 69-75)? Not therefore by that name can I address thee now, but as flesh and blood, and the child of man; for all that once was higher in thee has disappeared." In the question itself lies a plain allusion to Peter's vainglorious word, not recorded by this Evangelist, "Though all men shall be offended because of Thee, yet will I never be offended" (Matt. xxvi. 33). Peter understood his Lord better, and no longer casting any slight by comparison on the love of his fellow-disciples, is satisfied with affirming his own,[4] appealing at the same time to the Lord, the searcher of all hearts, whether, despite of all that miserable back-sliding in the palace of the High Priest, this love of his was not fervent and sincere. *He saith unto him, Yea, Lord, thou knowest that I love thee.* The Lord's rejoinder, *Feed my sheep, Feed my lambs,* is not so much, "Show then thy love in act," as rather, "I restore to thee thy apostolic function; this grace is thine, that thou shalt yet be a chief shepherd of my flock." It implies, therefore, the fullest forgiveness of the past, since none but the forgiven could rightly declare the forgiveness of God. The question, *Lovest thou Me?* is thrice repeated, that by three solemn affirmations he may efface his three several denials of his Lord (John xviii. 17; xxv. 27). At last, upon the third repetition of the question, *Peter was grieved;* and with yet more emphasis than before appeals to the omniscience of his Lord, whether it was not true that indeed he loved Him: *Lord, Thou knowest all things;* — confessing this, he confesses to his Godhead, for of no other but God could this knowledge of the hearts of all men be predicated (Ps. vii. 9; cxxxix.; Ezek. xi. 5; Jer. xvii. 10; 1 Kin. viii. 39; John ii. 24, 25; xvi. 30; Acts i. 24); and from this point of view the title *Lord,* which he ascribes to his Master, assumes a new signficance; — *Thou knowest that I love Thee.*

Many have refused to see any distinction between the two commissions, *Feed my sheep,* and *Feed my lambs.* To me nothing seems more natural than that by *lambs* the Lord intended the more imperfect Christians, the "little children" in Him (Isai. xl. 11); by the *sheep* the more advanced, the "young men" and "fathers"[5] (1 John ii. 12-14). The interpretation indeed is groundless and trifling, made in the interests of Rome, which sees in the *lambs*

---

[4] Augustine (*Serm.* cxlvii. 2): "He could not say aught but *I love thee:* he did not venture to say *more than these.* He would not be a liar a second time. It was enough for him to bear testimony to his own heart; it was no duty of his to be judge of the heart of another."

[5] Wetstein: "Those sheep at the time that they were committed to Peter were still tender lambs, new disciples who were to be attracted by Peter from the Jews and gentiles. When He commits unto him the sheep also He signifies that he will live to old age and see the Church constituted and regulated."

the laity, and in the *sheep* the clergy; and that here to Peter, and in him to the Roman pontiffs, was given dominion over both. The commission should at least have run, *Feed my sheep, Feed my shepherds,* if any such conclusions were to be drawn from it, though many and huge links in the chain of proofs would be wanting still.

But *Feed my sheep* is not all. This life of labour is to be crowned with a death of painfulness. The Lord will show him beforehand what great things he must suffer for his sake. *Verily, verily, I say unto thee, when thou wast young, thou girdedst thyself*—it is impossible to miss an allusion here to the promptitude with which Peter had just girt himself that he might the sooner join his Lord — *and walkedst whither thou wouldest; but when thou shalt be old, thou shalt stretch forth thy hands, and another shall gird thee, and carry thee whither thou wouldest not.* A prophetic allusion is here made to the crucifixion of Peter, St. John himself declaring that Jesus spake thus, *signifying by what death he should glorify God;* and no reasonable grounds exist for calling in question the tradition of the Church, that such was the manner of Peter's martyrdom. Doubtless it is here *obscurely* intimated; but this is in the very nature of prophecy, and there is quite enough in the description to show that the Lord had this and no other manner of death in his eye. The stretched-forth hands are the hands extended on the transverse bar of the cross. The girding by another is the binding to the cross, the sufferer being not only fastened to the instrument of punishment with nails, but also bound to it with cords. It cannot be meant by the bearing *whither thou wouldest not,* that there should be any reluctancy on the part of Peter to glorify God by his death, except indeed the reluctancy which there always is in the flesh to suffering and pain (Ephes. v. 29); a reluctancy in his case, as in his Lord's (cf. Matt. xxvi. 39), overruled by the higher willingness to do and to suffer the perfect will of God.

In this sense, as it was a violent death, — a death which others chose for him, — a death from which flesh and blood would naturally shrink, it was a carrying *whither he would not;* though, in a higher sense, as it was the way to a nearer vision of God, it was that toward which he had all his life been striving; and he then was borne whither most he would; no word here implying that the exulting exclamation of another Apostle, at the near approach of his martyrdom (2 Tim. iv. 6-8; cf. Phil. i. 21, 23), would not have suited his lips just as yell. It is to this prophetic intimation of his death that St. Peter probably alludes in his second Epistle (i. 14).

The symbolical meaning which we have found in the earlier portions of the chapter must not be excluded from this. To "gird oneself" is ever in Scripture the sign and figure of promptness for an outward activity (Exod. xii. 11; I Kin. xviii. 46; 2 Kin. iv. 29; Luke xii. 35; xvii. 8; 1 Pet. i. 13; Ephes. vi. 14); so that, in fact, Christ is saying to Peter, "When thou wast young, thou *actedst* for Me; going whither thou wouldest, thou wast free to work for Me, and to choose thy field of work. But when thou art old, thou shalt learn another, a higher and a harder lesson; thou shalt *suffer* for Me; thou shalt no more choose thy work, but others shall choose it for thee, and that work shall be the work of passion rather than of action." Such is the history of the Christian life, and not in Peter's case only, but the course and order of it in almost all of God's servants. It is begun in action, it is perfected in suffering. In the last, lessons are learned which the first could never have taught; graces called out, which else would not at all, or would only have very weakly, existed.

He who has shown him the end, will also show him the way; for *when he had spoken this, he saith unto him, Follow Me.* These words signify much more than in a general way, "Be thou an imitator of Me." The scene at this time enacted on the shores of Gennesaret, was quite as much in deed as in word; and here, at the very moment that the Lord spake the words, it would seem that He took some paces along the rough and rocky shore, bidding Peter to follow; thus setting forth to him in a figure his future life, which should be a following of his divine Master in the rude and rugged path of Christian action.[6] All this was not so much spoken as done; for Peter, *turning about,* — looking, that is, behind him, — *seeth the disciple whom Jesus loved* — words introduced to explain the boldness of John in following unbidden; him he sees *following,* and thereupon inquires, *Lord, and what shall this man do?* He would know what his portion shall be, and what the issue of his earthly conversation. Shall he, too, follow by the same rugged path? It is not very easy to determine the motive of this question, or the spirit in which it was asked: it was certainly something more than a mere natural curiosity. Augustine takes it as the question of one concerned that his friend should be left out, and not summoned to the honour of the same close following of his Lord with himself (2 Sam. i. 23). Others find a motive less noble in it; that it was put more in the temper of Martha, when she asked the Lord, "Lord, dost Thou not care that my sister hath left me to serve alone" (Luke x. 40)? ill satisfied that Mary should remain quietly sitting at Jesus' feet, while she was engaged in laborious service for Him. It is certainly possible that Peter, knowing all which that *Follow Me,* addressed to himself, implied, may have felt a moment's jealousy at the easier lot assigned to John.

It is plain that the source out of which the question proceeded was not altogether a pure one. There lies something of a check in the reply. These "times and seasons" it is not for him to

---

[6] Grotius here says excellently well: "As He had just taken previous events as signs of what was to be said, so now He expresses what He had said by a manifest sign. For the words, Follow Me, have not only the ordinary meaning to which also Peter was obedient at the moment, but a further and mystical one. For He is alluding to what He had said, Matt. x. 38."

know, nor to intermeddle with things which are the Lord's alone. *He* claims to be the allotter of the several portions of his servants, and gives account of none of his matters: *If I will that he tarry till I come, what is that to thee? follow thou Me* (cf. John ii. 4). At the same time this, like so many of our Lord's repulses, is not a mere repulse. He may refuse to comply with an untimely request, yet seldom or never by a blank negation. So it was here. For assuredly the error of those brethren who drew from these words the conclusion *that that disciple should not die,* had not its root in the mistaking a mere hypothetical *If I will,* for a distinct prophetical announcement. That *If I will* is no hypothetical case. As Christ did not mean, so certainly the disciples did not take Him to mean, If I choose that he should live on till my return to judgment, this is nothing to thee." Rather, even while He checks Peter for asking the question, He does declare his pleasure that John should *tarry* till his coming. Nor may we empty this *tarry* of all deeper significance. To *tarry* can be taken in no other sense than that of to remain alive (cf. Phil. i. 25; 1 Cor. xv. 6; John xii. 34).

But how could Christ thus announce that John should *tarry* till He came? We shall best interpret it by the help, and in the light, of Matt. xvi. 28; x. 23. The beloved disciple should *tarry.* He only among the Twelve, according to that other and earlier announcement of his Lord, should not taste of death, till he had seen "the *Son of man* coming in his kingdom." That tremendous shaking, not of the earth only, but also of the heaven, that passing away of the old Jewish economy with a great noise, to make room for a new heaven and a new earth (Heb. xii. 26, 27), he should overlive, and see the Son of man, invisibly, yet most truly, coming to execute judgment on his foes (Matt. xxiv. 34). He only of the Twelve should survive the destruction of Jerusalem, that catastrophe, the mightiest, the most significant, the most dreadful, and at the same time, as making room for the Church of the living God, the most blessed, which the world has seen; and *tarry* far on into the glorious age which should succeed.

Nor was this all. His whole life and ministry should be in harmony with its peaceful end. His should be a still work throughout; to deepen the inner life of the Church rather than to extend outwardly its borders. The rougher paths were not appointed for his treading; he should be perfected by another discipline. Martyr in will, but not in deed, he should crown a calm and honoured old age by a natural and peaceful death. This, which Augustine and others make the primary meaning of the words, we may accept as a secondary and subordinate.

He who records these words about himself notes, but notes only to refute, an expectation which had gotten abroad among the brethren, drawn from this saying inaccurately reported or wrongly understood, namely that he should never die. And is there not something more than humility in the anxious earnestness with which he repels any such interpretation? No such mournful prerogative should be his; not so long should he be absent from his Lord. There lies no such sentence upon him of weary and prolonged exclusion from that presence in which is fulness of joy (Phil. i. 23). Yet this explicit declaration from the lips of the beloved Apostle himself, that Jesus had never said of him that he should not die, failed effectually to extinguish such a belief or superstition in the Church. We find traces of it surviving long; even his death and burial, which men were compelled to acknowledge, were not sufficient to abolish it. For his death, some said, was only the appearance of death, and he yet breathed in his grave; so that even an Augustine

---

[7] *In Ev. Joh. tract.* cxxiv.: "We have the tradition . . . that, while accounted dead, he was actually buried when asleep, and will so remain until the coming of Christ, making known meanwhile the fact of his life by the bubbling up of the dust, which is believed to be forced by his breath, when asleep, to rise from the depths to the surface of the grave. I think it superfluous to contend against such an opinion. For those who know the place may see for themselves whether the ground there does or suffers what is said: because too we have heard it from men not without weight."

was unable wholly to resist the reports which had reached him, that the earth yet heaved, and the dust was lightly stirred by the regular pulses of his breath.' The fable of his still living, Augustine at once rejects; but is more patient with this report than one might have expected, counting it possible that a permanent miracle might be wrought at the Apostle's grave.